SACRED CLAIMS

STUDIES IN RELIGION AND CULTURE

Frank Burch Brown, Gary L. Ebersole,
and Edith Wyschogrod, *Editors*

SACRED CLAIMS

REPATRIATION AND
LIVING TRADITION

GREG JOHNSON

UNIVERSITY OF VIRGINIA PRESS
CHARLOTTESVILLE AND LONDON

UNIVERSITY OF VIRGINIA PRESS
© 2007 by the Rector and Visitors of the University of Virginia
All rights reserved
Printed in the United States of America on acid-free paper

First published 2007

1 3 5 7 9 8 6 4 2

Library of Congress Cataloging-in-Publication Data

Johnson, Greg, 1968–
    Sacred claims : repatriation and living tradition / Greg Johnson.
        p.   cm. — (Studies in religion and culture)
    Includes bibliographical references and index.
    ISBN 978-0-8139-2661-2 (cloth : alk. paper) — ISBN 978-0-8139-2662-9
(pbk. : alk. paper)
    1. Hawaiians—Funeral customs and rites. 2. Cemeteries—Hawaii.
3. Cultural property—Hawaii. I. Title.
DU624.65.J65 2007
363.6'909969—dc22

2007005472

The poem "Evolution" by Sherman Alexie is reprinted from
The Business of Fancy Dancing, © 1992 by Sherman Alexie,
by permission of Hanging Loose Press.

For Danny Berry (1967–1989),
who speaks from the past

CONTENTS

ACKNOWLEDGMENTS

Sacred Claims is the culmination of a decade of archival and ethnographic research and builds upon my doctoral dissertation, "The Terms of Return: Religious Discourse and the Native American Graves Protection and Repatriation Act" (University of Chicago Divinity School, 2003). While portions of several chapters have appeared in print previously, all chapters have been updated and otherwise revised and include new introductions. Parts of chapters 1 and 6 appeared as "Narrative Remains: Articulating Indian Identities in the Repatriation Context," in *Comparative Studies in Society and History* (47, no 3 [2005]: 480–506, © 2005 Society for Comparative Study of Society and History). Sections of chapter 2 appeared as "Naturally There: Discourses of Permanence in the Repatriation Context," in *History of Religions* (44, no. 1 [2004]: 36–55, © 2004 The University of Chicago). A brief section of chapter 1 and the central sections of chapter 3 appeared as "Tradition, Authority and the *Native American Graves Protection and Repatriation Act*," in *Religion* (32 [2002]: 355–81, © 2003 Elsevier Science). Portions of chapter 5 appeared as "Ancestors before Us: Manifestations of Tradition in a Hawaiian Dispute," in *Journal of the American Academy of Religion* (71, no. 2 [2003]: 327–46, © The American Academy of Religion).

Many people helped—directly or indirectly—to bring this book to life, whether by way of information, inspiration, care, or criticism (and in some cases all of these). I am profoundly grateful to all who helped me and apologize to those I have failed to mention. The usual caveats apply.

First, this book wouldn't exist had I not received a push into academics by Ed. L. Miller, whose off-the-cuff remark ("Mr. Johnson, you're not half bad") gave me confidence when I needed it most.

In the course of working on my dissertation, I received direction, encouragement, and criticism from Barbara Babcock; John MacAloon; Anthony C. Yu; and, most especially and formatively, Bruce Lincoln. I would also like to thank members of the Department of Anthropology at the University of Chicago, especially Jean and John Comaroff, Ray Fogelson, and Marshall Sahlins, who welcomed a religion student from "next door" and helped me to think more richly about the concept and realities of culture.

I received generous support for my research from the institutions with which I have had the good fortune to be affiliated and from the National Endowment for the Humanities, which gave me a summer research award in 2005. Annette Aronowicz, Stephen Cooper, and David McMahan were wonderful colleagues at Franklin and Marshall College, allowing disagreements to stand—but not stand in the way—and celebrating points of common vision. At the University of Colorado, the entire faculty in religious studies helped me to think and rethink aspects of my work in provocative ways. I am especially thankful to Sam Gill for a trenchant and challenging reading of the entire manuscript. Students at both schools have kept me happy and, when they could, on point.

Scholars in a number of fields have provided rich feedback concerning my research and writing. These include David Akin, Chadwick Allen, Pia Altieri, Garrick Bailey, Mansel Blackford, the late Vine Deloria Jr., Natalie Dohrmann, Steven Engler, Kathy Fine-Dare, Steven Friesen, Jeppe Jensen, Paul Johnson, Steve Lekson, Patty Limerick, Russ McCutcheon, Tim McKeown, Michael McNally, Glenn Penny, Michelene Pesantubbee, Frank Reynolds, Robert Segal, Winni Sullivan, Bron Taylor, Kocku von Stuckrad, and Robert Yelle.

In the course of my field research, I have had the opportunity to learn from a range of devoted, smart, and exciting people, including Foster Ampong, Victoria Atkins, Keola Awong, Malia Baron, Geraldine Bell, Bobby Camara, Lesa Hagel, Becky Hammond, Mel Kalihiki, LaFrance Kapaka-Arboleda, Guy Kaulukukui, Colin Kippen, Attwood Makanani, Kai Markell, Charlie Maxwell, Kunani Nihipali, Cynthia Orlando, Hoʻoipo Pa, Laura Schuster, Laʻakea Suganuma, and Larry Wiese. I especially thank Dana Naone Hall, who told and patiently retold her story to me; Eddie Halealoha Ayau, who was willing to talk at even the toughest times; and Uncle Kekuni Blaisdell, who opened his home and shared his wisdom many more times than I can ever repay.

I am very thankful to Gary Ebersole, both for his suggestion that I submit my manuscript to the Studies in Religion and Culture series and for his continued support. I would also like to thank Cathie Brettschneider at the University of Virginia Press for seeing this project through to its completion; Carol Sickman-Garner for a wonderful job of editing; and the outside readers, Joel Martin and

Gary Laderman, whose suggestions and criticism made this a much better book.

Finally, and most of all, I would like to acknowledge the love and support of my family, including Dad—the best research partner ever; Mom and Jack; Frank and Suzie; my siblings—in-laws and outlaws; and, at the center of my world, K, Hayden, and Soren.

A NOTE ON DIACRITICS

DIACRITIC USAGE in Hawaiian is a somewhat inconsistent phenomenon for a variety of historical reasons. I have not added diacritic marks when they did not exist in original sources. Otherwise, I have followed Pukui and Elbert, *Hawaiian Dictionary.*

SACRED CLAIMS

INTRODUCTION

SACRED CLAIMS AND RELIGIOUS ACTS

> We must not forget that an object is the best messenger of a
> world above that of nature.
>
> —Roland Barthes, *Mythologies*

View from a Sacred Mountain

EVEN FIRM faith looks for objective evidence to anchor itself. So it
was that I sought an extraordinary object, Noah's Ark. I was a young,
promising climber and had landed a spot on an expedition to Mount
Ararat with the famous astronaut-turned-biblical-explorer James
Irwin. While my father and I traveled as part of a tour group—not as
members of the research team—we were nonetheless scheduled to
climb the mountain and would have opportunities to explore it in
our own right. Looking around at the middle-aged group and assessing the stature of even the top climbers, I concluded that the Vegas
odds of finding the Ark were in my favor.

We spent several days organizing equipment at the base of the
mountain in Dogubayazit, an outpost town on the border of Turkey
and Iran. A certain spice was added by the utterly exotic surround-
ings and by the pack of wild dogs that nearly devoured me as I ran
back to town from an ill-advised warm-up hike in the hinterlands.
That episode, and the olives we were given for breakfast, hinted that
I was out of my element, in a place where my spiritual narrative for
being there did not square with the realities on the ground. If I had
any doubts about this, I was soon disabused of my pretensions to
postbiblical glory—not because I didn't find the Ark, which you've
probably surmised, but because I didn't even get a chance to look
for it. Nor, at the end of a rather prickly few days, did I want one.

Unfolding political drama had dispatched my aspirations altogether: I found myself on a terribly contested piece of ground.

A number of groups could be found on Mount Ararat during the summer of 1985, lending a seductive air of competition to the Ark-finding enterprise. While it occurred to me that it was odd for such manifestly religious groups to compete rather than cooperate in the quest for an object that would make the truth of their tradition plain for everyone to see, all of this turned out to be a sideshow. The real contestation was not between would-be Indiana Joneses but between Kurds and the Turkish government. In a struggle nearly as ancient as narratives about the Ark, Kurds had been fighting for political sovereignty over their homeland, divided and claimed by a number of nation-states in the modern period. Their presence in Iraq, of course, is now well-known, the U.S. government having celebrated them as freedom fighters for their resistance to the Iraqi regime under Saddam Hussein. In 1985, however, their political coinage vis-à-vis the United States and its citizens was a bit different: they were defined as "terrorists," known for their habit of threatening Westerners who encroached on the symbolic center of the disputed territory, Mount Ararat.

Only several days before we meant to ascend, we heard that Kurds had attacked a group of climbers, burned their equipment, and marched them off the mountain at gunpoint. Reports came in that they were promising to do the same to the "American spaceman" and us, at which point our Turkish military escort declined further involvement in the expedition. As the seriousness of the Kurds' threat and struggle hit me, my vision began to change. My narrative justification for being there suddenly seemed lifeless—fanciful—when compared to their entirely more concrete claims. Our group walked away, affording me a better view than any summit. I began to see that the world is shaped less by truths than by truth claims; less by the objective status of traditions than by people's reasons, means, and willingness to defend their claims to traditions and the identities for which they stand.

Some years later, as I began to study repatriation processes, I had the nagging feeling that I was back on the slopes of Mount Ararat. I wasn't looking for any arks this time, but I still couldn't shake the sense that many of those involved in repatriation—including legislators, scientists, and even some native representatives—were seeking objective truths and were therefore blind to cultural meanings and to the ways these live in and through subjects and subjectivities. That said, repatriation processes are object focused for good reasons:

unlike Noah's Ark, which I now take to have no physical reality, objects and histories in this context are painfully real. Thus, it was not the attention to objects per se that troubled me; rather, what nagged me was that the cultures, traditions, and religious systems to which the objects were said to belong—whether described in terms of the past or the present—were more often than not described as similar to the objects themselves: as stable, fixed, unchanging, existing above and beyond the political fray of the contemporary world.

This conception of tradition and religion strikes me as tragic insofar as it holds up fixed and fixating criteria for realities that are not objective, except as caricature. Tradition as an object is a mythical ark, and questing after it will always yield frustration and tremendous potential for misunderstanding. Tradition conceived as process or action, by contrast, is found in all of its human complexity and richness every time reference is made to the past in the name of the present and the future. This distinction—between tradition as static and tradition as dynamic—is, of course, not new. From at least the time of Franz Boas, scholars have made regular efforts to describe the relationship of tradition and change. Nonetheless, objective views of tradition persist outside the academy—often in consequential places, such as courtrooms—and even within it. In the latter case objective views of tradition are seldom advanced explicitly. Rather, they are often a product of old assumptions carried forward in new guises. Tradition as and in change is celebrated in many instances without its forms and consequences taken seriously enough. This tendency is most readily detected when persistent desires to locate authenticity surface in scholarly work. Frequently, the specter against which authenticity is measured is what critics might call "postured tradition," a shorthand means of suggesting that tradition expressed in political contexts is "merely political." I challenge this perspective by insisting that repatriation processes reveal how traditions become generative and alive in contexts of political and legal struggle. Far from merely posturing, representatives of tradition speak forth their identities with unrivaled vitality at such moments, frequently charting new relationships among past, present, and future in the process.

I argue for this view of tradition through presenting a range of repatriation case studies and theorizing the intellectual and social rewards of taking lived religion seriously. To this end the book attends more or less equally to three areas of focus: the legal history of U.S. repatriation deliberations, American Indian repatriation contexts, and Native Hawaiian repatriation disputes. As will become clear, these domains are not mutually exclusive in the analysis that follows. For this reason the book does not unfold in a strictly chronological way. While I present the history of certain developments and contexts in considerable detail, I have elected to retain a topical and case-study emphasis in order to illuminate the analytical issues central to appreciating the vitality of tradition in action.

Speaking Tradition

Sacred Claims is specifically focused upon the Native American Graves Protection and Repatriation Act of 1990 (NAGPRA), which was passed into law in 1990 and received its final rule and regulations in December 1995.[1] Fundamentally a form of human rights legislation, the law is largely redressive in intent: it provides a legal framework within which Native Americans can seek the protection of graves on federal land and the repatriation of human remains and certain cultural objects from federally funded institutions.[2] Since the early 1990s repatriations have been occurring at a significant rate. But as one might suppose, repatriation claims are often met with resistance—sometimes from the institutions holding the items in question but also, at times, from other Native American groups or factions within a particular group. In this respect, and in several other significant ways, the law is far from problem free.[3] In the fray of real-world implementation, one consistent feature of repatriation processes has emerged: when and where the law is stretched—here yielding exciting prospects, there faltering—religious and traditional claims tend to stand out in sharp relief. Attending to such moments, *Sacred Claims* explores the vibrant, revealing, and consequential intersection of legal processes and religious worlds.

Bones and other objects are at the heart of this study, as is the proposition that the meaning of such objects is not inherent. Rather, meanings—often multiple, shifting, and divisive—are assigned to bones and other objects by people in the present, almost always in the name of "tradition," be it indigenous, scientific, or otherwise invoked. This book, therefore, is about processes of meaning making in the present; it is about how various groups harness the symbolic to the material, the cultural to the natural, and the legal to the religious. I hope thus to demonstrate the ways repatriation processes provide windows into processes of cultural identity formation and living tradition.

Sacred Claims operates at the conjunction of two questions: what objects are in whose hands, and what words are uttered by whom?

In other words, this book investigates who lays claim to what, materially and symbolically. These questions are at once wide-ranging and pointed. So too is the analysis that follows. While at times I sketch issues in broad historical and theoretical terms, the core of this study is at the level of specific words and actions. My attention has been drawn to unexpected enunciations of religious language and perplexing claims to identity that illustrate how repatriation processes often run counter to legal, popular, and academic expectations in a variety of ways. What initially seemed to be a clear situation of native activism vis-à-vis nonnative interests and institutions in the early years of the repatriation movement has become an ambiguous arena of identity contestation unfolding at many levels. This shift remains drastically underanalyzed.

Consider the following episode, which transpired at a federal repatriation meeting on 18 September 2004, before the NAGPRA Review Committee, in Washington, D.C.[4] The Review Committee was hearing testimony regarding the notorious Kawaihae dispute (Forbes Cave), which has since gone to court and may become a test case for the law. The dispute had erupted in February 2000 when a prominent repatriation group, Hui Mālama I Nā Kūpuna 'O Hawai'i Nei (Hui Mālama), received eighty-three priceless ancient Hawaiian objects on loan from the Bernice Pauahi Bishop Museum of Honolulu (the Bishop Museum). Hui Mālama reburied these objects in the cave from which non-Hawaiians had excavated them in the early 1900s, sealing the entrance to the cave with rebar and concrete.[5] Subsequent to the reburial eleven other Native Hawaiian organizations asserted claims upon the objects, several announcing support for Hui Mālama's actions. A number of other groups, led by the Royal Hawaiian Academy of Traditional Arts, declared that they had not been alerted to the "repatriation" per law and demanded that the objects be removed from the cave and that authority regarding their disposition be reconsidered. Subsequently, the Review Committee recommended that the case be revisited. Hui Mālama rejected this advisory decision in July 2004. Thus, at the September meeting of the Review Committee, numerous Native Hawaiian representatives were providing compelling and conflicting testimony to the committee, creating a charged atmosphere. The tenor of the meeting escalated dramatically when, in the course of his introductory *pule* (prayer), Edward Halealoha Ayau of Hui Mālama, his voice rising and trembling, invoked the names of several rivals, including La'akea Suganuma, of the Royal Hawaiian Academy of Traditional Arts, imploring them to "e 'oki" (stop your actions). Tension mounted as

Suganuma responded to Ayau: "Let me say that I am a traditional person. I understand what has been said, and I return any negative thoughts to their sources tenfold."[6]

What renders this episode extraordinary and revealing is that both men are Native Hawaiian cultural experts who were testifying in an effort to gain protection for their *iwi kūpuna* (ancestral human remains) and various cultural objects. Why, then, were they pitted so fiercely against one another that they would invoke formulations suggestive of ancient sorcery (*'ānai*) in a highly visible public and political setting?[7]

This question becomes all the more complex when we consider what happened at the same meeting when a host of Native Hawaiian and non-Hawaiian representatives gave testimony concerning the Interim Guidance Policy of the Bishop Museum. In the spring of 2004, the Bishop Museum had asserted Native Hawaiian organization status, designed to enable Native Hawaiians' standing under NAGPRA. To assert such status is tantamount to claiming native identity for the purposes of the law. This move, if actualized, would have allowed the museum to assert cultural affiliation with objects in its collection and thereby deflect claims upon these objects asserted by other Native Hawaiian organizations. In the context at hand, what is notable is that Native Hawaiians did not form a univocal bloc in reaction to the policy. They spoke from diverse and seemingly polarized positions, invoking strong religious language to condemn and, alternatively, support the museum. Some argued that the museum is an honorable and responsible caretaker of and participant in Hawaiian traditions; others vehemently rejected this stance, casting the museum as the epitome of a colonial institution. After considering numerous presentations, some including poignant moments of ritual drama, the Review Committee was at an impasse, unable to weigh competing claims advanced in the tense idiom of religious accusation.

Much stands behind these episodes—or in front of them, as Native Hawaiians might say—not least the still-unsolved 1994 theft of remains widely held to be those of two ancestral Hawaiian kings (known as the *kā'ai*) from the Bishop Museum and their rumored reburial in the sacred Waipi'o Valley on the Big Island.[8] This event had sent shock waves through the Native Hawaiian community, catalyzing a debate over the status of tradition. Many Native Hawaiians regard their royal heritage—manifest in the *mana* (power/authority) of the bones of their kings and the *mana* of objects their ancestors used to engage gods and spirits—to be the cornerstone of their traditional identity. Disputes over the disposition of royal remains and religious relics are thus disputes over the location of tradition in the present. A number of contemporary Native Hawaiians argue that continued respect for ancestral burials and objects forms the proper link between past and present, even if this requires direct actions like taking objects and sealing caves. Others insist equally vehemently that remains and objects should be cared for and made available to the community through museum stewardship. Both camps agree that the disposition of ancient remains and objects is a religious issue, one that is pivotal for the health of Hawaiian tradition in the present. One can appreciate, then, why the Review Committee was so daunted by the testimony it was hearing.

Such testimony—while bringing the committee to a halt—propels *Sacred Claims*. This is a book focused on a seeming paradox: religious claims, the lifeblood of tradition in action, are the most powerful means by which repatriation processes are enabled and, alternatively, short-circuited. This dynamic, I suggest, often holds true in the cultural lives of modern democracies writ large: religion and tradition appear equally capable of both advancing and damaging group and cultural interests. While this point may seem obvious, illustrating this dynamic and theorizing its significance have for the most part proven elusive to scholars of religion. Here I do not aim to single out moments in repatriation disputes as "good" or "bad," so much as I strive to make clear that repatriation struggles, however one chooses to view their outcomes in political and moral terms, provide energy that enlivens traditions as process. Tradition is not located outside of disputes; it is a means and vehicle for waging them and is itself a product of them.

Places Low and High

My interest in repatriation processes began with objects. Having spent some time in the Four Corners region of the Southwest, I was perplexed by the range of ways nonnative inhabitants of the region made narrative—and often financial—sense out of "Anasazi" ruins and relics, which veritably dot the landscape.[9] I was temporarily living in a rather hardscrabble place, Dove Creek, Colorado, a town of seven hundred or so people, the majority of whom are dry-land bean farmers. Getting to know the habits and habitus of the local people, I was surprised to discover that ancient Anasazi remains hold a prominent place in their cultural imaginary and social practice alike. Pots, stones, and even bones are standard fixtures in many homes, and fields are rich in village sites and funerary mounds. And so I listened to farmers, ranchers, and miners talk as they walked a path linking prehistory to living history. Some narrative turns led to expected stories: of savagery giving way to civilization, of noble ways yielding to culture and cultivation.[10] Other stories related empathy for kindred souls who had farmed a hard land.

A number of farmers told me how they or their parents had plowed pueblos and kivas under in order to make land arable. In a similar mode I was shown places where crews had demolished ruins to make way for roadbeds and train grades. Locals even related that certain counties had utilized ruin sites as a source of rock to crush into road gravel. At a more everyday level, several people described how they or their relatives had "recovered" stones from ruins to use as building materials in their homes and gardens. And at a federal level, an entire valley of Anasazi sites had been flooded in the 1970s by the Department of Reclamation to make a reservoir. While often as not based on circumstantial practicality, these uses are linked by a view of Anasazi objects as raw matter—that is, as devoid of cultural significance.

Yet another historical mode of engaging Anasazi materiality is defined by a reinscription wherein native objects are treated as blank slates upon which European-American stories are written. Stories in this mode are as varied as their tellers' imaginations are lively. Narratives of "discovery" figure prominently here, with the Anasazi being sought—literally and figuratively—as terra incognita and found, over and over, as enchanted and enchanting remains of a world now gone.[11] As an ideological if not logical sequitur to this mythology, museum promoters and popular-press authors have commonly announced narratives of nationalism with vigor. By the late nineteenth century, the Anasazi were being cast as prehistorical embodiments of American exceptionalism at World's Fairs and museums and in the media.[12] In 1893, for example, a large American flag flew atop a faux Anasazi ruin on the midway at the Columbian Exposition.[13] In such narratives the Anasazi are peaceful, progressive agriculturalists of high scientific achievement, robust government, and sophisticated religion. They do not resemble modern Native Americans nearly so much as they do veritable New World Greeks and Romans. This romantic turn has fueled collecting appetites that continue into the present.

Indeed, relic collecting—taking Native American objects to sell on the art market—is a common practice in the region. Usually referred to as "pot-hunting" by critics and practitioners alike, this activity is for the most part legal when the objects are obtained on private land but illegal when they are collected on public land. As it happens, pot-hunting often entails digging in burial sites, as many sought-after objects—pots and figurines, for example—were interred with the dead as grave goods. Many families have a history of this clandestine activity going back several generations, to the time when a father or grandfather gained his skill at finding gravesites by working as a laborer for a nineteenth-century archaeologist.

One pot-hunting story in particular helped shape my research path. After several months knocking around the Four Corners interviewing people, I was fortunate to meet a man regarded by many locals as the most experienced pot-hunter in the region. When I described my interests, he turned to me with a smile and a squint: "You ain't a fed now, are you, Mr. Johnson?" After asking a few questions, he evidently concluded that I represented no threat to his livelihood and invited me to his home. Once there he led me down into his basement, which contained a display case full of rare ceramic effigy vessels. While I struggled to make sense of what I was seeing, he described his family history in the region. The members of his family had all been miners—of precious metals, uranium, and now desert rock. They had also used their tools and skills in Anasazi ruins, literally mining a heritage and minting one too. After a pause in the conversation, he beckoned me toward a door. We walked through a packed storage cellar and into a cavernous room with magnificently thick rock walls. My eyes adjusted to the dim light. As they did, he spoke: "Mr. Johnson, the feds have made me into an outlaw. But at the Apocalypse I will be safe, and these things will all turn to gold, providing for me and mine." It was then that I noticed the plethora of Anasazi objects embedded in the walls.

Two aspects of his announcement jarred against one another in my mind: his claim of persecution by federal authorities and his stunningly alchemical apocalyptic narrative. Past, present, and future seemed notably compressed in his sharp and pointed utterances. I needed to think more about laws, objects, and religious stories. My first order of business was to understand the laws that had made this man into an outlaw. My second task was to grapple with the linkage between law and religious narrative. My questions quickly led me to NAGPRA, which had only recently been passed. Reading the law and its provisions for religious claims shifted and defined my research agenda. To be sure, I remain fascinated by the story of the golden apocalypse and other narratives told by nonnative people in their attempts to describe their relationship to native objects. But reading the law, visiting native communities and representatives, and attending numerous federal meetings devoted to repatriation have further attuned me to the stories and lives of native peoples who seek protection and return of the human and cultural remains of their ancestors. They do not seek remedy in the distant future; they seek it in the present. Like the pot-hunter, they seek it through narrative; unlike the pot-hunter, however, the law is cast to include their narratives. My attention thus quickly turned to where these stories are told, to what audiences, and with what consequences.

Reading NAGPRA, I sensed a rich and complex history behind its protections, including early legal and professional attempts to curb the looting appetite of institutions and the public alike. But as history shows, many proposed remedies were predicated on the very worldview that enabled alienation and desecration in the first place.[14] Namely, they did not reach the threshold requirement of viewing and defending native histories, bones, and objects as being on equal terms with the same from the nonnative world. With the civil rights movement and other related developments in the 1960s, however, native people began to assert more vocally their human and cultural rights.[15] Native students attended law school in greater numbers, giving their communities much-needed leverage in legal environments. By the 1970s Native American voices were influencing policy in Washington, D.C. This was seen most visibly in the American Indian Religious Freedom Act of 1978 (AIRFA), a sweeping piece of legislation that sought to underscore and secure a wide range of native religious rights.[16] Celebration of AIRFA, however, was short-lived: two seminal cases, Smith and Lyng—the first concerning ritual consumption of peyote, the second protection of sacred land from development—demonstrated how easily the legislation could be undercut when confronted with competing government interests.[17] Realizing that AIRFA was too broad and lacked adequate means for implementation, native leaders regrouped in the late 1980s, deciding to promote specific and defensible legislation upon which to build for future battles. They focused, among other issues, on repatriation and graves protection, and this particular campaign resulted in the passage of NAGPRA.

Reflecting on this history, I am struck by how successful native advocates were at persuading politicians and the public of the seriousness and moral gravity of their position. A principal index of this perception is the ways and frequency with which legislators have described repatriation as a religious issue. Indeed, if we follow Susan Harding's account of the function of religious rhetoric, we might

come to the provocative conclusion that these politicians were con-
verted, albeit in limited ways, to Native Americans' religious and
moral perspectives. Harding argues that conversion is better understood as a mode of speaking and acting rather than as a mode of
belief. Specifically, she makes a case that conversion is registered as
a rhetorical capacity when listeners to a religious narrative become
active as speakers of that narrative.[18] In the context at hand, achieving this Herculean task—getting nonnative politicians to speak
their cause—required Native Americans to refashion the means and
meaning of tradition to reach new audiences and address new contexts. To read the history of NAGPRA with an eye for these dynamics is to see tradition in the making through the stretching of social
and narrative boundaries, the incorporation and utterance of new
vocabularies, and dexterous movements between and across identities. In these ways repatriation processes illustrate lived religion for
all to see.

Step into Liquid

This book unfolds as follows. Chapter 1, "Subjects, Stories, and
Strategies," opens with a discussion of my ethnographic experiences
with a key figure in repatriation disputes in Hawai'i. My point is
to suggest how my changing experiences with people involved in
repatriation processes have informed my understanding of lived tradition, while illuminating the awkward but sometimes productive
distances between analytical and normative uses of tradition. The
chapter then shifts to address theoretical concerns directly, attempting to specify the challenges indigenous speakers face as they seek to
make their claims audible and persuasive to nonnative audiences. I
advocate for a process-focused view of religious discourse, emphasizing modes of authentication and tradition in action.

Sacred Claims returns to concrete matters in the second chapter,
"Islands of Practice, Discourses of Permanence," to convey an on-the-
ground sense of repatriation politics. The examples here are drawn
from Hawai'i, an unexpected center of current repatriation discourse
and practice. I develop a theory of discourses of permanence as a
means to analyze the ways various Native Hawaiian activists and
religious practitioners have linked their positions and communities
to the past and all it stands for.

Chapter 3, "Writing the Law, Speaking the Sacred," entails a
close reading of the legislative history of NAGPRA. I argue that
Native Americans articulated a successful religious vocabulary and

rhetorical strategy in the process of consolidating their voice, recruiting allies, and responding to the authority claims (epistemological and moral) of their rivals. By emphasizing tradition-specific identity and authority, Native American representatives established that graves and objects are sacred; by invoking the notion of the sacred with a Western-cadence, they demonstrated to legislators and the public how these things are sacred—namely, they are inviolable and protected by commonly held human rights.

Chapter 4, "Tense Negotiations: Cultural Affiliation and the Limits of Identity," identifies "cultural affiliation" as the axial term of NAGPRA. As stipulated by law, evidence for or against "cultural affiliation" may take any number of forms, ranging from carbon-14 dating to oral history. The law does not offer guidance for how competing claims might be weighed or assessed beyond declaring that "cultural affiliation" may be demonstrated by "a simple preponderance of evidence." Addressing this problematic category and the rich debates it continues to foster, this chapter follows the concept's social life, examining a number of hearings and Review Committee meetings and paying primary attention to Native Americans' strategies for staging creative resistance to roadblocks placed before them by parties whose interests run counter to theirs.

The fifth chapter, "Ancestors before Us: Manifestations and Metaphors of Tradition in a Hawaiian Dispute," takes up a paradigmatic NAGPRA conflict to assess the ways tradition is metaphorically constituted. Pertaining to a rare and valuable wooden statue (ki'i), the dispute investigated here took place between the Roger Williams Museum and two Native Hawaiian organizations, the Office of Hawaiian Affairs and Hui Mālama. The Hawaiians' claims, as the chapter details, were particularly robust in their linkage of aspects of cultural history to present conflicts concerning land issues and sovereignty. I argue that Native Hawaiian claims about the object express the suppleness of tradition in ways that move beyond its mere invention.

Chapter 6, "Religious Voices and Social Borders," explores how NAGPRA-related religious discourse has functioned in the broader social arena. I seek to illuminate how expressions of identity have been recalibrated and refocused in response to the law, showing how such expressions sometimes, and for some purposes, expand and at other times retract. The chapter takes up two cases in particular: Cheyenne disputes over the repatriation of remains from the Sand Creek Massacre and Ute accounts of their relations to Anasazi remains and spirits. My discussion tracks particularly the ways Native

American representatives refocused the content of their religious discourse according to the audience being addressed and the social boundaries being marked.

The seventh chapter, "Dead Reckoning and Living Tradition: Sources of Power and Authority in the Divided Present," returns to contexts introduced earlier—the Kawaihae dispute, which pits numerous Native Hawaiian organizations against one another regarding the disposition of exceptionally rare Hawaiian artifacts; and the Bishop Museum's assertion of Native Hawaiian organization status. The chapter opens by situating the larger issues at stake in these conflicts, suggesting the ways discourse about ancestors, class status, and ritual protocol informs an understanding of tradition in action. The body of the chapter includes a detailed accounting of the Kawaihae conflict, meant to add texture to my assertion that repatriation processes have catalyzed a religious explosion in Hawai'i.

"Repatriation, Tradition, and the Study of Religion," chapter 8, concludes the book with final reflections on the Kawaihae dispute; the status of tradition as discourse and practice, as well as analytical category; and the relevance of repatriation processes for the general study of religion, with particular attention to suggesting guidelines for the study of tradition in action.

Linking the chapters of this book is a methodological approach intended to engage lived tradition as directly as possible. If my treatment of religion is occasionally irreverent, so too is my regard for disciplinary boundaries and the biases regarding sources these often entail. This book argues that lived tradition exists in a wide and surprising range of places and genres. To track its movements, expressions, and changes, I advocate for a path that jaywalks through the intersection of religious studies, anthropology, and cultural studies. In my research for this book, I consulted histories, historical ethnographies, legal archives, and popular media. In the field I attended numerous government meetings and hearings and repatriation workshops and conferences and conducted interviews with museum representatives, government officials, and Native Americans and Hawaiians across a wide spectrum. While I strive to situate each text and context with care and caution, I avowedly reject the assumption that some varieties of textuality and practice ought to count for more and others for less when we study lived tradition.

While my methods for collecting materials are eclectic, however, I strive for consistency in my interpretive approach. Indeed, the principles to which I adhere are the basic foundations of rhetorical analysis. I ask: Who speaks? To whom? With what expectations? With what results? When intentionality is elusive at the level of these questions, I attempt to illuminate the forms of cultural meaning, agency, and subjectivity behind and within expressions of tradition. Thus, my analytical frame shifts repeatedly from attention to individual performances to a focus on broader cultural movements in an effort to portray the fullest possible account of tradition in action.

1

SUBJECTS, STORIES, AND STRATEGIES

One either has the Elgin marbles or one does not, but scarcely any story exists in the absence of competing variants or alternative claims about what really transpired.
                    —Nicholas Thomas, *Entangled Objects*

From Text to Prisoner

THE ETHNOGRAPHIC component of my research has played a formative role in shaping my understanding of the meanings and stakes of tradition and repatriation. In order to convey aspects of my experiences and the insights I have derived from them, I would like to tell a story about my changing relationship with a central figure of this book, Edward Halealoha Ayau, leader of the extraordinarily active repatriation group Hui Mālama. As I write this, Eddie—I call him Eddie or Halealoha depending on the context—has emailed me to pass on some court documents and to complain about the tracking device on his ankle, which a federal judge ordered him to wear as part of his house arrest for contempt of court in the Kawaihae dispute. My relationship with Halealoha grants me perspective on Hawaiian conflicts, repatriation processes as a whole, and indeed on the nature of tradition generally. My realization here is, frankly, a fairly common one: life is defined by change, difference, and the struggle to render continuity and sense from these brute facts. But

contained in this ordinary insight is a link between tradition as lived
and tradition as a category of analysis. Both rely upon mechanisms
for perceiving and conceptualizing novelty in terms of the known.
Both rely on a metaphorical process, as well as a denial of this process (sometimes conscious, other times not) that reckons likeness
into sameness for purposes of stability and persuasion. This insight,
common though it is, is often lost in the study of religion. One clear
reason for this is that the study of religion has traditionally fixated
upon the past. Another reason is the willingness of scholars of religion to privilege insider accounts of traditions, which tend to imagine and construct stabilized pasts. Working in the present, however,
particularly in contexts of explicit struggle, disabuses one of both
of these tendencies. The price of thus relinquishing fixity is buying
into an economy of uncertainty; the benefit of doing so is that one
thereby gains a view of tradition in action.

Tradition in action, however, is lived by real-world people with
agendas, connections, faults, and feelings. So making the methodological choice to adopt a presentist focus does not relieve one of
analytical and moral conundrums. In some respects these grow. How
does one choose to engage the objects of one's research as human
subjects and as human beings? What are the analytical costs of drawing close to those whom one studies? What about cases like those
considered here, where the actions of the people one is studying are
also under the scrutiny of others, including courts? And what about
cases where research compels one to write about people in ways
they would not enjoin? These are all now-classic ethnographic questions that have been addressed in a range of ways since the 1980s,
chiefly in anthropological literature.[1] Too often, however, such questions are dismissed as self-referential indulgences. Such a position
commits the fallacy of assuming that our methodological choices
somehow stand apart from our analyses and findings. Anyone who
has conducted work "on the ground" knows this is not the case. On
the contrary, the choices we make shape the conclusions we reach.
This, again, may sound basic, but the ramifications of this reality are
not addressed often enough in the study of religion.[2] My interactions
with Eddie, however, have forced me to sift through such issues.

I first came to know Eddie Ayau as a name that appeared in the
legislative history of NAGPRA with some regularity. I knew him
through text. Then I witnessed him in the context of the ki'i dispute
as a powerful voice and presence (see chapter 5). I knew him through
performance. On my first research trip to Hawai'i, others spoke of
him frequently, some with admiration, others with disdain. I knew

him through reputation. Later in the same trip, he agreed to meet with me to discuss my research interests. I flew to his home island of Moloka‘i, and we had a conversation of several hours that weaved in many directions. He was taken aback, I think, to see a nonnative person interested in repatriation issues and was even more surprised to learn that I had followed the repatriation activities of Hui Mālama in considerable detail. He introduced me to various people and had his sister show me the Kalaina Wāwae footprints (see chapter 2). With this meeting matters had become more complex. I knew Eddie as a person. He was now an informant, a conversation partner, even a friend.

At about this time, in the summer of 2003, the Kawaihae conflict was boiling over in Review Committee meetings and in the press. It was becoming increasingly clear that Hui Mālama did not enjoy universal support. In the summer of 2004, then, I returned to Hawai‘i. I interviewed a number of the Kawaihae claimants and heard firsthand claims against Hui Mālama. Some accused Eddie of everything from inventing tradition to bullying and theft. Others represented him as nothing short of a saint who appeared ready to martyr himself in defense of the *kūpuna* (ancestors). My perspective on Eddie was becoming increasingly refracted, multiple, rich, and confusing.

That same summer I visited Eddie on Moloka‘i again, and he shared a number of documents and stories with me. We discussed NAGPRA issues in ways ranging from the practical to the highly theoretical. From his nice but humble home, I gained a sense that claims about him trafficking in artifacts were likely unfounded. From discussions about his religious commitments, I concluded that such trafficking accusations were almost certainly false. That same day we enjoyed and survived an epic spear-fishing expedition together, and he joked about his relief that Hui Mālama wouldn't have to conduct its first repatriation of a white guy. I knew Eddie as a partner in adventure.

At the end of this trip, I invited Eddie and two other members of Hui Mālama to visit me that fall. I was then teaching at Franklin and Marshall College, a liberal arts institution in southeastern Pennsylvania that sponsored Eddie and his colleagues to give a presentation describing repatriation law and their efforts under it. Now I knew Eddie by way of institutional and financial ties, as well as through growing personal experience.

On the same trip, in September 2004, I accompanied Eddie and his colleagues to Washington, D.C., for the twenty-seventh NAGPRA Review Committee meeting, mentioned at the beginning of this book. Both the Bishop Museum's Native Hawaiian organization status and the Kawaihae dispute were on the agenda, so I knew matters would be intense. I stayed with Eddie and his colleagues and accompanied them to the meetings. While I made a point of connecting with other Hawaiians at the meeting, it became clear to me that I was perceived by some as being affiliated with Hui Mālama. This impression was potentially enhanced when I spoke on the record against the Bishop Museum's proposed policy during the public-forum portion of the meeting. For my part, I spoke not as an ally of Hui Mālama but as a scholar and citizen who objected to the museum's position on legal and moral grounds.

A few months later an article based on my 2003 research appeared in the journal *History of Religions,* describing the Kawaihae situation up to that point and characterizing Hui Mālama as culturally sincere but aggressive. Now I knew Eddie through the awkward gap between some people's perception that I was an advocate for Hui Mālama and the nature of my published analysis of the group. Aside from the occasional email, a year went by without much contact from Eddie or other members of Hui Mālama. I was immersed in a move and in teaching and, quite frankly, was trying to sort out how best to approach and write about the increasingly contentious Kawaihae situation.

In November 2005 I met up with Eddie at the thirtieth NAGPRA Review Committee meeting in Albuquerque, where he argued for a reconsideration of the committee's previous finding that the Kawaihae objects should be returned to the Bishop Museum so that repatriation processes could be restarted. He immediately provided me with written versions of his testimony and a variety of other documents. A month later Eddie was incarcerated on the order of a federal judge for his refusal to disclose the location of the Kawaihae artifacts. Now I knew Eddie as a prisoner.

Today he keeps me abreast of developments when he can. I know him as a complex and changing person who is embattled, persistent, and immensely capable of transforming the latent energy of cultural symbolism into potent speech acts and drama.

The point of recounting my relationship with Eddie is not to suggest that he is the singular living embodiment of tradition and that getting to know him has afforded me a privileged understanding of it. Quite in another direction, I wish to convey that Eddie is one person among many whose actions in the present are contributing to a process of cultural foment. This process—not some imputed product, whether material or ideological—is what I describe as tradition in action. Ethnographically, engaging Eddie has enabled to me see more clearly how tradition resides in and in between human beings, not at some remove from them. So it is that I must interpret unfolding events in light of my experiences, simultaneously appreciative of the insights they afford me and cautious about the certainties they do not.

For all that I regard Eddie as a participant in tradition from my analytical perspective, I must likewise make sense of the normative positions of members of his own community when they assert that he is anathema to tradition. This disjuncture—between analytical frames and normative claims—continues to place stumbling blocks in my path as I strive to express a view of tradition across academic and cultural divides. My predicament here is one shared by all scholarly pursuits that employ analytical terms that are also "native" categories (e.g., religion, culture, society, and race). Indeed, most work in religious studies and anthropology shares in this quandary, whether or not scholars perceive and appreciate this fact. In order to address this tension, one option would be to recast my analytical language, reserving the term *tradition* for uses that refer only to insiders' normative enunciations. Other terms (e.g., *articulation*) hold out promise for greater analytical precision, and I use them to this end in some contexts. However, I am convinced that grappling with the disjuncture between uses of the term *tradition* is a worthwhile endeavor. If scholars sever ties of shared language with the communities we study, then we will truly be left talking to ourselves. The richest conversations are those in which community members, politicians, lawyers, museums, and scholars talk and argue over terms and the traditions that invigorate them, as in the disputes followed in this book.

Dispossession

Turning to theorizing the language of repatriation, we must acknowledge the full weight of a history of dispossession. Rather than add my own rendition to this history, I appeal to a poem by Sherman Alexie, a Spokane and Coeur D'Alene Indian poet from Welpinit, Washington:

EVOLUTION

Buffalo Bill opens a pawn shop on the reservation
right across the border from the liquor store
and he stays open 24 hours a day, 7 days a week

and the Indians come running in with jewelry
television sets, a VCR, a full-length beaded buckskin outfit
it took Inez Muse 12 years to finish. Buffalo Bill

takes everything the Indians have to offer, keeps it
all catalogued and filed in a storage room. The Indians
pawn their hands, saving their thumbs for last, they pawn

their skeletons, falling endlessly from the skin
and when the last Indian has pawned everything
but his heart, Buffalo Bill takes that for twenty bucks

closes up the pawn shop, paints a new sign over the old
calls his venture THE MUSEUM OF NATIVE AMERICAN CULTURES
charges Indians five bucks a head to enter.[3]

Alexie's voice—its edge, irony, and sentimentality—is that of a postindian warrior, to borrow Gerald Vizenor's provocative phrase.[4] With their words Alexie and other postindian warrior-poets are reclaiming their histories and representational entitlements, using acts of radical repossession to face down a history of dispossession. The movement is not only one of poets; postindian warriors are found elsewhere—in positions of power, in businesses, on reservations, in healing ceremonies, in bars, in Senate hearings. Though not always monolithic in vision or unified in force, these Indians are agitating for the right to be heard, to claim and assert their identities, and to prosper.[5]

Articulating Identities

Perhaps the clearest evidence of postindian warriors' successes may be found in the repatriation movement, which is linked to indigenous movements around the world.[6] From South Africa to South America, from Australia to Norway, indigenous peoples are working with—and sometimes against—museums and other institutions to facilitate the return of indigenous human remains and cultural objects to native hands.[7] Most obviously, repatriation enables native peoples to put their ancestors to rest and regain control over their material cultural heritage. Control over human remains and objects, however, cannot be understood apart from broader processes of indigenous self-representation, especially when viewed against the backdrop of modern liberalism–cum–emergent multiculturalism, which simultaneously shapes the possibilities and the limits of repatriation discourse. One revolutionary aspect of the contemporary repatriation movement is that it establishes conditions of possibility for the (re)articulation of indigenous narratives—these stories are about bones and objects, to be sure, but they are also always about identity in complex and thoroughgoing senses.[8] As Elazar Barkan has recently argued, "Negotiation of [group] identities often takes place through the medium of cultural property, such as art, religious and other artifacts, sacred sites, and even human remains."[9]

Repatriation policies and politics around the world share a common feature: in order to prevail, native representatives must speak forth narratives that persuasively link their selves and their communities to the objects in question.[10] The stories these narratives compose are frequently complex in fascinating and revealing ways. Most notable for our purposes, many repatriation narratives are deeply oppositional in that they mark and remark upon boundaries, differences, and antagonisms. What is more, the oppositional character of repatriation narratives is not always predictable. Exploring this unpredictability sheds light on several arenas, not least the unintended consequences of laws that attempt to settle matters concerning tradition, culture, and religion.[11]

For all that repatriation narratives defy predictability, however, media accounts, for the most part, have been drably formulaic. It is easy and attractive for journalists to reify the terms of repatriation disputes in order to cast such struggles as ones between nonnative institutions and native peoples, each side represented in monolithic and monochromatic terms. Scholars have done much better, but still there is a penchant for taking generalized views of the matter that cannot help but simplify and flatten the featured terrain. Typically, one group's interests (e.g., those of a tribe, a museum, or a cadre of physical anthropologists) are celebrated and endorsed—often implicitly and perhaps subconsciously—with the consequence that points of potential analytical interest are passed over or otherwise submerged.[12]

When repatriation implementation is viewed as narrative process, it becomes clear that it demands of orators something bordering upon the impossible at several interrelated levels.[13] In the most abstract sense, repatriation politics, defined at least in part according to the predilections of majority publics and polities, demand that indigenous orators articulate representations of themselves that are simultaneously premodern (precolonial identity) and high modern (identity announced according to the terms of law). In this respect repatriation politics constitute an especially vivid example of a general representational crisis faced by indigenous peoples world-wide whose legal and political campaigns hinge upon their ability to represent themselves at multiple levels and achieve a range of rhetorical effects.[14]

Indigenous speakers are compelled to present themselves on legal stages as "authentic" subjects/objects who, despite their manifest engagement in political processes, must maintain an appearance of disinterestedness, as signs of "interest" may be viewed by audiences as undercutting claims to authenticity.[15] To state this bind as a formula: natives = nature = neutral (or sacred = authentic = not profaned by engaging in politics). Successful self-narration in this legal context demands of native orators that they master the assets and liabilities of alterity, for it can gain them standing, protections, and entitlements, but it can also work against them if their claims are perceived as strange, inhuman, or otherwise beyond the pale of prevailing social constructs and habits.

At a more concrete level, indigenous representatives face the narrative impasse of articulating their communities' present connections to ancient objects and remains in the face of the objects' absence from the communities. For example, the definition of "sacred objects" under NAGPRA reads as follows: "Sacred objects shall mean specific ceremonial objects which are needed by traditional Native American religious leaders for the practice of traditional Native American religions by their present day adherents."[16] This formulation pushes us to ask: how can an absent object be central and essential to a tradition without the tradition ending or changing? With a view to the rhetorical demands such a conundrum establishes, one begins to appreciate the narrative challenge faced by native orators.

The weight of narrative expectation under NAGPRA is symptomatic of a tension in modern nation-state jurisprudence and constitutionalism with reference to nondominant subjects. Repatriation laws like NAGPRA cut against the grain of modern liberalism in two significant ways: first, their primary concern is with ethnic groups rather than with states or individuals; and second, in principle they affirm rather than reject the role of religion (and tradition) as a form of evidence. The conjunction of these features gives rise to many questions: When seeking to advance repatriation claims, how do native groups constitute and represent themselves? Who is included, and on what grounds? Who is excluded? How are these boundaries marked? How does religious rhetoric function in this context?

Religion and Authenticity

Seeking to address these questions, we begin to understand the specific ways religious narratives emerge in the context of repatriation claims if we assume that such claims are not different in kind from other sorts of religious discourse.[17] I am not arguing for an essentialized or protective view of religion. Instead, I maintain that it is analytically useful to assume that all religious claims are human and only human, emerging from the present for the purposes of the present, and are therefore ideological in the fullest sense.[18] My aim is not to dismiss religious claims; it is to appreciate the ideological load religious claims must shoulder and give to this task the analytical attention it deserves. Furthermore, my intention is not to suggest that indigenous religious claims are insincere. If we recognize that all religious discourse is human and ideological, then on what grounds can we reject some claims as politically opportunistic while unproblematically celebrating the content of others? This question is crucial, as accusations of fabrication and opportunism are frequently voiced by skeptical parties in response to native claims in the context of NAGPRA.[19]

Clearly, admitting religious claims as a form of evidence was a profoundly problematic move on the part of legislators. But they have done so. Now courts, indigenous representatives, and scholars must attempt to sort out the implications of this move. What will not suffice is equating "constructedness" with inauthenticity and the latter with deception.[20] For scholars especially, engaging in the discourse of authenticity is a poor start, amounting to participating in the very discursive domain we are attempting to analyze. It is far more productive to view religious claims as a kind of speech that must compete with other kinds of speech in the project of persuading audiences how to act. What needs to be specified is the particular quality—the specific rhetorical purchase—of religious speech in the contexts with which we are concerned. If we assume that religious claims are constructed at and as the boundary with the "other" (though not always in a conscious fashion), then we see that religion is productively viewed as the maximum amplification of "tradition"—for here claims to identity harness the persuasive force of claims to transcendent authority. In repatriation contexts this move is of central importance. In codifying this narrative possibility, legislators afforded native representatives the opportunity to challenge nonnative claims with religious claims that are by definition nonfalsifiable. This has given rise to myriad procedural problems of the apples-and-oranges variety. Whose claims should be weighed more heavily, especially as NAGPRA holds that competing—and even mutually exclusive—forms of evidence such as carbon-14 dating and myth shall be held equal? Native representatives have been quick to understand the nature of this impasse. They understand as well that religious speech has a greater range of rhetorical possibilities than Western discourses of science and legalism. Whereas the latter are resolutely literal, religious language is defined by its playfulness; its metaphoric capacities; and, in short, its sheer capacity for narrative innovation.[21]

Tradition and the Political Arena

In a pressing way the political/legal arena has taken on one of "our" old chestnuts: the nature of culture, the traditionalism of tradition. What, we should ask, can we learn when such a debate goes public and has dramatic manifestations and consequences? My intention here is to suggest some observations that might help us begin to chart the course navigated by Native Americans who have worked around and with this tension to assert the meaning of tradition. My analysis builds on what many Native American witnesses have demonstrated: tradition is a resource, a fund of cultural values, energies, and interests that can be invoked and evoked by various authorities to address contemporary and future needs of the people; tradition is registered as a culturally distinct and politically engaged mode of being contemporary.

We can speak of tradition, then, not as a collection of objects on museum shelves but as the spirit of the people who seek to animate these objects in the present. In this way, following Jocelyn Linnekin and Richard Handler, we can say that "tradition is a process of interpretation, attributing meaning in the present through making reference to the past."[22] Specifically, claims to traditional status entail processes of metaphorical interpretation wherein selected and valorized aspects of the past and present are likened to one another. It must be added, however, that the metaphorical aspect of tradition is usually denied or not perceived by insiders to a tradition; literal truth, of course, is the typical status assigned to tradition by insiders.

Another way to advance the point I'm trying to make is to suggest that historicizing traditions entails as a first move that we reframe our study of tradition as the study of representations of traditions.[23] Thus, attention now is focused not on authenticity as a set of objects

or identities; instead, attention is focused on modes of authentication and on authenticators—authenticity and tradition are therefore
understood as processes rather than as products. Building on this
shift in perspective, it is analytically helpful to approach traditions
as rhetorical expressions that, like all forms of rhetoric, seek to be
persuasive.[24] When we cast our efforts in this direction, comparative
insights begin to emerge.

The Coproduction of Authority

Here I wish to direct attention to the legal arena as a site of the
"production" of tradition.[25] Native Americans' use of legal and academic categories is quite real and consequential, signaling one of the
central ways native peoples emerge from their engagements with
modernity to appear, paradoxically, more like their "traditional"
selves. In other words, through acts of legal representation, native
witnesses engage in a creative (even procreative) process. It is incum-
bent upon scholars, then, to recognize the genre of legal/political
representations of tradition, attending to its formal qualities and
its adversarial features in particular.[26] In short, this amounts to a
microhistoricization of the matters at hand, foregrounding specific
issues: Who is seeking what? Against what counterdiscourses do
they advance their position?

No longer passive objects of legal machinations and mystifica-
tions, Native Americans have learned to wield and capitalize upon
resources of the Western legal system: if outcomes still seldom favor
them, they are nonetheless reaching broader audiences in more compelling ways than ever before, adding momentum to ongoing shifts
in popular sentiment regarding the value and place of their cultures.
And perhaps more than anything else, political/legal contexts such
as the legislative history of NAGPRA motivate Native Americans
to remember, research, and articulate their traditions. In this way
defending traditions sustains and invigorates them. Coming full
circle, this momentum has at times had direct legal ramifications.
Laws such as NAGPRA, at least by way of legislative intention if not
always in practice, champion contemporary Native Americans and
explicitly embrace and celebrate "culture," "tradition," and "religion" in ways that often resonate with indigenous interests. In this
way legislators and the processes they enable become coproducers
of native cultural resurgence. It is not merely that they create legal
forums in which cultural disputes can be heard. More radically, legislators, wittingly or not, establish and endorse the grounds from

which myriad revived and revised traditions spring. If not by way of collusion, then at least by way of conjunction, Indians and legislators become coauthors of cultural claims.[27] The result of this process is the construction of a highly formalized authorizing sphere. In short, laws such as NAGPRA offer a template upon which authority can be constructed and enacted, specifying who can speak, at what times, and in what ways so as to be recognized as culturally and legally authoritative.[28] In the chapters that follow, I seek to demonstrate how this process is conducive at times to promoting the speech of some "traditional religious leaders" above rival voices.

2

ISLANDS OF PRACTICE, DISCOURSES OF PERMANENCE

Massive Native Hawaiian men, just standing there. The afternoon before, they had gone to the National Museum of Natural
History of the Smithsonian where all these green boxes are,
and they had made an appointment and very politely asked to
see all their dead relatives. Box after box was brought to them.
When the tables were filled with the boxes, they picked up all
the boxes and said, "We'll be taking them home now." And
they just left. They didn't wait for permission, they didn't wait
for a law, they just left. The next day, when they came and
stood in that hearing room, there wasn't a native person in the
room who didn't know that we owned the world, and that anything that we were going to do was charmed and blessed
and that we would win.

—Suzan Shown Harjo, "American Indian Religious
Freedom Act after Twenty-five Years"

People of the Bone

NOWHERE HAS repatriation law been stretched further and more cre-
atively—perilously close to the breaking point, in some cases—than
in Hawai'i. And nowhere have repatriation issues entered public discourse to the extent that they have in Hawai'i, where discussions of
kuleana (responsibility) for the *kūpuna* (ancestors) and their *moepū*

(grave goods) are common topics in the press and on the street. In the wake of recent repatriation activities, Hawai'i has a new generation of saints, martyrs, heroes, and heretics. Who assigns and receives these designations is, of course, hotly contested and continuously shifting.

It is somewhat surprising, therefore, that observers of NAGPRA-related processes have largely neglected to describe or analyze adequately the fact that Hawai'i is at the forefront of repatriation politics.[1] Consulting NAGPRA-related federal meeting records, one sees immediately how frequently Native Hawaiian representatives register their voices. And even a cursory look at the history of the NAGPRA Review Committee reveals how much of its energy has been devoted to mediating Native Hawaiian disputes. Furthermore, Native Hawaiians have been involved in federal court proceedings more than any other group, beginning with an early test case, *Na Iwi v. Dalton*, wherein fourteen Native Hawaiian claimants sued the U.S. Navy over the removal of human remains from Mōkapu Point, O'ahu. Thefts, untimely deaths, political shakeups, and intense secretism have long been features of this landscape.[2] Ominously, Native Hawaiians are the only group that has had one of their members incarcerated for his repatriation activities.

All of this does not amount to "mere politics." Sometimes in radical ways, other times in practical ways, occasionally with broad-based accord but just as often with sharp discord, NAGPRA is catalyzing religious action across Native Hawaiian communities. This chapter explores several Native Hawaiian examples of NAGPRA-inspired religious action, illustrating how repatriation processes frequently follow unexpected contours that reveal both lines and fractures of group identity and interests.

The Spirit of Aloha

My initiation into Hawaiian repatriation issues was just as stimulating as my epiphany on Mount Ararat, if not as unconventional. Struggling to find contemporary material to inform my teaching, I attended a conference on indigenous sovereignty issues in the mid-1990s. One presentation in particular struck me as powerfully related to themes I had been addressing in class: an impassioned and articulate speech by Kekuni Blaisdell, a soft-spoken research physician by day and a hard-hitting Kanaka Maoli (Native Hawaiian) activist by night. Innocently enough, I approached Kekuni to ask if he would be willing to address my class the next day, which he agreed to do. His presence in my class remains a highlight of my teaching life to date, his style providing a humbling lesson on how to reach students. Afterward, Kekuni gave me his card and told me to contact him if I ever made it to Ka Pae 'Āina (Hawai'i—in this usage the nation, not the state).

I filed his card away. Only a few months later my research revealed how prominent Native Hawaiians had been in the legislative history of NAGPRA. Then, shortly thereafter, I attended a NAGPRA Review Committee meeting that featured a Native Hawaiian dispute. My interest in Hawaiian repatriation by this time was keen, but it was principally limited to archival analysis of legal and political documents. In 2003, however, I was fortunate to spend a summer in Hawai'i conducting research on mounting repatriation disputes. I found Kekuni's card and decided to contact him. To my surprise and delight, he remembered me and invited me to visit his home and sit in on his monthly sovereignty group meetings, which are attended by a fascinating assemblage of activists, religious practitioners, and academics. At the first meeting I described the nature of my interests and my desire to meet and interview Native Hawaiians active in the repatriation movement. I left inspired, holding a list of names and numbers.

Thus began several years of visits to Hawai'i that allowed me to meet and interview many key figures in the repatriation movement. I have been struck most of all by the range of voices I have heard—by the divergence of opinions but the unanimity of passion for the ancestors.[3] My research has given me many pleasurable moments: long sessions of "talking story" with repatriation leaders; visiting Pu'uhonua o Hōnaunau, Pu'u Kohalā, the Waipi'o Valley, and other sacred sites; and a tranquil 'awa ceremony in a hale (traditional house) with grassroots legend Attwood Makanani. I have also, on the other hand, visited the plowed remains of former burial sites and seen Disney-style resort approaches to native heritage.

My most jarring experiences, however, were also my most instructive. At such times I witnessed—often in highly public settings—people I had come to know struggle over the terms of their tradition, a tradition that is, in a seeming paradox, both deeply shared and fiercely contested. I would suggest that what may seem unusual or unfortunate in such circumstances might better be viewed as exemplifying the nitty-gritty of culture and community in action. Because I view such moments as the pulse of cultural and religious life—not the hemorrhaging others might imagine—I am committed to analyzing these episodes as directly as possible. As I draw attention to such instances of cultural conflict, therefore, my analysis may come across at times as distant or harsh. For this reason I wish to make clear at the outset that I have observed nothing but profound (if competing) sincerity on the part of those people I have had the privilege to encounter. Thanks, then, to Uncle Kekuni and others who welcomed me and tolerated the *maha'oi* (nosy) questions of a *haole* academic, I am able to tell the stories that follow.

Indian Law and Polynesian Realities

A word about how Native Hawaiian issues figure into NAGPRA is in order here. Most observers associate NAGPRA with American Indian contexts for very good reasons, not least the title of the law; its emergence from American Indian claims against museums and archaeologists; and such high-profile disputes as those pertaining to Iroquois wampum, Zuni war gods, and Kennewick Man. From its outset, however, NAGPRA was drafted to also include Native Alaskan and Native Hawaiian claims, thus rendering "Native American" a geopolitical category referring to people indigenous to the United States. Many factors warrant this inclusionary aspect of the law. Hawaiian and Alaskan native people suffered colonial and collecting histories very similar to those of American Indians.[4] Moreover, Native Hawaiians function in the Pacific sector of the modern American imaginary much as Indians do, as a tour through the magnificent Bishop Museum in Honolulu will make clear to any visitor familiar with the iconizations of Indians in places like the National Museum of the American Indian. Additionally, contemporary Native Hawaiian and Alaskan communities face many of the issues germane to American Indian communities, including protracted struggles for religious freedoms. For all these groups such issues are linked directly to care for the land, ancestors, and sacred objects. Furthermore, for Native Hawaiians as for American Indians, the repatriation movement is part and parcel of a larger contemporary cultural renaissance. In Hawai'i this renaissance has taken a variety of forms, including a revival of open-ocean sailing; restoration of native lands and sustenance practices; renewed interest in hula, chanting, and Polynesian martial arts; the practice of precontact religious rituals such as the Makahiki ceremony; publicly visible emphasis upon a traditional method of dispute resolution known as *ho'oponopono*; and production of a rich and widely read Native Hawaiian literature.[5]

But nonetheless, for all the ways that contemporary Hawaiian traditions resemble those of American Indian groups, the inclusion of Native Hawaiians in NAGPRA is fraught with difficulties, primarily centering on issues of political and ethnic organizations and how the nation-state relates to them. For one thing, Native Hawaiians are not organized as tribes, and this is the operative category of both NAGPRA and federal Indian law generally.[6] Nor do they enjoy "federally recognized" status as forming a semiautonomous government.[7] While this status derives from several sources in federal Indian law, it ultimately hinges on whether a tribe has a history of treaty making with the government, whether the tribe agrees to be recognized, and whether its recognized status was ever "terminated"—itself a terribly complicated issue. A further complicating matter is that tribes determine their own membership and do so in a wide variety of ways, particularly with regard to blood requirements.[8]

Congress has been debating for several years the merits of the Native Hawaiian Government Reorganization Act (also known as the Akaka bill), which would provide for Native Hawaiians to self-govern and to manage various assets and programs, on the model of the federal government's relationship to Indian tribes. As of the summer of 2006, this bill had failed to move forward in Congress, but its supporters are numerous and vocal, and a reintroduction is widely anticipated. Though far from unanimously supported by Native Hawaiians, such legislation is considered urgent by some, as a litany of recent court rulings has undercut various Native Hawaiian entitlements, including the native-only policies of the Office of Hawaiian Affairs and the Kamehameha Schools (e.g., *Rice v. Cayetano; Doe v. Kamehameha*).[9] If such legislation passes, there will be a much clearer analog between Native Hawaiian and American Indian forms of political organization. Until and unless this happens, however, their differences will continue to hinder implementation of NAGPRA.

Thus, while Congress recognized important commonalities among native peoples across the United States in drafting NAGPRA, the law's mechanisms do not reflect or account for their real differences. Addressed principally and clearly to federally recognized American Indian tribes, the law entails correspondingly vague ways of defining and addressing Native Hawaiian groups. The relevant portion of the statute reads:

(10) "Native Hawaiian" means any individual who is a descendant of the aboriginal people who, prior to 1778, occupied and exercised sovereignty in the area that now constitutes the State of Hawai'i.

(11) "Native Hawaiian organization" means any organization which
(A) serves and represents the interest of Native Hawaiians, (B) has
as a primary and stated purpose the provision of services to Native
Hawaiians, and (C) has expertise in Native Hawaiian Affairs, and shall
include the Office of Hawaiian Affairs and Hui Malama I Na Kupuna
O Hawai'i Nei.[10]

Just who fits this definition, and from whose perspective, is both a
rich matter for analysis and a seriously troubled and troubling issue
on the ground, for Native Hawaiians and the government alike.

Nothing Simple about Concrete Situations

The action described below—at once religious, cultural, and political
—pertains to three examples of what I will call "discursive permanence." Our point of entrance into these examples comes through
stories set in stone and in stone's semantic and modern proxy, concrete. We will begin on Maui, then move to Moloka'i and the Big
Island. The broad proposition to be explored through these examples
is that permanence is not a condition but an aspiration that reveals
cultural priorities.[11] I argue that scholars of religion and repatriation alike may gain new perspectives on their subject matter when
analysis shifts accordingly. In this mode questions about speech
conditions and agency replace ontological ones: Who invokes the
discourse of permanence? To what audiences? For what purposes?
To what symbolic resources do these people appeal in their constructions of permanence? In the repatriation context discourses of
permanence, anchored in enduring symbols of fortitude, have been
pivotal in native efforts to shift the burden of disputes away from the
need to demonstrate historical continuity through the techniques of
Western science. Permanence and battles over it—some entrenched,
others ephemeral—also play a role in entirely more local ways.

GUT INSTINCTS AND CONCRETE ANSWERS

Our first example takes us to Maui, where the Hawaiian grave-
protection movement was catalyzed in the late 1980s. The point
here is twofold. First, I want to illustrate how far the grave-protection
movement has come in the short space of fifteen years. Second, I
wish to describe how some Native Hawaiians, working with seemingly meager traditional resources, have developed exceptionally
concrete solutions to the problem of permanence.

While Native Hawaiians have been at the forefront of repatriation and reburial issues since the late 1980s, they did not emerge on the repatriation scene ex nihilo. Native Hawaiians have strong cultural traditions pertaining to caring for the remains of the dead.[12] Like Native American mortuary traditions, these practices were disrupted by colonization. Missionary pressure in the nineteenth century and development pressure in the twentieth conduced to a double crisis wherein traditional mortuary practices fell into decline and existing burial sites faced desecration. By the 1980s this crisis was acute, especially for traditional Hawaiian religious practitioners, as Hawaiian religion (temple and posttemple) has always been defined by relations to the ancestors.[13] In many respects attracting and manifesting *mana* (power) is the goal of Hawaiian religion. *Mana* is understood to be regulated by deities, many believed to be deified ancestors or ancestral *'aumākua* (spirits).[14] The *'aumākua* must be cared for properly if one hopes to receive *mana* from them, and such care begins with proper mourning and burial rituals. If thus cared for, the *'aumākua* are believed to grow out of the *iwi* (bones) to nurture the *'āina* (land) and the people.[15] As Hui Mālama argued in a written statement before the Senate Committee on Indian Affairs: "Hawaiians are not whole until the ancestors and the living are *lokahi* (united). We live off the nourishment that the bones of our ancestors provide to the land."[16] Conversely, improper burial and desecration of burial sites are believed to disrupt this cycle, with possibly dangerous consequences. Thus, one can begin to appreciate the scope of the potential crisis that loomed in 1986 when the Kapalua Land Company, a subsidiary of the Maui Land and Pineapple Company, obtained governmental approval for the construction of a luxury resort for the Ritz-Carlton Corporation on top of a very large ancestral burial site at Honokahua, on the northwestern side of Maui.[17]

At the time, however, there was no visible repatriation and grave-protection movement in Hawai'i. While Native Hawaiians had long been offended and incensed by developers' tactics regarding burial sites, no groups or laws existed to challenge them. This would change, however, as a result of the conflict at Honokahua, which represented a case of critical mass at the right time and the right place. By *critical mass* I mean several things. First and most significant is the sheer number of remains at Honokahua: more than nine hundred individuals were excavated there. Second, tremendous public attention was focused on the site. Third, as a function of the first two factors, key players involved in the development project altered building plans to avoid further disturbing the burial site.

This change marked a radical departure from the status quo of development and cultural politics in Hawai'i. Various native representatives joined forces in this conflict and, in the process, developed protocols for reburial. Many of the central people involved then moved forward to focus on repatriation and reburial issues, including Dana Naone Hall, a poet and activist for Native Hawaiian and environmental issues. The story of the trajectory of Hall's engagement is one that I would like to tell, as it highlights significant changes of the past twenty years concerning the protection of ancestral remains and the contemporary articulation of Hawaiian religious discourse and practice.

In 1986 grave-protection issues were not of primary concern to Dana Naone Hall.[18] Her energy at the time was, however, devoted to the relationship of the living and the dead. Specifically, she and the group she belonged to, Hui Alanui O Makena, were in the heat of battles concerning public access to shoreline. By law all beaches in Hawai'i are open to the public. In practice, however, developers had abused the law during the building boom on Maui in the 1970s and 1980s. Local people were dissuaded from using choice beaches by developers who provided little or no public parking at their resorts and made physical access to beaches circuitous and generally difficult. For example, they built inland roads that ran well away from the shore. This was the issue that held Dana Naone Hall's attention in 1986. Traditional Hawaiian identity, she argued, was linked directly to the ocean and to beaches. Without this link people's ability to be Hawaiian would be in jeopardy. A system of trails and paths had always connected Hawaiians to the shore.[19] Until the time of resort development, then, Hawaiians could literally walk in the footsteps of their ancestors as they approached the ocean. Hui Alanui O Makena had been formed specifically to address a case wherein this link was being threatened by the development of the Prince Hotel in Makena, Maui. Its efforts were largely successful, the Prince Hotel agreeing to preserve for public access one section of an ancestral trail that bisected the multimillion-dollar property.

After this victory Hall and her husband, Isaac Hall, learned of a proposed hotel on the northwestern shore of Maui that would threaten portions of another ancestral trail: the Ritz-Carlton project at Honokahua. At this time the Halls also learned that the project area included a burial site that had been identified by state archaeologists in the early 1970s and confirmed by the developer's archaeological consultant. Upon investigating the path and site, Dana Naone Hall and several others saw fragmented human skeletal remains on the surface of the dunes at Honokahua. The developers formed a plan for removal and reinterment of the remains in the burial site. However, momentum was building quickly on the native side, as more and more remains were being unearthed daily. As its members became convinced of the need to protect the *kūpuna* (ancestors), Hui Alanui O Makena redirected its energies. In the process it came into contact with longtime activists Leslie Kuloloio and Ron Makaula Dela Cruz, who had had a poignant and pivotal experience at a ceremony at Honokahua on Good Friday 1987. They had gone to Honokahua because Cruz felt strongly that he had to take a *ho'okupu* (offering) to the *kūpuna*. Although he had never done so before, he felt guided by the *kūpuna* to prepare a traditional offering of food (salted fish and taro) and clothing (*tapa* cloth, traditionally used in mortuary rituals). Once on the site the men "ate with the ancestors." After burying their offering in the sand, the men, feeling very relaxed, were facing west toward Moloka'i when they saw a dark cloud traveling toward them. At this moment a big wind behind them startled them. They jumped up to face the dune and began calling out their genealogies. According to Cruz, they then witnessed the appearance of a *kupuna* dressed in a cape and helmet, the traditional garb of the *ali'i* (chiefly or aristocratic class). After a while the men proceeded to walk around the burial site, later reporting their sensation that "the ancestors were watching." Once away from the burial site, they realized it had been raining all around, but not on them. Their experience was so powerful that its recounting enhanced the *hui*'s growing conviction that it must stand by the *kūpuna*.

But protecting the ancestors would prove difficult in many realms. Legally, laws still favored developers, and public sentiment had yet to shift. Culturally, Hall and the *hui* were faced with the unknown: no protocol existed for the task at hand. As she expressed it, activists and religious practitioners pooled their knowledge of mortuary customs, appealing to the *kūpuna* for revelations in order to establish a provisional approach to reinterment. As much as anything, Hall said, this process was one of following their "gut instincts," an idea to which we will return below. Along with Kuloloio, who acted as an onsite cultural monitor, Hall kept a vigil by visiting the site weekly to observe the archaeological excavation and care for the *kūpuna*. "We realized," she said, "that if the kupuna were going to come out against their will and against our will, that we had a duty to stay with them, to comfort them as they were exposed."[20]

As more and more bones were revealed, the public became aware of the magnitude of the burial site. Protests were taking place by

October 1988, and by December more than nine hundred confirmed remains had been found. The protests then moved to the state capitol in Oʻahu and the ʻIolani Palace, gaining tremendous visibility, and the public responded with an outpouring of sympathy for the activists, Governor John Waihee calling for a halt to the development. Under pressure, and at the encouragement of the state and county governments, the project developers decided to change their plans, agreeing to a state subsidy designed to defray costs to the company. Plans for the Ritz-Carlton were then redrawn so that the burial site would remain in place as a cultural site in perpetuity. Thus, walking the path of the *kūpuna,* Dana Naone Hall and her group prevailed against a strong foe; they would ride this momentum into the future.

While a number of Hawaiian reburial and repatriation activists now operate at the federal and state levels, Hall has stayed on Maui, and her engagement with these issues is decidedly local. For example, in 1998, a mere ten years after Honokohua, Hall was no longer staging protests and hoping for action. Now, as a member of the Maui-Lanai Islands Burial Council, she was helping to advise builders on how to proceed in culturally sensitive ways, paying particular attention to preserving the integrity of in situ burials. The particular 1998 project I am interested in here entailed the construction of a road through an area of scattered burials near Wailuku. The council recommended that the road be moved to a path that would affect the fewest burials. This was done, but a number of burials would still be covered by the roadway. With their suggestions to mitigate this situation, Hall and the council managed to propel Hawaiian mortuary customs into the present with precisely engineered detail. First, they directed that beach sand be packed around all of the burials. Second, they instructed the builders to construct a four-inch-thick concrete barrier above the burials. Over this was placed nondegradable utility tape marked with the words "ancestral Hawaiian remains." More sand was then packed over the tape and concrete, and finally the road itself was built. This example of the council's work is not atypical: during the summer of 2006, I attended a council meeting during which a number of cases received similar attention.[21] In several instances the council recommended to developers that they construct various walls, platforms, and plant barriers to protect burials. The level of detail proffered was amazing: at one point the council deliberated over which subvariety of native grass was most appropriate to a specific location. In all cases developer representatives appeared to pay close attention, indicating the degree of respect the council commands.

The burial council's interventions—their technologies of permanence—might best be understood as the products of a telling and elegant contemporary innovation. When I asked Dana Naone Hall how she envisioned protocols for the burial described above (using sand, concrete, and utility tape), she told me it came to her *na'au* (guts) from the *kūpuna;* in other words, it was a "gut feeling." As we have seen, she had expressed the same idea in the Honokahua context. Furthermore, such language is frequently used by other Native Hawaiians involved in repatriation issues. Edward Halealoha Ayau, for example, said the following in the context of one 1990 repatriation: "The inventory list and one of the iwi kupuna, a skull, do not match. Which is wrong? Should we ignore it and just take the iwi home? What if it belongs to an ancestor from another tribe? But our na'au (guts) tell us that this skull is that of a Native Hawaiian."[22] Or consider this description of *na'au* from repatriation leader Pualani Kanahele:

> One of the senses that we utilize is the sense of feeling. We feel from our *na'au*, from our gut. Maybe this starts at birth, maybe it starts before. This sense of feeling is something we must cultivate because it is the pulse that makes us sensitive to the unseen world. It gets us going toward adulthood and leads us, hopefully, to become one with the *'aumakua*. But because we live in this world, somewhere along the way the people eliminate this sense of feeling and become very logical. There is always an explanation for it, but we forget about this fundamental sense called feeling.[23]

According to *Nānā I Ke Kumu*, a widely regarded source of commentary on Hawaiian language and tradition, na'au refers to the "intestines, bowels, gut" and, by association, to emotions, character, and intelligence.[24] However, the authors of *Nānā I Ke Kumu* distinguish between knowledge that comes from the na'au and knowledge that comes by way of the 'aumākua, which they locate in the head.[25] My point here is to suggest that the claims Hall and others make for spiritual revelation by way of na'au represent a relocation of tradition—from a place, time, and organ where it was comparatively codified and protected by a priestly class to a place, time, and organ where it is felt, intuited, and engaged through direct action. The seat of Hawaiian religion, as it were, has shifted from the head—from priestly authorities of days long gone—to the gut of contemporary activists.

In celebrating the dead—reconsecrating them—Native Hawaiians are reclassifying them in a twofold way. First, the dead thus become citizens of the present moment, citizens whose human rights and cultural space are recognized in the present and protected for the future. Second, through ritual attention even commoners, through their bones, are treated like nobility. Thus, Kanaka 'Oiwi (people of the bone, a common self-designation of Hawaiian natives) can stand proudly with their ancestors, facing up to and against the prevailing status quo.

CARVED IN STONE

We were standing on the shore of Moloka'i at Mo'omomi Bay, watching the waves, when a local educator and activist related the following story to me. The stone we were looking at, known as the Kalaina Wāwae, had been carved by a sixteenth-century Hawaiian prophetess, Kuuna. She declared that someday men with clad feet would conquer Hawai'i, taking the land of the native people. To depict her vision, the prophetess carved into the stone the naked imprint of feet, with a set of booted feet, marked by pointed toes and sharp heels, coming from the sea and trampling them.[26] This prophecy was met with incredulity and hostility, and the prophetess was subsequently stoned to death. Several hundred years later Captain Cook arrived, the prophecy was realized and remembered, and the stone became a venerated site. Colonization, as foretold by Kuuna, then gripped the islands. In the nineteenth century the land containing the stones became part of Molokai Ranch, and the hooves of cattle began to destroy the carvings. To preserve the stone, the manager of the ranch cut a section out and sent it to the Bishop Museum. The stone was stored there until the summer of 2003, when it was repatriated to Hui Mālama.[27] With help from the students of a Hawaiian-language and -culture immersion school, the stone was then placed on a newly constructed *heiau* (temple) in the bay on Hawaiian Home Land property, along with interpretive signs and a native garden. It was cemented into place, though reversed from its historical orientation, the pointed boots now facing out to sea.

This story continues to fascinate me, and much might be said about it at this juncture. We might venture into a discussion of Hawaiian prophecy, which has a long tradition on Moloka'i.[28] Certainly, we would want to call attention to the missionary history of the island, which has long been host to a plethora of Christian churches.[29] Another important aspect of this history concerns the "Great Mahele," the land policy of the late nineteenth century that alienated many Native Hawaiians from their land in much the same way as the Dawes Act did American Indians on the mainland.[30] Indeed, Kuuna's prophecy seems to speak directly to this. Also germane is the fact that not everyone agrees that the stone impressions are the result of deliberate human activity. For example, George P. Cooke, the ranch manager who removed a section of the stone for the Bishop Museum, wrote that the markings are remnants of human footprints preserved in sand that subsequently hardened.[31] Finally, we might track the ongoing dispute between Hui Mālama and the Bishop Museum, as the repatriation process itself was far from smooth, and issues with regard to title remain unresolved.[32] This, in part, explains the use of concrete to secure the stone to the *heiau*.

While all of the foregoing merits further attention, I will limit my focus to the symbolic space of Moloka'i as the terrain from which this case of discursive permanence has emerged. In much tourist-focused media today, Moloka'i is celebrated as "the most Hawaiian Island." In some respects this is accurate, though not in the ways marketing gurus intend. Moloka'i has by far the highest percentage of native peoples, native-language speakers, and native landowners of any island.[33] Several historical factors are behind this demographic. First, Moloka'i was regarded in pre-European times as an island of great and potentially dangerous spiritual power and thus was believed to stand apart from the other islands. Second, Moloka'i was subjected to colonial powers and settlement later than most of the other islands. Some early European visitors pronounced it a wasteland, and others were rightfully intimidated by its sea cliffs and the dangerous ocean currents surrounding it. Third, when it was colonized, it became home to the Kalaupapa leper colony, which was founded in 1864 and made famous by the martyrdom of Father Damien.[34] Needless to say, this fact alone kept non-Hawaiian development interests to a minimum. Fourth, the island has relatively few open beach spots of the sort prized by developers. Finally, because the island has remained primarily in native hands, there is now vocal opposition to any attempts at nonnative development, currently expressed as antipathy to proposed visits by cruise ships.

But "the most Hawaiian island" has serious social problems, too. The island lacks significant institutional infrastructure, most of which is administered out of Maui. While not impoverished, the people of Molokaʻi do not have immediate access to basic social services or a diversity of educational resources. While these problems are real enough, however, the people I spoke with tended to emphasize one problem in particular, a problem that is at once a symptom and a cause of violence, sexual abuse, robbery, and apathy. This is the prevalence of crystal methamphetamine, or crystal meth. By all accounts its use is nearly epidemic among some groups of adolescents. Families and police have had little success in curbing the problem. With the abuse of crystal meth, then, the colonial malaise purportedly predicted by Kuuna has reached its nadir.

On Molokaʻi cultural activists, a number of whom live on the island, are now facing the challenge of crystal meth and the erasure of identity it simultaneously represents and enacts. Groups like Hui Mālama are getting youths involved in their projects, hoping to confer to them a sense of responsibility for their history and place, to give them a cultural foundation on which to stand so that they can face forward and participate in the ongoing shaping of Hawaiian identity. It is here that yet another meaning of the prophecy stone can be found: recounting, revising, and reacting to prophecy enables Native Hawaiians to take narrative control of colonial history and assume agency in the unfolding of their lives, symbolized by pointing the booted feet back out to sea. Permanence here thus operates in the form of cultural aspiration. What better to stimulate this than tracks etched in stone?

FACING FUTURES

The Kawaihae dispute, described earlier in the book, is also proving pivotal for NAGPRA-implementation processes and for the contemporary face of Native Hawaiian religion. According to Dana Naone Hall, "Kawaihae is like Honokahua: the ancestors are speaking in the present. The question is, what path will we follow?"[35] I would like to add some details to my account of the Kawaihae dispute, thus shedding additional light on the future-looking component of a discourse of permanence. Unlike the case of the Kalaina Wāwae, the point here is less about the future of Native Hawaiians and Hawaiian identity in monolithic terms and more about the ways a plurality of voices are engaged in an ongoing and sometimes contentious process of articulating Native Hawaiian identities. The Kawaihae dispute has had serious ramifications at a variety of levels: both Hui Mālama and the Bishop Museum have experienced serious leadership crises in the course of the dispute; conflicts of interest have been provoked among and across various Native Hawaiian organizations; and the status and effectiveness of NAGPRA have come under fire from a number of directions. What provoked this crisis?

Recall that bricks, mortar, and rebar did. Using these materials, Hui Mālama fortified its claim to sole authority over a set of eighty-three artifacts that had been "loaned" to them by the Bishop Museum in February 2000. But why should such measures be necessary, and why have they resulted in such strong reactions? At an economic level we can look to the extraordinary rarity of the objects and the price such goods command on the antiquities market, which is in the millions. This alone, however, does not adequately account for the passions the issue has stirred in the Native Hawaiian community. To better understand this context, then, it is important to gain a sense of the symbolic power of the objects and the area around the cave in which they were interred. Indeed, one basic point should be clarified at the outset: the objects, the cave, and the cave's general location are linked in a variety of ways for many Native Hawaiians to Kamehameha the Great and all he stands for, including political prowess, cultural genius, and religious integrity.

Forbes Cave is located near the town of Kawaihae on the Kohala Coast of the Big Island.[36] Just up the coast from the cave are the site of Kamehameha's birthplace and several important religious and historical sites related to his life. Most poignant, very near the cave is one of the most imposing *heiaus* (temples) in Hawai'i, Pu'u Kohalā. Here Kamehameha fulfilled sacrifices and performed other acts that had been prophesied as requisites for his achieving the goal of uniting the islands under one ruler. In a very real sense, this *heiau* is the religious center of the living Hawaiian nation, at least as it is imagined in cultural terms by sovereignty-minded Hawaiians. It should also be noted that the objects in the cave point to Kamehameha's time and possibly to Kamehameha himself.[37] Many Hawaiians regard control of Kamehameha's material heritage as a direct claim upon the inheritance of his symbolic power as well. For these reasons, among others, Native Hawaiians are passionate about the objects' disposition.

After word of Hui Mālama's actions had spread, a number of other Native Hawaiian organizations emerged to announce claims of affiliation with the objects. Initially, three additional groups came forward, then seven, then twelve. But these groups' claims were asserted after the thirty-day grace period stipulated by NAGPRA had passed. The Bishop Museum was then caught in a difficult situation. It recalled the "loan," but Hui Mālama balked. Opting for another

path, the museum declared that the objects had been legally repatriated to Hui Mālama. A number of the other claimants pushed the
matter, insisting that no legal repatriation process had taken place.
These claimants drafted a "Document of Truth and Agreement,"
which was sent to the museum in August 2001.[38] The museum responded that the matter was settled from its perspective. At this
point the claimants requested that the NAGPRA Review Committee evaluate the dispute. The Review Committee agreed, and the
dispute was heard in May 2003.[39] Now the museum conceded that
there had been errors in the repatriation process and expressed an intention to revisit the process in consultation with the thirteen total
claimants.[40] In a finding published on 20 August 2003, the Review
Committee recommended this approach.[41]

Several of the groups claiming affiliation appeared pleased with
this finding. Hui Mālama and its supporters were not. Along with
one member of the Review Committee, Rosita Worl, it argued that
the repatriation process was complete and, according to the statute,
could not be revisited. Edward Halealoha Ayau declared that Hui
Mālama would not return the artifacts.[42] Kunani Nihipali, another
member of the group, echoed Ayau's position with strong and revealing language:

> It is not for us, who live at this time, to decide the fate of these ob-
> jects. The decision was made long ago when the personal articles were
> placed in the cave. As Hawaiians of today, our function is simple: it is
> to see that the initial decision is realized and respected. Let's respect
> the wise practices of our ancestors as we hope that our progeny will
> see the wisdom of our decisions and practices. . . . Maintaining the
> *kuleana* to care for the *iwi* and *moepu* is a profound expression of our
> cultural identity as *Kanaka 'Oiwi.*[43]

The storm of energy sparked by this impasse heated an already
steaming dispute into a tempest of cultural and legal conflict, to
which we will return later in the book (see chapter 7).

For our present purposes some basic observations from this developing story can be distilled regarding discourses of permanence.
Hui Mālama's actions with regard to Kawaihae may be viewed as
an attempt to protect its present dominance of repatriation issues
and identity politics and project it into the future. From the late
1980s, when NAGPRA was debated in Congress, to the present,
Hui Mālama has been at the center of Hawaiian repatriation activities, accumulating tremendous cultural and economic capital in the

process. Now, like some tribes in the Southwest, it occasionally uses its clout and accumulated legal acumen against other groups that assert repatriation claims. Some representatives from other Native Hawaiian organizations feel that Hui Mālama has been inconsistent, sometimes dominating local repatriation and grave-protection issues, sometimes "chasing the limelight" (i.e., pursuing only cases with high media visibility or grant-generating prospects).[44] Others suggest that Hui Mālama has lost sight of the relationship between repatriation concerns and more general processes of cultural rejuvenation, though I would suggest that the Kalaina Wāwae case cuts against this view. More radical critics of Hui Mālama accuse the group of capitulating to the federal government by accepting limited control of repatriation activities in lieu of real agitation for cultural autonomy predicated on political sovereignty in a maximal sense. From this sketch of local responses to Hui Mālama, what should be clear is that repatriation is every bit as complex and contentious at the local level as it is at the level of native engagement with nonnative institutions and states. Such complexities point further to tensions inherent in the relationship of liberal democracies to nondominant groups that must struggle (often with one another) to express identities that match their aspirations in ways that are plausible to legal bodies and, simultaneously, persuasive at the local level.

To defend and fortify itself in this context, Hui Malama has asserted and buttressed its position of strength with rebar and concrete, working from future consequences back to the present, as it were. In the words of Edward Halealoha Ayau: "The efforts of Hui Mālama serve to restore the ancestral foundation in hopes of unifying our people both past and present, to form the walls of the Hawaiian nation. Imua kākou. Forward together!"[45] But this act—of closing off the cave—is also a naturalizing discourse insofar as it quite literally cements the relationship of a specific group to the ancestors and the earth itself. In this way Hui Mālama's words and actions convey a dual message that reveals much about discursive permanence articulated in the construction and patrolling of external as well as internal boundaries. On the one hand, Hui Mālama asserts that all Native Hawaiians, in principle, stand united with symbols of ancestry against the debasing forces of colonial modernity. On the other hand, Hui Mālama has made it abundantly clear that in practice it will be the group that determines, over and against the wishes of other groups, the disposition of ancestors and cultural objects. Politics of repatriation, alas, are not immune to internalized struggle and the prospect of cultural bullying. It does not suffice, however,

for scholars, courts, or the public to reject claims of groups like Hui
Mālama on the grounds that they foment tension and evince political motives. For all that they might plague the Review Committee
and courts, diverse agendas and actions define rather than negate the
presence of "culture."

Naturally There

It is my view that the discourses of permanence we have considered
should be viewed as forms of religious discourse, not merely as staged
performances of religion. These cases are vivid examples of identity
construction that are not different in kind from the sorts of phenomena usually studied by historians of religion. I make this point despite the manifestly political and legal contexts of these cases. The
challenge of my view, then, is to understand these cases by way of
terms and categories employed in the study of religion. To this end
I argue that the Kalaina Wāwae repatriation, the Maui grave-protection cases, and the Kawaihae dispute all exhibit a basic structure of
territorial mythology with the following components: the intersection of past, present, and future in a way that transcends and eclipses
competing histories and historiographies; the intersection of ancestors, the current generation, and future progeny as "the people"; and
the intersection of people with territory (held, desired, or imagined),
so that people and place are forever coextensive. This ideal nexus
must be understood as informed by local cultural concepts and categories, for Native Hawaiians speak of *mana*, not *wakan*. However,
discourses of permanence, while culturally configured in each specific articulation, are also always a product of opposition advanced
against potentially antagonistic others (including internal others)
who assert, as a route to legitimation or conquest, deeper or alternative claims upon genealogies, places, and history itself.

We should view the discourses of permanence I have described as
dynamic components of identity formation rather than as last-ditch
efforts to shore up "the" identity of a people. Here the example of
Kawaihae is germane. One view would entail considering the dispute surrounding Hui Mālama's actions (sealing objects in the cave)
and the subsequent reactions of other native groups as evidence
of the absence of a defined and defining Native Hawaiian culture.
Another view, which I urge, understands the plurality of voices in
this context as constitutive of "culture" itself—a domain of contestation wherein groups work to advance their interests in ways
that sometime intersect with and sometimes oppose the interests of

other groups in the larger context of common history, territory, and self-identification.[46] If we embrace this view, we can generalize from the Hawaiian context to see the ways present disputes over cultural heritage and ethnicity are not divergent or categorically different from processes of identity articulation found through time and across cultures. Colonial contexts and engagement with the apparatuses of nation-states (e.g., NAGPRA) undoubtedly amplify and accelerate the dialectics of identity articulation, as political resources are terribly uneven in such contexts. But this dynamic should not predispose scholars or courts to view claims advanced in such contexts as less "religious" (e.g., as merely opportunistic) than "religious" claims advanced in settings that are not explicitly political or legal. In the next chapter I apply this argument to a quintessentially legal and political context, the legislative history of NAGPRA.

3

WRITING THE LAW, SPEAKING THE SACRED

As we proceeded in the evolution of this bill, one question
popped up quite constantly. That was: is it appropriate for the
Congress of the United States to define the word "sacred"?
— Senator Daniel K. Inouye

Stacks of History and Living Words

I HAD set out with a plan to read the legislative history of NAGPRA,
but I had no idea of the magnitude of this task. Sheet upon sheet
of microfilm revealed the long, rich, and at times perplexing life
story of the bills and debates that would eventuate in NAGPRA. No
mere updating of existing legislation, this was a process replete with
proverbial hair pulling, teeth gnashing, and soul searching for all involved, including politicians, scientists, museum professionals, and
native representatives. Several years of federal meetings and hearings were devoted to deliberation, and hundreds of pages of documents were generated along the way. The result is a grand narrative
with many subplots and fascinating turns.

On my first read through this inspired corpus, two of its qualities
captured my attention. First, it became clear to me that repatriation
was regarded by most of the involved parties as metonymic of the
relationship between the nation-state and native peoples. Repatriation was cast as a raw-nerve issue that simultaneously exposed the
wounds of history and offered prospects for healing them. Lands and

lives would not be restored by repatriation, but many participants argued that dignity and trust could be. At no time in the history of the United States has Congress, which has plenary authority over Native American issues, invested so much energy in crafting legislation intended to rectify past wrongs in ways that do not entail major trade-offs on the part of the people it is designed to serve. As the enormity of this history dawned on me, I began to sense the weight, burden, and promise of repatriation processes and all that they stand for. Concomitantly, I began to appreciate the classic conundrum that faces legal interpreters: the distance—sometimes negligible, occasionally galactic—between the letter and the intent of law.

The second feature of the history that dazzled me was the realization that I had in front of me a veritable archive of contemporary Native American religious speech. Native American involvement in the process was no token affair. Scores of native leaders from across the country—including national figures such as Vine Deloria Jr. but also local elders who had never before been to Washington, D.C.—testified at length as to the significance of repatriation and grave protection for their communities. Over and over again their presentations focused on religion and tradition. Their words were direct, impassioned, and full of tremendous detail. In order to persuade politicians of their positions, these representatives described their cultural worlds in ways that linked past atrocities to present hopes with pathos and conviction. Historical narratives were recounted with texture that would make a champion ethnographer jealous. When pressed by agenda-driven politicians, native representatives frequently launched into impromptu theological discussions, striving like contemporary Black Elks to make their words and worlds ring true in foreign ears. As the legislative history unfolded, these speakers and their audiences grew familiar. They closed some gaps and broadened others. In the process a truly remarkable record of Native American religious perspectives was recorded.

This record is also a public one, a fact that is crucial to the spirit of the analysis that follows. For many understandable reasons research pertaining to indigenous peoples is today increasingly controlled by the people themselves. Tribes routinely review research proposals, seeking to discern ways a project might misrepresent the tribe or otherwise damage its interests. Researchers who pass this vetting process are often asked to modify their work in order to focus upon an issue determined by the tribe. More problematically, many indigenous groups monitor the findings and arguments of researchers and exercise editorial oversight with regard to publications. This is especially the case when religion is involved. Some tribes, including the Hopi, have banned research on their religions and have even requested that teachers refrain from addressing their cultures. As much as my sympathies are with people who have long been abused by the academic arm of colonialism, I believe that rigid control of access to and dissemination of knowledge and perspectives will inevitably lead to increased, not diminished, misunderstandings across cultural worlds. A public archive of religious speech is therefore a wonderful and much-appreciated resource for the work to which I am committed.

Legislative History

The legislative history of NAGPRA began in February 1987, when the Senate Select Committee on Indian Affairs (SSCIA) met for a hearing concerning bill S. 187, the Native American Cultural Preservation Act. The record of the hearing opens with a statement by Senator Daniel Inouye, chairman of the committee. He introduced the bill by saying, "We gather to discuss a proposal which would accommodate the interests of historical preservation and scientific inquiry while responding to concerns of Native Americans regarding their sacred artifacts and skeletal remains."[1]

According to the text of S. 187, it was designed "to provide for the protection of Native American rights for the remains of their dead and sacred artifacts, and for the creation of Native American cultural museums."[2] Here we have the incipient leverage point of Native American advocates: the guiding language that identifies the intent of the legislation springs from human rights discourse, which manifestly pertains to the present even when it refers to the past. Such human rights language becomes even more explicit in the "Findings" section of the bill:

Sec. 2. The Congress finds that—

(1) numerous museums, universities, and government agencies have considerable Native American collections that include artifacts of sacred nature and human skeletal remains that morally should be returned to the families, bands and tribes;

(2) these artifacts and remains are extremely important to Native Americans.[3]

If we take these findings at their face value, the legislation appears to have a moral impetus: specifically, it is meant to relieve a moral burden that is the product of improper possession. We also see a modest but telltale present-tense verb in the second finding: artifacts *are* important. Artifacts matter in the present. This idea was given ample expression by various Native American witnesses at the hearing. Consider, for example, the words of Chief Earl Old Person, chairman and chief of the Blackfeet Tribal Council:

> I think in the early 1950's people were very reluctant—even in the late 1940's—to really practice their Indian way of religion because of the things that had happened to them by the governments, by the people that come and try to keep us from practicing our Indian way of gathering, religious ceremonies. But in the early 1970's I saw where people became very strong, and they came on very strong, in their belief. That is why I believe you see today that they have gone back to wearing their hair long, in braids, and dressing in their native way of life. It shows they want to come back, and they want to retain—they want to bring back and live that life to the best they can, to keep up that ritual, to keep up that religion because our way of life in those days—and hopefully today—we escape to a spirit, hoping they will give us that guidance and a way of life.[4]

As Chief Old Person presented it, the matter here concerns not only the continuity of tradition but also the self-conscious resurgence of it. In this process religious revival is part and parcel of thoroughgoing cultural revitalization.

With more issues before them than they might have anticipated, legislators turned their attention to another group of witnesses, the representatives of various museum and archaeological interests. Matters became less clear as new fronts of contention were opened. In particular, some witnesses challenged simple views of the past, problematizing the relationship of present groups to the remains in question. The issue, as represented by one federal witness, was "deciding on the point at which somebody—a group—had a legitimate cultural interest in the remains in question."[5] Other expressions of resistance were registered as well, reiterated throughout the legislative history. First, there was no need for federal legislation on the issue, as repatriation matters could best be addressed at the local level. Second, repatriation efforts must be weighed against the "scientific" interest in whole, coherent collections. And third, the various remains in question were part of universal human heritage and should not be subjected to the wishes of individual groups.[6]

S. 187 met with challenges on several fronts, not the least of which focused on the breadth of its definitions and the unlikelihood of its feasible implementation. A year and a half passed before the next significant event in the legislative history of NAGPRA, when the SSCIA met on 29 July 1988 for a hearing concerning a revised version of the bill, now entitled the Native American Museum Claims Commission Act. In general, the language of this version of S. 187, as revised by Senator John Melcher, is much tighter than in its previous incarnation, though the intent appears largely unchanged.

At this hearing witnesses for museum and archaeological groups continued to express opposition to the legislation.[7] Senator Melcher, surely frustrated that his revised bill was meeting resistance, became agitated by the Smithsonian's position. He had this exchange with the museum's representative, Undersecretary Dean Anderson:

> MR. ANDERSON. Well, the intent of the legislation, Senator, is something we endorse wholeheartedly.
>
> SENATOR MELCHER. Well, I'm glad to hear that, because that's what Congress has to deal with—what's proper and correct.
>
> I find it distasteful to have the Smithsonian say, on the one hand say we're in favor of it and on the other hand say we don't think it's necessary. The question of whether it's necessary or not is not one for the Smithsonian or some other museum; it's for Congress to decide. There's plenty of evidence that we have reviewed that indicates all too often the tribes are thwarted . . . by the museums, pushed aside by some procedure.
>
> You have 18,000 skeletal remains, I believe, of Native Americans; is that not correct?
>
> MR. ANDERSON. That's correct.
>
> SENATOR MELCHER. Well, I'm glad you're in favor of the intent because I think that's what Congress has to determine in their own judgment, whether or not we're going to follow the same procedure as we would with anybody else.
>
> Surely, Mr. Anderson, if it were your grandparents or great grandparents that were involved, you would feel that your family had some rights to reclaim the remains; would you not?
>
> MR. ANDERSON. Yes, indeed, and we are actively—
>
> SENATOR MELCHER. Thank you.[8]

Apparent here is Senator Melcher's growing conviction regarding the human rights aspect of repatriation, the implicitly universal values upon which his claims are based. Native American representatives took up this position in strikingly persuasive ways, amplifying these sentiments and reflecting them back to legislators in ways that illustrate the joint moral authorship of the emergent legislation.

However, parties antagonistic to the legislation were not prepared to concede the moral ground. Consider the testimony of Cheryl Ann Munson, a Society of American Archaeologists (SAA) representative, who extended opponents' arguments against the legislation in new directions: "Archaeological research provides a voice for peoples and their cultures who would otherwise be silent, yet whose stories enrich our understanding of humanity. Archaeology talks about those peoples who were here before written history or were not interesting to those people writing early accounts."[9] We see in Munson's claim an emergent theme that would become increasingly central to opponents of the legislation: a morally based narrative voice that is intended to respond to the religious cum moral narratives of Native Americans and the legislators who champion them. Munson's written testimony is a classic of this genre. She expresses concern with regard to the future; speaks of national heritage; and, most innovatively, invokes language that echoes the vocabulary of religious-freedom discourse: the role of archaeology is "unique and indispensable" and "essential" to an understanding of the history of the United States.[10]

Nevertheless, following this hearing, the SSCIA prepared a report to the Senate recommending that the bill pass. Written by Senator Inouye, the report suggests that Native American representatives were successful in persuading legislators of their positions. In fact, much of the substance of the report relies upon a document provided by a leading Native American advocacy group, the Native American Rights Fund (NARF).[11] In its report the committee set forth several key legal principles in favor of Native Americans: (1) museums have no legal interest in objects taken without Native American consent; (2) common law demonstrates no ownership interests in human remains; (3) Native Americans have paramount rights to control remains when reasonable identification can be found; (4) oral ("traditional") evidence must be accorded appropriate weight alongside other forms of evidence; and (5) in resolving issues surrounding objects, the burden should rest on the nonnative party to demonstrate "right of possession."[12]

This report met with vigorous rejection by representatives of the SAA, the American Association of Museums (AAM), the Smithsonian Institution, and the American Tribal Art Dealers Association (ATADA), all of which were vocal in communicating their positions to their political representatives. Perceiving the unfavorable climate, the committee decided to pursue a yearlong dialogue on the matter involving central figures from both sides of the dispute. This dialogue resulted in the *Heard Museum Report,* a seminal document that helped determine the fate of future NAGPRA legislation.

The legislative history of NAGPRA resumed on 14 May 1990 with another hearing before the SSCIA. At this juncture it seems that opponents of the legislation initiated a dual strategy of both seeking compromise and battling to gain ground within the terms of the bills. The compromise component was expressed in public statements affirming the human rights sentiment of the legislation; the battling meant challenging its every definition and mechanism. Representative of many groups that had resisted repatriation legislation heretofore, Jerry Rogers, associate director of cultural resources at the National Park Service (NPS), opened the hearing by stating that the Department of the Interior and the NPS wanted to "make it clearer that we are willing to deal with this as a human rights issue."[13] Even as he conceded the human rights impetus of the legislation, however, Rogers stated unequivocally that the departments he represented had considerable anxiety regarding "culturally unidentifiable remains."[14] Indeed, this issue remains a primary stumbling block in the implementation of NAGPRA. The issue's relevance here is that it impinges directly upon "tradition." As we will see later (chapter 4), this category concerns the boundaries drawn around traditions and the kinds of knowledge deemed legitimate when drawing these boundaries. What seems on its face like a credible scientific category—"unidentifiable remains"—is at times instead invoked as a device meant to preclude "oral tradition" as relevant knowledge, to exclude all nonscientific information from speaking to the deep past, thereby limiting the claims of Native Americans to only a shallow span of time.[15] Consider also the testimony of Willard Boyd, president of the Field Museum of Chicago, who spoke favorably of the legislation in general but moved to challenge the category of "cultural patrimony," saying that the term "has a different meaning than we are used to in the museum field and begins to blur into a great number of other objects."[16] At stake here is the taxonomical range of the category; anxiety centers on the mileage Native American claims might gain from nebulous definitions that imply but do not fix boundaries.

Native American representatives were quick to respond with strong statements. Among these the testimony of Walter Echo-Hawk of NARF stands out:

When fundamental human rights are at stake, Congress has never hesitated in the past to enact laws to protect Constitutional rights. Policies, Mr. Chairman, are no substitute for laws when it comes to these matters.

Protective legislation is even more appropriate in this instance in order to carry out Federal trust responsibilities for Indian tribes and dependent Native communities. Congress has never ceded its guardianship over tribes to non-governmental entities when tribal property rights are at issue or when tribal sovereignty over domestic affairs is threatened.[17]

Adding force to Echo-Hawk's point, the next witness, Norbert Hill, executive director of the American Indian Science and Engineering Society (AISES), made the following impassioned plea:

It is strongly urged that these very significant bills be passed to demonstrate that equality of all races exists in the United States and that we, as a nation, will be entering the 21st Century with respect, honesty, and integrity as fundamental truths.

The heart of the Indian people lives in the spirit of the past, the past that wells within our hearts and reminds us of the heritage when our ancestors lived in tribes and were close to the Earth. As related by Chief Joseph of the Nez Perce in the hour of his father's death in 1871: "'My son, never sell the bones of your father. When I am gone, think of your country. You are chief of these people; they look to you to guide them. Always remember that your father never sold this country. You must stop your ears whenever you are asked to sign a treaty selling your home. A few years more, and white men will be all around you. They have their eyes on this land. My son, never forget my dying words. This country holds your father's body. Never sell the bones of your father and your mother.' I told him I would protect his grave and he smiled and passed away to the spirit-land. . . . A man who would not love his father's grave is worse than a wild animal." Thank you very much.[18]

The point to note here is the way human rights discourse shapes possible responses to it.[19] Such claims demand assent if one is to be considered human; conversely, those who do not assent are "wild animals." Casting their claims at this level—insisting upon their universal relevance—was the enabling move of the Native Americans' position. Opponents of such discourse, I submit, are not anti–human rights; rather, they sense the power of such discourse and are reluctant to embrace it on the grounds that to do so would subsequently undermine their ability to wage coherent resistance to the legislation.

Despite the affective power of Native American presentations, however, all was not won. The next group of witnesses also presented firm resistance to the bill, even challenging the view that human rights were at stake. Representatives of the SAA and the AAM continued to try to constrict the range of "sacred objects," "cultural patrimony," and "cultural affiliation." Clearly alarmed about the role of the cultural imagination in the present, these groups were concerned that objects might be newly imagined, that "tradition" might suddenly rupture its institutional bubble. Further, a previously quiet group expressed similar trepidation. Private art collectors and dealers spoke to legislators in the cadenced lingo of a remarkably authoritative kind of speech: the rhetoric of the bottom line. The concern of this contingent, here represented by Sotheby's, was with retroactive "inventions of tradition." They demanded that the legislative definition of "sacred object" be far more limited in order to disallow "subjective" revaluations of objects. This specific concern led them to reject the legislation as a whole.[20]

Matters moved to the House of Representatives on 17 July 1990 for a hearing on three repatriation bills.[21] At this time opponents of the legislation pushed for constraints upon the criteria and breadth of "cultural affiliation" so as to leave "culturally unidentified remains" as a correspondingly larger category.[22] Other pressure against the bills again came from art collectors and dealers. These were among the only groups explicitly to address the issue in constitutional terms, arguing that the bills would lead to violation of the establishment clause of the First Amendment. James Reid, vice president of the ATADA, asked: "Are these materials to be lost to the larger world because they are considered important by a specific group? Is their history not our history, too? And are Native American groups less prone to political abuse than public institutions? Does the history of Native American business ventures suggest that individual tribal entities might better care for the common cultural heritage than the established museum system? And with what broad brush are things painted sacred, and by whom?"[23] Reid concluded by making a comment intended for Native Americans as well as legislators, saying that they must recognize that "the past cannot be rewritten by the present."[24]

WRITING THE LAW, SPEAKING THE SACRED

The next event in the legislative history was Senator Inouye's submission of a report recommending that the bill pass in an amended, substitute form entitled the Native American Graves Protection and Repatriation Act (NAGPRA). A key victory for proponents of the legislation is found in the report's discussion of "cultural affiliation," where the SSCIA addressed a major stumbling block: how to interpret the purported continuity of various traditions. Its statement is revealing, opening an avenue toward the past. Specifically, the report states that Native American claimants need not establish cultural affiliation with "scientific certainty."[25] They need only demonstrate this relationship by a "simple preponderance" of evidence. Most crucial for the ongoing debate surrounding NAGPRA, the report has this to say regarding kinds and standards of acceptable evidence:

> The types of evidence which may be offered to show cultural affiliation may include, but are not limited to, geographical, kinship, biological, archaeological, anthropological, linguistic, oral tradition, or historical evidence or other relevant information or expert opinion. The requirement of continuity between present day Indian tribes and materials from historic or prehistoric Indian tribes is intended to ensure that the claimant has a reasonable connection with the materials. Where human remains and funerary objects are concerned, the Committee is aware that it may be extremely difficult, unfair or even impossible in many instances for claimants to show an absolute continuity from present day Indian tribes to older, prehistoric remains without some reasonable gaps in the historic or prehistoric record. In such instances, a finding of cultural affiliation should be based upon an overall evaluation of the totality of the circumstances and evidence pertaining to the connection between the claimant and the material being claimed and should not be precluded solely because of gaps in the record.[26]

Crucially, tradition here is not assumed to be seamless or preserved in amber. Discontinuities, we are told, should not be taken as necessarily undermining traditional claims. Indeed, the SSCIA language suggests that a modicum of discontinuity is to be expected in repatriation claims—the claims, after all, are pursuing remains that have been missing. Native American representatives had to be pleased with this document, which echoed and affirmed many of their hard-fought positions, even while it made select concessions to the opposition.

A similar report was submitted to the House of Representatives. Regarding the definition of "sacred objects," this report clarifies the committee's intent with regard to the continuingly vexing issue of renewal:

> The definition of "sacred objects" is intended to include both objects needed for ceremonies currently practiced by traditional Native American religious practitioners and objects needed to renew ceremonies that are part of traditional religions. The operative part of the definition is that there must be "present day adherents" in either instance. In addition to ongoing ceremonies, the Committee recognizes that the practice of some ceremonies has been interrupted because of governmental coercion, adverse societal conditions or the loss of certain objects through means beyond the control of the tribe at the time. It is the intent of the Committee to permit traditional Native American religious leaders to obtain such objects as are needed for the renewal of ceremonies that are part of their religions.[27]

In October 1990 NAGPRA was debated in both the House and the Senate.[28] Minor amendments were proposed and generally accepted, and the bill was signed into law by President George H. W. Bush on 16 November 1990.

Traditional Warriors, American Soldiers

We leave off historical narrative at this point to take up a closer analysis of the rhetoric of Native American witnesses at formative moments in these hearings. Native witnesses, in their testimony, sought to persuade the congressional audience of two claims that do not, prima facie, reside comfortably together: first, that speakers have tradition-specific authority; and second, that speakers' claims have universal moral relevance and thereby exact a redressive response from the U.S. government with regard to repatriation. Proponents of the legislation (not necessarily in concert or always consciously) thus developed a persuasive dual rhetorical inflection of tradition that allowed them at turns to resolve, harness, and repress this tension. The first category of claims, centering on speakers' tradition-specific authority, consists of appeals to culturally specific knowledge, heritage, entitlements, and history. I will call such claims, which above all emphasize religious authority, *minority-specific claims*. The second category, hinging on assertions of citizenship, includes much broader, even universalistic claims. I will call these claims, which convey an unmistakable moral appeal, *majority-inclusive claims*.

MINORITY-SPECIFIC CLAIMS

Minority-specific claims serve to establish localized authority.[29] Discourse about the sacred in this key meets a number of expectations (popular and academic) regarding how "natives" might speak: we find here richly textured expressions of identity, the narrating of history according to ancestors and places rather than by time and events, reflections upon the coherence of community as the highest religious value, expressed desires for balance. For all of its "otherness," such speech should not be taken as wholly disinterested remembrances of what was, as nostalgic recounting of "traditional life." On the contrary, this is an oppositional rhetoric, and it casts native cultural and religious authorities over and against Western discourses of authority and their authors. Such speech seeks to establish the highest claim upon a limited but precious resource: the people's heritage (as both material remains and narrative authority).

The classic indication that a speaker is about to orate in this capacity is when he or she addresses the audience in a native (though not always native to the speaker) language.[30] Together with speaking in a native tongue, witnesses at the hearings often chanted or offered brief prayers, gestures that have instantaneous emotional effects and that constitute a formal reconfiguration of the criteria of authority: they did not merely speak *about* their religious authority as witnesses in a hearing; rather, they co-opted the genre of the hearing, temporarily putting its typical constraints at bay, so as to speak *in* authority, to speak religiously.[31] In this same mode speakers often demonstrated and enacted their putative authority by displaying physical emblems, often testifying in regalia and brandishing ritual paraphernalia.[32]

Another indicator that this genre is operative can be seen in the rehearsal of lineages, which establishes relationships to places, ancestors, and the authority vested in these. Reciting lineage is a sine qua non of Native American speech in the public sphere: it allows the speaker to narrate him- or herself into context, into an authoritative position. William Tall Bull of the Northern Cheyenne Tribe, for example, situated his testimony with reference to the heritage of the Dog Soldier Society and his family's multigenerational association with it.[33] Patrick Lefthand described his familial connection to the Jump Dance, a ritual he purports to be fourteen thousand years old.[34] Another classic example can be seen in the opening comments of Michael Haney, repatriation officer of the United East and Southern Tribes: "I am an enrolled member of the Seminole Nation of

Oklahoma, and a member of the Newcomer Band. I am a member of the Alligator clan. It is our clan's responsibility to assist with the preparation of the final resting place of our deceased tribal members. I am familiar with the ethical treatment of the dead of our people and the ceremonies used for burial."[35]

Beyond individual accounts of lineage and associations, tribal representatives frequently presented situating narratives on behalf of their people. Consider, for example, this letter from the Wanapum Indian Tribe to Senator Inouye regarding S. 187:

> From time immemorial we, the Wanapum people (river people), have dealt [sic] and still live, along the Columbia River that stretches from the well above Priest Rapids to the mouth of the Snake River.
>
> Since prehistoric times we have buried our dead along the lands adjacent to the Columbia River, the lower reaches of Crab Creek, the Yakima River and the Snake.
>
> Without our permission, consent or notification our dead have been excavated and their remains taken to distant lands.
>
> *It is our deep spiritual and religious belief that the remains of our ancient ones be returned to the land from which they were taken.*[36]

Another characteristic of minority-specific rhetoric is storytelling. This genre asserts an epistemological and moral authority that purports to spring from sources untarnished by the modern world and its mechanisms for assessing truth. And yet the magic of storytelling is found in the way the stories themselves usually harbor no explicit threat to the outside world; it is the *way* the stories are told, the authority the speaker asserts over his or her audience, that makes the most powerful claim. Well-told stories elicit a kind of assent that is subtle and mild, asking listeners simply to imagine another kind of world. And the very act of listening—which provides a forum and an audience—accords significant authority to the speaker, especially when the forum is a congressional hearing and the audience legislators.[37]

Perhaps the most obvious and persuasive way Native American witnesses established their authority was through rendering accounts of specific traditions and objects (e.g., Zuni war gods, Pawnee and Native Hawaiian mortuary rituals, Haudenosaunee wampum). Consider, for example, William Tall Bull's moving description of the role of the Dog Soldier Pipe in Cheyenne culture:

> I come to you as a member of the Dog Soldiers Society, one of the four warrior societies that guard and protect the covenants and that have

responsibility to make sure that the rituals are carried out from beginning to end, that everyone comes together at the time of the rituals,
that everything is properly in its place, with the fact that the rituals
are exacting, are in sequence, and there are no substitutions.

When a ritual takes place and it is determined that an item is missing, it is a duty of the warrior society to seek out that item. If that
item cannot be present so that the ritual can continue, then the ritual
stops. It has to be determined at this point whether the ritual can continue without this item. If the ritual continues without the item, it
is demoralizing to all people that are present in the camp. This is the
situation which we find ourselves in.[38]

From chanting and speaking native languages, to storytelling
and reciting ritual needs, minority-specific discourse was pivotal in
gaining sympathy for repatriation legislation. Such discourse had a
structural effect in this context, entailing the revaluation of key categories by way of transposition. That is, before the NAGPRA debate,
legislators, I assume, valued (at least tacitly) modern, Western claims
to knowledge and authority over putatively "traditional" ones. This
can be schematized as a categorical opposition:

| (−) | (+) |
| Non-Western knowledge | Western knowledge |
and values	and values
Tradition	Science
Myth	History
Orality	Textuality
Inalienable property	Alienable property

After the debate, however, as evinced by the human rights language
of various legislators and expressions of legislative intent to this
effect, these same categories were in place, but their valuation had
been reversed with reference to repatriation. In this way minority-
specific claims were rendered authoritative (or publicly embraced as
authoritative) to a majority audience, if in a limited and politically
defined way.

As effective as they may be at establishing authority and revaluing
structural oppositions, minority-specific claims rely on a strategy of
differentiation and segmentary separation and on an affirmation of
cultural relativity (of some variety) on the part of the auditors. In and
of itself, then, this sort of appeal is incomplete in political terms;

while carving out a niche of authority and place, it risks alienation, misunderstanding, and apathy from a Western audience. An encompassing strategy would instead balance minority-specific assertions with complementary gestures of affiliation with—indeed, inclusion in—broader society. And this is precisely the unexpected inflection many Native American witnesses gave their testimony.

MAJORITY-INCLUSIVE CLAIMS

Majority-inclusive claims open an umbrella, extending localized authority by way of various moral appeals to impugn and make demands upon broader society. These appeals, however, are cast in terms of affiliation and are therefore meant to be perceived as an internal criticism of American society. In this way, shifting from segmentally separated claims of authority to segmentally associated claims of morality, witnesses bridged a daunting divide and mobilized support for their repatriation efforts. Whereas I describe minority-specific claims as operating by means of transposing categorical valuations, I would characterize majority-inclusive claims as achieving categorical revaluations by remarking and remaking boundaries of identity. Here Native American witnesses asserted claims as American citizens, as (at times) Christians, as human beings. Emphasizing their position and status in these terms allowed witnesses to wage critiques of the majority in the majority's terms, to speak, ultimately, of repatriation as a matter of human rights.

To make their case persuasive, Native Americans first had to elaborate upon putatively universal values regarding the dead before they could demonstrate that American government and society have historically and continually violated this "truth." NARF's attorneys led this charge, making repeated arguments concerning the universal sacredness of the dead and linking this to their assertion that common law historically has found no property interest in the dead.[39] Beyond NARF's quite academic argument, other witnesses expressed the same basic idea. Norbert Hill, of the AISES, phrased the matter in this way: "The reburial and repatriation issues are simple questions of humanity and morality, of reconciling Western scientific ideology and Indian spirituality, and of religious freedom. Based on this the AISES feels that the dead of all races and nations are entitled to protection from arbitrary disturbances and treatment which is offensive to the rights and sensibilities of living communities. All graves and cemeteries should be regarded with a strong presumption of inviolability."[40]

Other witnesses developed this line of presentation specifically to address Christianity, arguing, in effect, that Christian and universal values are in agreement with regard to treatment of the dead. In this way universal, Christian, and national values were represented as homogenous in principle, though national values were described as being the most prone to historical corruption. Thus, if the nation was demonstrated to have fallen short of universal values, it had likewise violated foundational religious principles. Edward Lone Fight of the National Congress of American Indians expressed this sentiment in the following terms: "In a Christian nation that reveres the sacredness of death and the rituals that surround the end of life, it is a sad commentary on how we, as a people, continue to be viewed in our own land."[41] Here, and in the following statement by William Tall Bull, we see sharp critical force achieved by witnesses reflexively wielding Christian imagery:

> In the only terms that the majority of this country may be able to understand, from the standpoint of antiquity, we refer you to the Bible, the First Book of Samuel, Chapter 4, verses 1–22: "And she said, 'the glory has departed from Israel, for the Ark of God had been recaptured.'" The loss of the Covenant of the Ark resulted in the slaughter of 3,000 Israeli soldiers, so greatly were they demoralized. . . . When medicine bundles and graves are desecrated and objects used in rituals and ceremonies are missing, to that extent the tribe is severely weakened and demoralized. . . .
>
> In extolling the virtues of some religious practices, we hear one persistent theme: "the family that prays together stays together." How can the extended families of the Cheyenne stay together for lasting mutual benefit and progress until those objects which we used to pray with are returned to us?[42]

Having presented an account of purportedly universal—and Christian—values regarding the dead and the sacred, witnesses next looked to the national context in order to point out the country's relative failings. But before witnesses could criticize the values of the nation as insiders, they needed to establish their insider status. Here, of course, they spoke in the discourse of citizenship:

> There is a situation in this country where we practice, I believe, among the American people—a belief that we have as our honor system. Over across the river, in Arlington, we pay great respect and tribute to missing soldiers, to people who have served the country in one way or

another, and there is a lot of respect and honor bestowed on the dead.
We would like to see a commission where the honor can be shared and
enjoyed by all peoples. We practice such things as saluting the flag; we
pledge allegiance, we do a number of things that express honor, and we
would like to have that honor shared so that all people can enjoy it in
their own respective manners.[43]

Further, witnesses demonstrated not merely that Indians are citizens but that they include the most dedicated kind of citizen, soldiers. Testimony regarding the history of Native American participation in the U.S. military and its engagements worldwide cemented witnesses' claims to inclusion in American society. In effect, they said: we have proved our affiliation with you by fighting your wars, being at your side in battles, pursuing freedom and human dignity with you, dying with you. Consider, for example, this description of the Pawnee Scouts, which was a central component of NARF's testimony:

> By most accounts, Pawnee Scouts provided an invaluable service to the
> American people. While serving in uniform under white officers, the
> Scouts performed vital military assignments with dignity, honor, and
> heroism, paving the way for white settlement in the Great Plains. . . .
>
> The Scouts established a tradition of military service that is carried
> on today. Hundreds of Pawnee men and women have followed in the
> footsteps of their ancestors by serving in the armed forced during the
> nation's times of need. . . .
>
> Five died while in combat during World War II. . . .
>
> During these wars, Pawnee servicemen received numerous combat
> awards, including purple hearts, bronze stars, and distinguished service medals.[44]

To invoke military-related sentiments was to call upon a variety of claims nearly as unassailable as religious ones. Museums and scientists, in contrast, could not thus speak to American honor, pride, and duty.

Once they had established their affiliation with and commitment to the United States as soldiers, Native American representatives were in a position to wage their criticisms of the society in earnest. They were prepared to call in debts owed them by the United States, to press their soldierly status one notch further. Their claim, then, was that if soldiers express the highest honor that can be given to a country, then the highest honor a country can bestow on a soldier is proper and dignified burial. Conversely, the most disturbing indignity, to both the individual soldier and the national conscience, is to let a body remain "missing in action" (MIA). Their rhetoric was thus turned home with a profound conclusion by way of analogy: Native American remains are MIA. Consider the moving testimony of Arlouine Gay Kingman, executive director of the National Congress of American Indians: "This past week we learned that the government of Kampuchea, known previously as Cambodia, has offered the United States passage into their country to search for remains of brave servicemen who lost their lives there during the Viet Nam era. Our nation will accept that offer, and at great expense we will seek those remains for return to their grateful homeland. The grieving relatives of those MIAs must surely understand and appreciate how we Native Americans feel about the repatriation of the remains of our ancestors."[45] This argument is persuasive because it entails a proposition wherein assent to the most broad positive value— human rights—becomes assent to the specific cause in question. In effect, the rhetorical question is the one so famously posed by Chief Joseph: are you human?

Naturalized Citizens

In the context of NAGPRA's legislative history, Native American representatives persuasively legitimated their specific authority and, thus, the basis for their claims upon human and cultural remains, while simultaneously invoking affiliation with broader American society in religious, moral, and civic terms. Emphasis upon tribal religious authority and cultural identity established *that* Indian graves and objects are sacred; invoking the notion of the sacred with a Western cadence demonstrated to legislators and the public *how* these things are sacred: they are inviolable, protected by commonly held human rights. And though the moral and religious discourse of American society was adopted at times, this serves to highlight not Native Americans' acquiescence to a kind of colonialism but their persistent agency in seeking political, cultural, and religious autonomy. As we have seen, then, it is in part Native Americans' ability to traffic in sacred Western images that has come to serve as an antidote to Western trafficking in theirs.

In this way NAGPRA's legislative history illuminates broad theoretical issues concerning tradition, authority, and identity. In a recent work on social poetics, Michael Herzfeld argues that "ultimately, the language of national or ethnic identity is indeed a language of morality. It is an encoded discourse about inclusion and exclusion."[46] Furthermore, Herzfeld insists, we should not imagine social boundaries to be fixed or stable. They can and do shift, expand, collapse, or otherwise reconfigure themselves with surprising frequency and suppleness, particularly in contexts of dispute.[47] In order to avoid lapsing into another kind of essentialism, then, we should resist reifying any single line of dispute (e.g., Indianness v. Americanness) as a definitive boundary. As we have seen, even settings that appear oppositional or unified in stark terms may well involve multiple possible lines along which antagonisms and allegiances can be expressed. Another way to state this is to acknowledge that boundary-marking discourses may well have typical patterns, but patterns, however recurrently imprinted, should not be taken as the "natural" form of social realities. In other words, marking in and marking out are never simple acts of reproducing "tradition." Similarly, we should reject the impulse to assign or accept singular imputations of identity, whether couched in terms of tradition, religion, or ethnicity. As our analysis of NAGPRA-related rhetoric demonstrates, Native Americans inhabit multiple identities and are able to enact these in multiple fields simultaneously. Most specifically, Indian representatives have successfully reconfigured "traditional" boundaries through their uses of minority-specific and majority-inclusive authority in order to embrace and challenge "Americanness." They have done so precisely because they are Dog Soldiers who fight American wars; they are Indians and citizens who can speak within, between, and against two worlds as inhabitants of both.

4

TENSE NEGOTIATIONS
CULTURAL AFFILIATION AND THE LIMITS
OF IDENTITY

> A traditional religious leader from the Cheyenne River Sioux
> Tribe states that the eleven pipes, six pipe bags, two pipe
> tampers, four rattles, two eagle bone whistles, and one webbed
> shield spoke to him and asked to be brought back to the Lakota
> Nation.
> —*Federal Register*, 4 March 1997

ON ITS FACE quite a simple thing, cultural affiliation seems to be a
commonsense way to state and demonstrate relationships of the living to the dead, of things to their rightful owners. As with so much
surrounding NAGPRA, however, cultural affiliation is a category
that is astoundingly vague in practice and equivocally embraced
by competing interests. Because it is the mechanism of NAGPRA
that, in the absence of claims by lineal descendants, enables groups'
standing to speak for bones and objects, cultural affiliation is the
law's axial term. Claims to cultural affiliation assert identity and
may be announced over and against rival claims emerging from
within the same group, from other native groups, from institutions,
or from legal rulings. It is fair to say that the life history of NAGPRA
has depended and will continue to depend on how various audiences
read and react to this vexing term.

Following the story of cultural affiliation from its earliest appearance in repatriation discourse to the present, it is clear that the

concept has functioned much like a Trojan horse. Various parties have sought to co-opt the term and construct it to their advantage, loading it with unseen rhetorical warriors, each believing that it has been appropriated by opposing groups and is being wielded surreptitiously to undermine their interests. This is a classic rhetorical contest with all the trappings of an epic: battles won and lost, revealing side skirmishes, abandoned fronts, surprise attacks, and the marshalling of spiritual forces. This chapter will investigate this struggle.[1]

Legislative History

As we saw in the last chapter, the legislative history of NAGPRA began in 1987 with the Senate's consideration of S. 187, the Native American Cultural Preservation Act. This bill itself contains no discussion of "culturally unidentifiable human remains," the category against which "cultural affiliation" obtains its paramount relevance in the law. It would be a few years before this terminology, and the categorical distinction it signifies, would become an explicit point of legislative consideration. Indeed, even "cultural affiliation" appears as an undefined and therefore implicitly self-evident term in the bill.[2]

While legislators may not have foreseen the ramifications and complications involved with determining cultural affiliation, representatives of Native American groups and scientific institutions were quick to focus upon the term, seeking to direct its usage in ways that would advance their respective interests. Incipient lines of the ensuing rhetorical battle were drawn at the Senate hearing regarding the bill. Since "cultural affiliation" was not defined in the bill, the term itself was not so much at issue at this point. Rather, its conceptual load attracted attention, the language in play including discussions of "cultural relationships," "cultural affinities," and "legitimate cultural interests." The latter notion was first invoked by Thomas King of the Cultural Resource Preservation Office of the National Park Service: "As I read the bill, it would apply at least to any remains to which an Indian tribe could make a plausible claim of cultural ancestry or descent. . . . What really gets tricky for most archaeologists is deciding on the point at which somebody has—a group has—legitimate cultural interest in the remains in question."[3] Setting aside for the moment the nagging question of plausibility, here we see that cultural affiliation is implicitly indexed by time depth as a determining criterion. This issue, which emerged at the center of discussions of cultural affiliation, continues to be problematic in the current implementation of the law.

One of the primary "players" in cultural-affiliation issues is the Society for American Archaeology (SAA), an active scientific interest group that has sought to preserve a category of scientifically valuable human remains against repatriation efforts. At the same time it has long supported NAGPRA and has been consistent in seeking ways to render it legally defensible. At this early stage in NAGPRA's legislative history, its strategy was like implementing a controlled burn, wherein a fire is promoted in a designated area precisely to prevent it from erupting elsewhere. The SAA appears to have decided early on, in conjunction with other scientific interest groups, effectively to abandon attempts to retain control over those items perceived to have a high cultural value for Native Americans—and high visibility in national museum collections—namely, historically recent human remains and purportedly sacred objects. Not coincidentally, these same remains and objects have a relatively low scientific value. What are of value to scientists are the Native American skeletal remains that make up the majority of the osteological collections in the United States. The SAA thus affirmed Native American sentiments concerning repatriation of the former category of objects, while simultaneously and strenuously blocking skeletal collections from the repatriation process. Time depth was then promoted as the categorical boundary—the effective fire line.

Consider the testimony of SAA representative Mark Leone: "If it was felt that the vast majority of the remains that were of concern were 100 years old, or there were an age limit on that, that would certainly relieve us a lot. I don't know that it would turn us around with regard to the bill; but as long as the entire population, skeletal population, prehistoric population is not challenged, that's a different matter."[4] While proffering this line of reasoning, the SAA sought also to alert the Senate to potential Native American reactions to their position. Specifically, Leone addressed the issue of kinship assertions: "Among lots of Native American groups, kinship has no limits. It includes lots and lots of people."[5] This position was echoed immediately thereafter by Robert Adams, secretary of the Smithsonian Institution, who declared that "there are Indian groups who sincerely believe that they are a part of a unity with their entire past, and . . . they would certainly seek to press those claims."[6]

As the legislative and implementation course of NAGPRA unfolded, both of these assertions proved true. Various Native American and Hawaiian representatives pursued precisely such claims to eliminate rhetorically the categorical possibility of unaffiliated remains. We will take up the ramifications of and responses to these claims as they emerge, for they reveal much about the power of identity and authority assertions. Here we turn our attention to the immediate response of Native American representatives, specifically to the influential position of the Native American Rights Fund. NARF's strategy, like that of scientific interest groups, was initially to exert pressure on the concept of cultural affiliation, though it sought to push the boundaries in the opposite direction by way of a legally couched argument wherein it claimed that skeletal collections are neither "archaeological resources" nor "property of the federal government." Rather, as we saw in the previous chapter, NARF argued that these remains are *human* remains and must be treated in accordance with universal principles regarding treatment of the dead. This argument took the provocative path of invoking property rights: "We firmly believe that where cultural affinity can be demonstrated, a tribe or tribal group has property rights in human remains and associated grave goods superior in the law to the asserted property rights of either federal government or public or private institutions."[7] This basic premise was subsequently embraced by legislators, fueling political winds that would threaten to blow the controlled burn in unpredicted directions.

The next development in NAGPRA's legislative history was the 1988 proposal of a revised S. 187 bill, now entitled the Native American Museum Claims Commission Act. Here "cultural affiliation" was still undefined, though the bill was more sophisticated with regard to the complexity of issues at stake. The testimony of the representatives of various scientific groups at the Senate hearing concerning the bill suggests that they were willing to compromise on "historical" remains but were becoming increasingly defensive of their "scientific right" to control the disposition of skeletal remains. Meanwhile, NARF kept up its push for the rhetorical upper hand, recasting the struggle as one over basic principles of epistemology, lobbying for the inclusion of nonscientific forms of evidence in the process of rendering determinations under the proposed law: "As an evidentiary matter, appropriate weight must be given to tribal oral traditions, and to traditional law, custom or practice, and to applicable traditional Native religious cultural practices or beliefs, regarding relevant ownership, burial and mortuary, and descent and distribution issues, where such a body of traditions, laws, customs or practices controlled at the time the sacred object left native hands or was interred by Native next of kin."[8] NARF also asked that the burden of proof in resolving ownership issues rest upon non-Indian parties. Manifestly, NARF's lobbying was effective, as the Senate report on the bill included its position statements almost verbatim.[9]

The next event in the legislative history was the presentation of the penultimate generation of NAGPRA bills, S. 1021 and S. 1980. S. 1021 established cultural affiliation in ways that directly impinge upon the realm of "prehistoric" remains:

> Sec. 5.(b) Any skeletal remains and grave goods of a Native American for whom the heirs cannot be ascertained, and any sacred ceremonial objects, that are found on Federal or tribal land shall be considered to be owned by the Indian tribe—
>
> (1) which has jurisdiction over the reservation on which such items were discovered,
>
> (2) which aboriginally occupied the area from which such items were discovered,
>
> (3) in the case of remains and grave goods, of which the Native American was a member,
>
> (4) in the case of grave goods or sacred ceremonial objects, from which such grave goods or object originated, or
>
> (5) which can show cultural affiliation with such items.[10]

Here, in effect, cultural affiliation presents an avenue that allows Native American claimants to bridge the gap between history and prehistory, between traceable lineal descent and claims of cultural relationship. The space afforded by this gap, as we will see, became the locus of Native American mobilizations of tradition in the present.

The hearing concerning S. 1021 and S. 1980 was pivotal. Here we find specific development of the notion of "culturally unidentifiable human remains," the categorical negative of "culturally affiliated remains." The American Association of Museums (AAM) registered its voice and in doing so aligned itself with the SAA, specifying its frustration with the concept of cultural affiliation.[11] Moreover, the AAM expressed support in its written statement for the more rigorous standard of "blood relative" in place of "cultural affiliation" for claims upon human remains and associated funerary items. The SAA was again present at the hearing, this time represented by its president, Keith Kintigh, a professor of anthropology at Arizona State University. He celebrated the idea of repatriation, at least with regard to historical objects, commending the Senate for its bold actions. However, with reference to S. 1021, Kintigh had strong words regarding the bill's effective collapsing of the category of culturally unidentifiable remains: "The Society for American Archaeology's most strenuous objection to the current draft relates to finding 2(b)(4) and its implementation in Sec 6(a)(3)(D). While we accept the need to provide for return, on request, of culturally affiliated remains, we do not believe that it is appropriate to dictate the return of all culturally unidentifiable remains."[12] Kintigh offered up an alternative rhetoric, invoking the discourse of universal human heritage: "Turning over such remains of any group would be, in our view, an unwarranted destruction of our human heritage."[13]

The SAA's attempt to defend the notion of "culturally unidentifiable remains" was seriously challenged by the findings of the Heard Dialogue Panel. Its report was summarized for the Senate, Heard representatives stating that the panel supported the reburial of all Native American human remains, including culturally unidentifiable human remains.[14] However, the panel was not unanimous in its findings, and the dissenting voice is revealing in its alignment with the principles of the SAA and the AAM. A document drafted by dissenting members, all Smithsonian-affiliated scientists, reads:

> In our opinion, although the Panel's majority indicated their desire to request reburial of unaffiliated remains, we do not believe that this issue was adequately examined and considered. We note that the three dissenting members of the Panel on this portion of the National Dialogue report were the only members with extensive experience in working with human remains and the problem of affiliation.
>
> There are many portions of S. 1980 that are important and will go a long way toward resolving past injustices; the issue of unaffiliated remains needs additional consideration and discussion. We respectfully ask that the portions of S. 1980 that include references to unaffiliated remains be removed from the Bill.[15]

Even as the AAM, the SAA, and the dissenting Heard Panel members sought to constrict the range of cultural affiliation, Native American and Hawaiian representatives at the hearing were set to expand it to ever-greater dimensions. Native Hawaiians would take their place as leaders in this rhetorical charge. In a direct retort to the SAA, they declared that all Hawaiian human remains are familially related and also made an attention-getting claim upon all Polynesian remains: "As Native Hawaiians, we are descended from Southern Polynesian ancestors, many who came from New Zealand, Tahiti, the Marquesas, the Society Islands, and Samoa. They truly are our ancestors and we must care for them. . . . Language could include simple notification of the fact that ancestral remains are in the hands of museums and institutions . . . and are available for repatriation."[16] Various Native American groups offered testimony in a similar key. For example, the Association on American Indian Affairs, Inc., submitted a letter stating that all burials are sacred and all human remains related to the people of the present.[17] Emerging here is the application of religious language to the category of culturally unidentifiable human remains.

The next major event in the legislative history was a hearing before the House Committee on Interior and Insular Affairs on the final round of NAGPRA bills, including H.R. 1381, H.R. 1646, and H.R. 5237. H.R. 5237, its text and the debate surrounding it, is what concerns us here, as this bill most closely embodies the substance and intent of the law. In H.R. 5237 "cultural affiliation" receives an explicit and revealing definition:

> Sec. 2.(2) The term "cultural affiliation" means that there is a reasonable relationship, established by a preponderance of the evidence, between a requesting Indian tribe or Native Hawaiian organization that the Native Americans from which the human remains or other material covered by this Act are derived, regardless of age or antiquity, which can be evidenced or inferred by geographical, kinship, biological, archaeological, anthropological, linguistic, folkloric, oral tradition, historical, or other relevant information or expert opinion. In the absence of clear and convincing evidence to the contrary, there shall be a presumption of cultural affiliation between an Indian tribe or Native Hawaiian organization and human remains or funerary objects, sacred objects, and objects of inalienable communal property which were obtained, discovered, excavated, or removed from the tribe's or organization's tribal or aboriginal homelands.[18]

This definition is a notably flexible construction of the term and its potential breadth. Much of the qualifying language that NARF had insisted upon is incorporated here, including broad evidentiary possibilities, a clause regarding time depth, and a clear expression that the burden of proof shall not rest on Native American groups.

At the hearing concerning the proposed legislation, the SAA, again represented by Kintigh, asked for a reinstatement of the definition from a draft substitute for S. 1980, which stipulated that groups attempting to demonstrate cultural affiliation must show a "continued group identity through time."[19] This sentiment was affirmed by the AAM, whose representative anxiously declared that "the phrase 'cultural affiliation' is defined in very general and almost limitless terms."[20] Its written testimony specifies the source of the organization's misgivings, illustrating once again what kind of rhetorical storm was brewing: "the definition contemplates use of folkloric and oral tradition evidence for the determination of such a relationship. Such evidence may not be necessarily grounded in fact and therefore may have minimal relevance to such a determination."[21]

Finally, before the legislation was passed, final reports were submitted to Congress: S. 101-473 and H.R. 101-877. These documents are crucial to the life history of this contentious process, including detailed accounts of the contested terms; they have subsequently been looked to as the most concrete expressions of legislative intent on these matters. S. 101-473 provides this consequential discussion of "cultural affiliation":

> The requirement of continuity between present day Indian tribes and materials from historic or prehistoric Indian tribes is intended to ensure that the claimant has a reasonable connection with the materials. Where human remains and funerary objects are concerned, the Committee is aware that it may be extremely difficult, unfair or even impossible in many instances for claimants to show an absolute continuity from present day Indian tribes to older, prehistoric remains without some reasonable gaps in the historic or prehistoric record. In such instances, a finding of cultural affiliation should be based upon an overall evaluation of the totality of the circumstances and evidence pertaining to the connection between the claimant and the material being claimed and should not be precluded solely because of gaps in the record.[22]

This way of describing "cultural affiliation" amounts to a compromise of sorts. The SAA's concern with demonstrating continuity of group identity is included, though the broad possibilities for evidence and a moderate standard of proof are retained. What is not elaborated here is the former directive that the burden of proof shall not rest with Native Americans. Why this omission occurred at this stage of the legislative history, and where Congress intended the burden of proof to rest, remain central points of contention to the present.

H.R. 101-877 is significant because it includes a description of the Review Committee's responsibilities:

> One of the responsibilities of the Review Committee is to compile an inventory of culturally unidentifiable human remains and develop

a process for their disposition. There is general disagreement on the proper disposition of such unidentifiable remains. Some believe that they should be left solely to science while others contend that, since they are not identifiable, they would be of little use to science and should be buried and laid to rest. The Committee looks forward to the Review Committee's recommendations in this area.[23]

This passage is central for locating congressional intent (or lack thereof) with regard to the disposition of culturally unidentifiable remains. The matter is addressed as one fraught with conflict, with differing viewpoints that Congress did not care to reconcile at the time. Deferring, then, Congress appealed to the Review Committee to address these volatile issues. We now turn to this history, following the Review Committee in its attempt to fulfill its dubious charge.[24]

Implementation History

Beyond the high-profile Kennewick Man dispute, to which we will return, implementation of NAGPRA has centered on the activities of the Review Committee. A remarkable percentage of the committee's time has focused upon the nexus of intractable tensions we have been chronicling. For nearly fifteen years not a single meeting, hearing, or significant publication of the Review Committee has failed to address cultural affiliation and its categorical other, culturally unidentifiable remains.

In the spring of 1992, the Review Committee met for the first time and immediately confronted these troublesome issues.[25] Committee members were then in an awkward stage, just becoming familiar with the statute and with the tendencies and interests of one another. With regard to this process of tactical position staking, the minutes record the following exchange: "Dr. Sullivan posited that he felt the affiliation of nearly 90% of some collections would be determinable. Dr. Walker disagreed, thinking the percentage of affiliated human remains to be much lower."[26] Whatever else we might observe at this juncture, it is most relevant here to note the clear disparity in perceptions of committee members concerning this core issue of NAGPRA. In order for the committee to function as an interpretive community, such distances will need to be addressed and surmounted, however provisionally. The question becomes, then, how might a tentative consensus emerge? How might committee members agree—or at least present the appearance of consensus—on volatile issues when the constituents they represent are poles apart?

The details of this process began to emerge at the committee's second meeting as it self-consciously struggled with its role as an interpretive community. Committee members, it seems, were taken aback by the demands placed upon them to elaborate upon the statute in ways that their diverse audiences (e.g., the scientific and academic communities, various Native American and Hawaiian groups, the Department of the Interior, and the Justice Department) would find generally acceptable and workable. Committee members latched onto an interpretive strategy that would gain them a modicum of latitude: asserting that they desired to be responsible to both the letter and the intent of the legislation. As a principle this seems admirable; in practice it often leads to potential breakdowns: Whose intent? Which hearing? Whose reading of "the letter"?

The committee, in its deliberations, took on "cultural affiliation" by way of addressing the bedeviling phrase "shared group identity." Appealing to the letter of the law yielded little insight, as the phrase is unelaborated in the statute. Recourse to legislative intent was also problematic; the issue hinged on forms of evidence to demonstrate shared identity, and it is unclear how these are to be weighed. In other words, does legislative intent imply a hierarchy of evidential forms? Discussions circled around these issues without any decisive assertions being forwarded until a Native American representative, Tessie Naranjo, stated that she would like to see biological evidence prioritized over cultural evidence, asserting that "blood" is what matters most to Indians.[27] Considering the context of NAGPRA debates, this position is puzzling, as claims about blood could be manipulated in any number of ways, particularly in ways that could cut against native understandings of kinship. Many Native American representatives would subsequently recognize this and reframe their stance accordingly.

At its fourth meeting the committee heard its first dispute, between the Native Hawaiian organization Hui Mālama and the P. A. Hearst Museum of the University of California, Berkeley. This dispute forced committee members to articulate a position with regard to cultural affiliation and culturally unidentifiable remains. Timothy White represented the Hearst Museum, while several self-described Native Hawaiian cultural and religious leaders represented Hui Mālama. The dispute hinged on determination of the "cultural affiliation" of two sets of skeletal remains found on an Oʻahu beach a century ago and since then held by the museum. The museum argued that the skeletal remains were unidentifiable ethnically and therefore should not be open for repatriation. Presenting its case, the museum emphasized the scientific value of its osteological collection and the importance of maintaining its coherence. To support its claims, it invoked the rhetoric of keeping remains available for "future" science. Hawaiian representatives responded that "spirituality" was being left out of the museum's considerations. Edward Halealoha Ayau related how he and his wife had received "spiritual feelings" from the bones when they visited the Hearst Museum, implying that such feelings should constitute evidence under NAGPRA. When pressed on why no affiliation had been determined by the museum, White responded that the bones did come from Hawai'i, according to acquisition records, but that biological and other scientific information was indeterminate with regard to ethnicity. Ayau responded by asserting that the museum was attempting to hold the committee to a higher standard of scientific proof than is demanded by NAGPRA. He reiterated his feeling that the bones had asked to "come home."[28]

In considering the dispute, the committee acknowledged that the Hearst Museum was asking, in effect, what constitutes a "preponderance of the evidence." Committee members expressed a need to represent the "intent" of the law and recommended that the remains be repatriated. In its discussion of a draft finding concerning the dispute, the committee set a major precedent by according weight to the Hawaiians' spiritual evidence.[29] For a precedent-setting first time, authorizing mechanisms that were constructed and legitimized under the sacred-objects and cultural-patrimony portions of the law (e.g., the testimony of "traditional religious leaders" and religious claims generally) had been utilized by native representatives with regard to remains previously categorized as unidentifiable. In this way the vague notion of "expert opinion" was reinscribed, in practice, with authorizing language from other sections of the law. In its published finding the committee formalized its position, declaring that a "shared group identity" exists between Hui Mālama and the remains in question.[30]

The next major event in the implementation of NAGPRA was an oversight hearing before the Senate Select Committee on Indian Affairs regarding the statute's implementation, on 27 May 1993. The day following the hearing the Department of the Interior (DOI) published a draft of the proposed rules for NAGPRA's implementation. The relevant section appears as follows:

10.14 Lineal Descent and Cultural Affiliation.

(d) Evidence. Evidence of a kin or cultural affiliation between a present-day individual, Indian tribe, or Native Hawaiian organization and human remains, funerary objects, sacred objects, or objects of cultural patrimony must be established by using the following types of evidence: Geographical, kinship, biological, archaeological, anthropological, linguistic, folklore, oral tradition, historical, or other relevant information or expert opinion.

(e) Standard of proof. Lineal descent of a present-day individual from an earlier individual and cultural affiliation of a present-day Indian tribe or Native Hawaiian organization to human remains, funerary objects, sacred objects, or objects of cultural patrimony must be established by a preponderance of the evidence. Claimants do not have to establish cultural affiliation with scientific certainty.[31]

At its fifth meeting the Review Committee added a crucial paragraph to this definition upon the suggestion of Timothy McKeown (NAGPRA group coordinator for the NPS). He suggested that the following paragraph be added to reflect legislative intent: "10.14(d) findings of cultural affiliation should be based upon an overall evaluation of the totality of circumstances and evidence pertaining to the connection between the claimant and the material being claimed and should not be precluded solely because of some gaps in the record."[32] The committee accepted this suggestion; the language was added to the *Final Rule and Regulations* in 1995 and has since been central to the direction of NAGPRA implementation.

At the sixth meeting of the Review Committee, a momentous idea was embraced by both sides of the debate surrounding unidentifiable remains. Native Americans and scientists began to suggest that regional consortiums of tribes be organized to address repatriation in concerted, regionally specific ways. The concession on the part of scientists was based in the hope that regional consortiums would be amenable to allowing future research on collections, something individual tribes had been largely unwilling to grant. Indian representatives seem to have entertained the idea for a range of reasons, most notably an acknowledgment that Native Americans have historically been very mobile in ways that make strict geographical claims complex and contentious. In any event, this signal development has resulted both in hopeful moments of compromise and in episodes of acrimony wherein unlikely antagonists have emerged to pursue their interests in unpredicted ways.

Also of note here is the fact that this meeting saw for the first time the presence of a henceforth outspoken and influential Native American group, the North Dakota Intertribal Reinterment Committee (NDIRC). The NDIRC became a champion of two related causes: it regularly defended and invoked "spiritual evidence," and it argued uncompromisingly for the repatriation of all culturally unidentifiable human remains. One of its representatives, Ronald Little Owl, suggested to the committee "that Indian tribes had their own ways of identifying the cultural affiliation of human remains and cultural items."[33] Pemina Yellowbird, another NDIRC representative, made a provocative gesture by stretching this authorizing claim to its limits, indicating "that the North Dakota Intertribal Reinterment Committee would accept responsibility for the care of all culturally unidentifiable and unclaimed human remains."[34]

At the seventh meeting of the committee, William Tall Bull, now a committee member, revisited rhetoric he had honed during the legislative battle five years earlier, speaking of Native American remains as MIA and concluding that they should be returned and reburied at once and with honor. Thomas Bullhead of the NDIRC sought to maintain the momentum of this sentiment by declaring that the current condition of unidentifiable remains was causing illness that was afflicting his people. Deanna Francis, a representative of the Passamaquoddy Tribe,

> explained to the Committee how her people are able to identify some remains. She talked about the remains of two individuals brought back from the Maine State Museum. Tribal representatives asked the two to "identify yourselves. They did. One was an elderly woman. The other was a young woman who was very scared. We got the paper work some days later from the museum. The young woman had an unhealed trauma in her chest . . . according to the archaeological data, she had been killed." Ms. Francis stated, "There are no unclaimed remains. All human remains will be claimed."[35]

At the end of the meeting, the NDIRC exemplified the rhetorical dynamic at work in these claims, wherein localized authority constructions based on assertions of inspiration are extended to assert authority in an entirely more general and nonlocal sphere (national museum collections of nondescript bones). In this case the NDIRC representative invoked the popularized Lakota saying "we are all related" as a claim substantiating cultural affiliation to unidentifiable remains.

Another crucial moment in the implementation history of the law came on 1 January 1995, when the committee published its long-awaited "Draft Recommendations Regarding the Disposition of Culturally Unidentifiable Human Remains." These recommendations, granting heavy favor to Native American interests, did not go unchallenged by the scientific community. The document's central passage reads: "Although the disposition of culturally 'unidentifiable human remains' is left open in NAGPRA, there is a firmly established principle in the act that assigns responsibility for what happens to human remains and associated funerary objects to lineal descendants and culturally affiliated tribes. This general principle should be followed in determining the disposition of culturally 'unidentifiable human remains' that are known to be ancestral Native Americans."[36]

Shortly after this document was published, the committee held its ninth meeting. Initially, there was much discussion concerning the fate of non–federally recognized tribes; in a pattern that would repeat itself many times, the committee considered alternative channels for such groups' claims without reaching a workable solution.[37] The majority of the meeting, however, was again devoted to the disposition of unidentifiable remains. In these discussions the committee began to adopt the looser term *affinity* to express the relationship of unidentifiable remains to the proposed tribal consortiums, signaling in yet another way that the categorical boundary between "affiliation" and "unidentifiable" had been breached, if not erased. Once again the NDIRC was present, and once again it stretched its claims into unforeseen territory. Its representative, Tim Mentz, "recommended the Committee take a position that all ancient human remains are Native American human remains regardless of the amount of information associated with them . . . and added that Native Americans are compassionate enough to rebury remains determined to be non–Native American."[38]

At its tenth meeting the committee addressed reactions to its "Draft Regulations." Many people had written formal responses; few supported the draft. At the outset of the meeting, committee member Dan Monroe "suggested that the Committee focus on the issues raised in the comments by the following comment in the draft recommendations—'Ultimately decisions about what happens to the human remains of Native American individuals from anywhere in the U.S. and associated funerary objects should rest in the hands of Native Americans'—and stated that the majority of the comments against this statement came from the academic community."[39] Other commentators advocated scientific rights in a variety of ways, underscoring that consensus had not been achieved on this turbulent issue. The committee reacted by responding to requests that *affinity* be dropped and replaced by the former designation, *affiliation*.

Not long after the tenth meeting of the committee, the DOI published the *Native American Graves Protection and Repatriation Act Regulations, Final Rule*.[40] Despite its title, however, the document is far from "final." Several significant sections of NAGPRA, including 10.11 (regarding culturally unidentifiable human remains), were reserved for future determination. Still, even with regard to reserved sections, the document is revealing. In the preface to the regulations, the NPS provides a summary of public commentary on a section-by-section basis. From these comments it is clear that "culturally unidentifiable human remains" was singled out by many groups as the most contentious terrain covered by the law. Many comments were also submitted regarding "cultural affiliation," particularly from the scientific community. Commentators suggested, for example, prioritizing scientific evidence, eliminating folkloric evidence, and requiring that cultural affiliation be established with scientific certainty. Despite these comments, the description of criteria for determining cultural affiliation was retained from the 1993 draft regulations.

Next was a Senate hearing before the SSCIA that was virtually consumed by seesaw testimony concerning the categorical boundaries of "unidentifiable remains." First to speak were Native American groups, including the NDIRC, the American Indian Ritual Object Repatriation Fund, Keepers of the Treasures, NARF, the Pawnee Tribe, the Navajo Nation, Hui Mālama, the Standing Rock Sioux, and the Cheyenne River Sioux. The latter group offered this interpretation of "expert opinion": "Expert opinion without definition enables non-Indians to seek out, authorize and utilize other non-Indians as experts who can interpret tribal history and traditional cultural mores, activities, and spiritual beliefs of a people [with] whom they have no shared ethnicity. . . . The term must either be dropped from the clause, or, it must be defined to state that expert opinion means: *Oral testimony of traditional tribal elders of the Indian tribe submitting the repatriation request*."[41] The Nez Perce Tribe presented especially compelling testimony, offering a mythical charter for contemporary claims upon unidentifiable remains. The myth recited begins in this way: "In the beginning, Grandfather Creator and Mother Earth blessed we Nez Perce or Nee Mee Poo. All other Indigenous people were also blessed. The creator and Mother

Earth provided for all our relations. I am one with your relations, we are all related, everything is connected according to Earth Law."[42]

Caught between the positions of various constituents, the Review Committee teetered, trying to find elusive ground on which it might regain its balance. The committee was still in this uncomfortable state as it embarked on its eleventh meeting in the summer of 1996, the same summer the nine-thousand-year-old remains of so-called Kennewick Man were discovered.[43] The committee opened the meeting by acknowledging that the scientific community was very anxious about the draft-proposal language. Two points were especially hot: first, how ancient is ancient (i.e., how far back cultural affiliation can be pushed); and second, the committee's underlying assumption that Native Americans should control decisions regarding disposition. The committee drafted and presented the following revised definition of shared group identity: "Shared group identity means a relationship between a present-day Indian tribe or tribes and an earlier group based on: (1) direct historical links and/or (2) a combination of geographical, temporal, and cultural links. Geographical, temporal, and/or cultural links may be established through biological, archaeological, linguistic, folkloric, oral traditional, or other relevant information or expert opinion."[44]

Elaborating on the new definition, committee member Dan Monroe stated that in some cases the conditions of shared group identity will not be met by evidence under the first clause but might nevertheless be met by evidence under the second. In this way, then, the committee continued to affirm the precedent set by the Hui Mālama v. Hearst Museum finding. The committee also affirmed the use of "spiritual" and "artistic" evidence under the rubric of "cultural traditions and lifeways."

The fourteenth committee meeting brought a changing of the guard: four members had ended their terms, and four new ones had been appointed.[45] It was not long before the new committee members weighed in with their opinions, attempting to shift the committee's course. The fifteenth meeting saw the beginning of this process when the committee heard the case of the Me-wuk, a nonrecognized tribe seeking repatriation of pre-Columbian remains. John O'Shea, nominated to the committee by the SAA, reacted to this request with a blanket assertion that he did not see the validity of "cultural affiliation" claims with regard to ancient remains, a perspective that would shortly weigh heavily on NAGPRA. O'Shea then elaborated upon his position, declaring that he did not agree with the previous committee position that "ultimately the decisions on repatriation and disposition of human remains and cultural objects should rest in the hands of Native people."[46] James Bradley, nominated to the committee by the AAM, concurred with O'Shea's position. The factions solidified as three Native American committee members, Tessie Naranjo, Armand Minthorn, and Lawrence Hart, registered their affirmation of the earlier committee stance. Minthorn, who was directly involved in the unfolding Kennewick Man case, announced his conviction that unidentifiable remains are "holy, sacred and deserving of respect."[47]

At its sixteenth meeting the committee heard a presentation concerning a consortium of twelve Southwestern tribes that were seeking a joint repatriation of culturally unidentifiable human remains from Carlsbad Caverns National Park. The consortium invoked oral tradition and geographical location as its primary sources of evidence for establishing its claim. The Review Committee expressed support for this effort and agreed that repatriation should move forward. However, despite this recommendation, the committee also signaled some trepidation, declaring that the remains were still unidentifiable for purposes of NAGPRA.

Yet another presentation from a consortium of tribes was also heard at this meeting, this dispute centered in the Great Plains region. The consortium, headed up by the NDIRC, was working with the University of Nebraska, Lincoln, to repatriate 152 sets of human remains. The university representative explained to the committee that the remains in question were "formerly thought to be unidentifiable on the basis of an initial reading of NAGPRA wherein affiliation seemed to refer to the status of a single tribe."[48] With group claims, she said, the situation had changed dramatically. Though this case was structurally similar to the former one, here Native Americans' claims were more general in scope and contained less detail. Perhaps most significant, this case concerned a far larger collection of remains, one that was academically held. Nevertheless, the majority of the committee recommended repatriation, although O'Shea expressed his reservations.

On 20 April 1999 a Senate oversight hearing was held before the SSCIA. At the hearing, convened to address difficulties in the implementation of NAGPRA, the disposition of unidentifiable remains was predictably central. When asked to testify, Keith Kintigh, of the SAA, directly attacked the Review Committee's interpretation of cultural affiliation:

Cultural affiliation is a cornerstone of NAGPRA because it provides legitimacy for most repatriation claims. A critical problem is the expansion, in practice, of the statutory definition of cultural affiliation beyond any legally defensible limits. While the law requires evidence demonstrating cultural affiliation, frequently little or no evidence is presented. Procedural shortcuts and distortion of the definitions have already led to problems such as that of the Kennewick Man and have the potential to lead to many more problems, disputes, and ultimately, lawsuits.[49]

In his written testimony Kintigh specified one area as especially problematic—claims for joint affiliation:

Joint affiliation is now being used in ways that clearly extend beyond the statutory definition of cultural affiliation. Using this strategy, joint affiliation is asserted between a prehistoric cultural group that may be thousands of years old with a broad collective of tribes that may be very different or even traditional enemies. This argument has been used to broaden the concept of cultural affiliation to the point that all remains become "culturally affiliated," which is clearly inconsistent with the definition employed by the statute.[50]

Kintigh's mention of Kennewick Man is notable here: the increasingly visible and problematic dispute over this particular set of remains was one instance of a joint claim that relied heavily upon claims of oral tradition to establish cultural affiliation. It is extraordinary, in retrospect, that the Review Committee and the DOI were wading so deeply through the thickets of cultural affiliation when Kennewick Man emerged on the scene, quite literally falling out of a riverbank to bring a palpable edge to the law. Because of his antiquity and Caucasoid features, his effect was extreme, presenting a threshold case to test NAGPRA. A veritable circus ensued as various interest groups rallied around the remains. Many in the scientific community seemed thrilled to have a test case that, in their view, would lay bare the patent absurdity of NAGPRA's evidentiary allowances. Many Native Americans were cautious, sensing that the time and conditions were not ripe for such a test. Others jumped right in, taking cultural affiliation as far as anyone imagined possible. Even the Asatru Folk Assembly, a group devoted to purportedly European tribal traditions, asserted a claim. In this fragile context Kintigh's testimony may be read as a prescient attempt to salvage the law in the face of impending judicial and public critique.

Many Native American representatives were in attendance at the Senate hearing where Kintigh spoke. Tex Hall, chairman of the Three Affiliated Tribes, next spoke to the senators. His written testimony provides a succinct account of his position and a pointed retort to Kintigh:

> According to our teachings, there is no such thing as culturally unaffiliated Native remains, since we believe that we are related to all that lives, and this teaching includes peoples of other indigenous Nations. Some relationships are closer than others, of course, but our oral histories teach us not only who our relatives are, but where we lived, with whom we shared our aboriginal homelands, and when we occupied certain lands and territories. Our teachings regarding the ancient remains taken from our collective aboriginal homelands tell us we have a responsibility to each ancestor, no matter when they lived or died. Our teachings also tell us that subsequent curation and scientific study has caused grievous spiritual abuse and suffering to our ancestors. It is for these reasons that we have been fighting for the return of all remains, and any deviation from our original instructions concerning their treatment will have a devastating impact on their spiritual peace and rest.[51]

The debate at this point appeared as intractable as ever, but only days later it would take a novel twist, at the seventeenth meeting of the Review Committee.

At this meeting, in May 1999, the committee considered a dispute involving the Hopi Tribe and Chaco Culture National Historic Park (Chaco). At issue here was the fate of numerous ancestral Puebloan ("Anasazi") remains and objects. The Hopi Tribe disagreed with cultural-affiliation determinations that had been made by Chaco, notably taking issue with the "implicit assumption that nearly all southwestern Indian tribes are affiliated with the Park."[52] The Hopi Tribe asked instead for compliance with the "letter of the law" to determine "genuine" cultural affiliation, asking that "geographical association" be eliminated as a form of evidence for determining affiliation.[53] The Hopi position was then endorsed by a Pueblo of Zuni representative.[54] Next, a Hopi religious leader presented mythological evidence for the Hopi Tribe's affiliation with the Chaco region and with other Puebloan tribes in the region. The Hopi then brought out an archaeological expert, Linda Cordell of the University of Colorado, to give "scientific" evidence for their claims of affiliation. Her presentation would reveal the core of the dispute.

Cordell proposed a distinction between "cultural affiliation" and "cultural relationship," then described Hopi relations to Chacoan remains in terms of the former and Navajo relations to Chacoan remains in terms of the latter. The national park's determination of affiliation included the Navajo, and this was the source of anxiety for the Hopi Tribe. Aspects of this dispute may be read as a contemporary inscription and playing out of long-simmering tensions between the Hopi and Navajo tribes. Particularly since the late twentieth century, their relationship has been strained at various levels, especially with regard to Peabody Coal and the uncertain fate of jointly used lands.[55] In this case NAGPRA became a means by which each tribe sought to symbolically and legally lay claim to the Southwest and its ancient history. Notable for our analysis is the fact that we can see here how some Native Americans have attempted to use NAGPRA to limit the claims of other Native Americans. The irony is that such moves serve overall to constrict the category of "cultural affiliation" in ways that run counter to many Native Americans' expressed interests, instead serving nonnative interests in shrinking the scope of identity claims under the law.

After the Hopi presentation Navajo representatives were given a chance to state their case, advancing a variety of forms of evidence to substantiate their claims. They presented their own academic representative, anthropologist David Brugge, who summarized his paper entitled "Navajo Religion and the Anasazi Connection." Then the Navajo introduced another scientist who presented biological and genetic arguments drawing a connection between the Navajo and the Anasazi. Finally, a Navajo traditional religious leader addressed the issue by reciting a Tower of Babel–like narrative that depicted Chaco as the originary center of many cultures, from whence Hopis, Zunis, Navajos, and others dispersed in prehistoric time.

The committee, seemingly bewildered by this dispute, revisited it at its eighteenth meeting. The Hopi, led by Leigh Kuwanwisima, continued to argue that Chaco, despite a nine-year consultation process, had reached faulty conclusions regarding cultural affiliation. Specifically, the Hopi argued that all determinations of cultural affiliation should have been made on a case-by-case and tribe-by-tribe basis so as to prevent blanket findings of cultural affiliation that include all Southwestern tribes. Apparently sensing a developing quagmire, the committee unanimously recommended that Chaco reassess its determination of cultural affiliation, "weighing all available evidence."[56] At this juncture Kintigh "commended the review committee on their recommendation . . . and stated that the precedents set by that recommendation should help preserve the integrity of the definition of cultural affiliation in the statute and help address the issue of culturally unidentifiable remains."[57] Notable here is the convergence of some native strategies with the interests of an influential nonnative group, a dynamic also occasionally seen in Hawaiian contexts.

The status of culturally unidentifiable remains was addressed again at the committee's nineteenth meeting.[58] Native people pressed hard for elimination of the category; other voices—principally from archaeological and museum groups—argued that preservation of the category would be necessary for the law to weather judicial scrutiny. Developing aspects of the Kennewick Man case seemed to bear this position out. Secretary of the Interior Bruce Babbitt had determined that the nine-thousand-year-old remains were affiliated with a coalition of Northwestern tribes on the basis of oral tradition, causing some observers to suggest that he had implemented a sense of cultural affiliation far softer than that contemplated by NAGPRA.[59] One commentator, Vincas Steponaitis, who would soon become a committee member, invoked the same distinction advanced by the Hopi to distinguish their claims from those of the Navajo, suggesting that the secretary had relied on a vague notion of cultural relationship versus a defensible demonstration of cultural affiliation.

In May 2001 the committee convened in California for its twenty-first meeting. Given the historical situation of Indians in California, where few groups have federally recognized status, the committee heard considerable testimony regarding the perils and challenges facing nonrecognized tribes, thus continuing to address thorny issues in the implementation of the law. Increasingly apparent, however, was the larger-order issue of the constitutionality and coherence of the statute itself. Again, Kennewick Man served as the catalyst for these issues, pressing hard on foundational issues: how far may cultural affiliation be extended, and on what grounds? Friends of America's Past, a nonprofit group that advocates for the scientific study of prehistory, warned that Secretary Babbitt had run afoul of the Constitution and the law in his handling of the Kennewick Man controversy and admonished the committee to adhere to a stricter basis in determining cultural affiliation.[60]

The committee, however, moved in quite a different direction at its next meeting, where it heard testimony regarding Spirit Cave Man, a set of remains also estimated to be nine thousand years old.

Here, then, was a case similar to that of Kennewick Man, particularly with regard to how the claimants, the Fallon Paiute–Shoshone Tribe, relied on oral testimony and religious claims to state their affiliation with the remains.[61] Whereas John O'Shea was against finding cultural affiliation, the majority of committee members found in favor of the tribe, despite "gaps" in the record.[62]

On 30 August 2002 U.S. District Court judge John Jelderks issued his opinion in the Kennewick case, *Bonnichsen et al. v. the United States*.[63] Moving in a direction wholly opposite to the Review Committee's recent tendencies, he found no cultural affiliation between the remains and the coalition of tribes claiming them. Judge Jelderks took issue with the oral-history evidence advanced by the tribes and the fact that the claim was coalition based, expressing considerable misgivings about the statute generally. Addressing cultural affiliation at its outer limits, Judge Jelderks ruled, in a stunning blow to the tribes, the DOI, and the law, that the remains were not Native American as defined by the statute. His ruling focused on the statutory definition of "Native American": "of, or relating to, a tribe, or culture that is indigenous to the United States."[64] Jelderks's finding, emphasizing the present tense of the definition's verb, continues to define NAGPRA deliberation. Thus, if the Review Committee had reduced the scope of "culturally unidentifiable remains" by extending the range of "cultural affiliation," Jelderks did just the opposite —and did so more definitively—by parsing language that would sever claims in the present from things of the past.

Native Americans were quick to react, doing so vocally at the twenty-fourth meeting of the Review Committee. Various Native American representatives, including James Riding In and Rebecca Tsosie, argued unequivocally that all remains of early peoples of North America are Native American, that all remains are culturally affiliated, and that all remains should therefore be repatriated.[65] In this tense context both the government and the tribes appealed Jelderks's decision.

In February 2004, then, the Ninth Circuit Court ruled on the U.S. government's appeal in *Bonnichsen*, affirming Jelderks's opinion: "The 9th Circuit held that the Secretary erred in defining Native American in the regulations and concluded that NAGPRA requires that human remains bear a 'significant relationship' to a presently existing tribe, people, or culture to be considered Native American and that NAGPRA does not apply to the Kennewick remains."[66] According to a representative of the Department of the Solicitor,

"the decision may render provisions concerning culturally unidentifiable human remains meaningless or extremely narrow because in
those cases there would be no ability to show a present-day culturally affiliated claimant under NAGPRA."[67]

In seeming defiance of Jelderks's opinion, however, the Review
Committee made two findings of affiliation with reference to previously unidentified remains at its twenty-seventh meeting.[68] One
recommended repatriation of remains from Effigy Mounds National
Monument to a coalition of thirteen tribes.[69] The other recommended
repatriation of remains from Colorado College to the Southern Ute
Tribe.[70] Further discussions were also devoted to proposals focusing
on culturally unidentifiable remains, including one for a "Tomb of
the Unknown Indian."[71]

Shortly after this meeting, on 23 September 2004, Senator Ben
Nighthorse Campbell of Colorado introduced S. 2843, "A Bill to Make
Technical Corrections to Laws Relating to Native Americans."[72]
This bill pinpointed the loophole in NAGPRA that had allowed
for Jelderks's opinion: the present-tense verb *is* in the definition of
"Native American," which Jelderks had read literally. S. 2843 responded by adding two words: *or was*. While tagged as a "technical"
correction, this change would effectively undo Jelderks's opinion.
Tremendous attention thus came to bear on these most humble
words as museum professionals, physical anthropologists, lawyers,
Native American representatives, and Review Committee members
became overnight experts in the devious semantics of apparently
self-evident language. In an interesting and telltale move, the DOI
did not comment on the bill: observers might have surmised at this
juncture that a shift in the government's view of cultural affiliation
was afoot.

And indeed, one year later, on 28 July 2005, this shift was rendered
explicit at a hearing before the SSCIA regarding yet another version
of the proposed amendment to NAGPRA.[73] The hearing opened with
a statement by Paul Hoffman, the DOI's deputy assistant secretary
for fish and wildlife and parks. In a reversal of the position it had
maintained throughout the Kennewick Man dispute, the DOI now
declared that it did not support the amendment. Following Judge
Jelderks's reasoning in *Bonnichsen*, Hoffman conveyed the new
position of the DOI: "We believe that NAGPRA should protect the
sensibilities of currently existing tribes, cultures, and people while
balancing the need to learn about past cultures and customs. In the
situation where remains are not significantly related to any existing

tribe, people, or culture they should be available for appropriate scientific analysis. The proposed legislation would shift away from this
balance."[74]

The DOI's position, however, was firmly challenged by other
speakers at the hearing. Paul Bender, of the Arizona State University
College of Law, who had long been active in the legislative history of
NAGPRA, argued:

> Bonnichsen v. United States seriously undermines the scope of Con-
> gress' broad remedial purpose. The decision construes the central
> provision of NAGPRA—the provision defining the materials to which
> NAGPRA applies—in a way that is not only plainly incorrect as a
> matter of statutory interpretation, but that frustrates NAGPRA's im-
> portant human rights objective of including Indian governments and
> groups in decisions about whether materials are Indian-related and
> about the treatment and disposition of such materials.[75]

Strong testimony by NARF attorney Walter Echo-Hawk echoed Professor Bender's argument. Perhaps more surprisingly, the SAA also
supported the amendment, Keith Kintigh arguing that "requiring
demonstration of a relationship to present-day Native peoples in order to categorize remains or items as Native American is contrary
to the plain language of the statute, is inconsistent with a commonsense understanding of the term, and would lead to the absurd result
of excluding from the law historically documented Indian tribes that
have no present-day descendants."[76]

The most colorful testimony of the day came from Paula Barran,
an attorney representing Friends of America's Past. With hyperbolic
rhetoric that seemed to set the clock back to pre-NAGPRA days,
Barran attempted to scare the committee: "If you pass this amendment," she declared, "the scientists of the future will inevitably be
taught by foreign schools, and foreign-trained scientists will become
the faculty of the future."[77] Taking another tack, she beseeched the
committee to "consider the consequences to the dead. Do they not
have a right to have their stories told and preserved for future generations to learn from?"[78] Barran probed for that most sensitive nerve
of the body politic: "This country has always held itself out as the
one place in the world where totalitarian thought control does not
happen. The proposed amendment is the ultimate form of thought
control."[79]

Who would have guessed that the verb *was* could hold such a threat? In these times of tense negotiations, the fate of the future hinges, once again, on what Congress will decide about the past.[80]

A Long Road

So things stood in November 2005 as I drove Interstate 25 south from Denver on my way to the thirtieth meeting of the Review Committee in Albuquerque, New Mexico. On the long drive my mind wandered across the strange terrain of NAGPRA's history. I also wondered about the present. In the wake of *Bonnichsen* and the subsequent proposed amendment, what kinds of attitudes would I find at the meeting? When I did walk into the meeting, one thing at least was clear: NAGPRA still matters to lots of people in lots of ways. The large room was packed and alive, buzzing. Many, many Indian attendees were present, clearly there to seek specific repatriations and assurances regarding their culture and history, not to haggle over legalese. This became especially vivid during a dinner hosted by the Pueblo Council in honor of NAGPRA's fifteenth birthday, where my attention was drawn to the myriad Native Americans from around the Southwest and beyond who had traveled to Albuquerque to learn about a law they had heard could help them get their ancestors back. Many of the people with whom I chatted knew or cared little about the most recent SSCIA meeting or *Bonnichsen*; they cared about how to set things right. Exemplifying this relationship to NAGPRA, an elderly man from Jemez Pueblo described to the audience how he had worked for the momentous repatriation of thousands of Pecos remains from the Peabody Museum: "I told them I didn't know much about their fancy law or their fancy language. I told them I was a simple man who wanted to care for my ancestors. They seemed to understand that."

5

ANCESTORS BEFORE US

MANIFESTATIONS AND METAPHORS OF
TRADITION IN A HAWAIIAN DISPUTE

> It is our obligation and our duty to question the untested regulations set forth by NAGPRA in 1990. . . . The support figure represents the first such case to involve any object other than human remains. Based on the guidelines issued by the National Park Service, we believe—and always have believed—that the support figure is not a sacred object but a practical, utilitarian piece that holds no religious significance. I am confident that we will successfully clarify, in court, the language set forth by NAGPRA and set the precedent for future cases of this kind.
>
> —Vincent A. Cianci Jr., mayor of Providence, Rhode Island

Standing Up for Tradition

ON THE PLANE to Norman, Oklahoma, for the thirteenth meeting of the Review Committee, I wondered what would transpire over the next several days. Given the location of the meeting, I knew there would be a tremendous Indian presence. I suspected we would hear from Plains tribes and from tribes that had been relocated to "Indian Territory" in the nineteenth century, such as the Cherokee and the Choctaw. The latter groups were indeed especially well represented, hosting a wonderful evening for all attendees at the meeting. As at the thirtieth meeting in Albuquerque, food, conversation, and cultural presentations did as much as the meeting proper to foster the kind of cross-cultural communication that lies at the heart of NAGPRA. At the opposite end of the spectrum were accusations leveled between members of the Southern Cheyenne Tribe regarding the repatriation of remains from the Sand Creek Massacre, a topic to which we will return in the next chapter. The centerpiece of the meeting, however, did not pertain to Oklahoma Indians or even to mainland Native Americans. Rather, Hawaiians again captured the attention of the Review Committee, this time in a dispute with the Roger Williams Museum of Providence, Rhode Island, over a carved statue, or ki'i. In the course of their presentation, Native Hawaiian representatives from Hui Mālama and the Office of Hawaiian Affairs (OHA) demonstrated their remarkable ability to convert bureaucratic proceedings into jaw-dropping cultural performances.

Much of my understanding of tradition in action was shaped—one might say awakened—by the Hawaiians' testimony in Norman, where Native Hawaiian claimants set their arguments over and against those of the museum in stark fashion. Doing so, they did not rely solely on mere words to fight words; rather, they evoked an entire cultural sensibility, establishing a deep history of human identity and connecting it to the present in the course of several hours of testimony. This involved genealogical recitations, chants, and prayers. The Hawaiians' words became performances, speech acts of the highest order. Quite apart from referring to the sacred, they sought to participate in it, to incarnate tradition through ritual in the present. In this manner they transcended the parameters of the law even while they sought the relief it could offer. I would characterize their efforts as the metaphorical extension of tradition for its maximum—here legal—application. Whether or not courts find such mobilizations of tradition persuasive, my interest is in the process wherein tradition is stretched, amplified, and refocused in the course of being so defended. As I argue earlier, this modality of lived tradition is not categorically distinct from "status quo" or apparently stabilized forms of tradition. Traditions must change to survive. Depending on political stakes and resources, some must engage in dynamic reformulation more deliberately and explicitly than others. But doing so—rising to speak forth—illustrates the most human but frequently forgotten aspect of traditions: they exist and survive only insofar as people act them out and hold them up.

The dispute over the ki'i thus provides us with a remarkable example of tradition in action. Most likely manufactured in the late eighteenth or early nineteenth century, the object itself is a stout anthropomorphic figurine that stands about two feet tall, has a smooth blue head, and once had eyes of inlaid mother-of-pearl. Art historian Edward Dodd describes the object as follows: "This curious, though undoubtedly authentic pre-European piece is a triple spear rest for an Hawaiian chief, designed to be lashed to the gunwhale [sic] of his war canoe. Its singularity is that the body is carved in a style traditional to god images, and one would not expect a god to be performing such menial labor even for a great chief. But the head is more reminiscent of the menehune tradition which would be quite appropriate. This then seems to be a mixture of traditions; something quite rare in Polynesia."[1] The object was clearly designed to be a canoe-mounted support apparatus of some sort, as it incorporates a sizable triple rack. But just what it carried is at the heart of the dispute: did it bear fishing poles or sacred spears? This distinction is, of course, metonymic of a larger issue: was the object designed and used for secular or religious purposes?

The dispute first erupted in 1996, when Hawaiian representatives learned that the museum was attempting to sell the object via Sotheby's.[2] The claimants invoked NAGPRA, specifically asserting that the law affords triple protection of the object as a funerary item, an item of cultural patrimony, and a sacred object. The first two claims failed to move forward, but the third claim largely succeeded. Specifically, Hawaiians argued that the ki'i was a vessel for 'aumākua, ancestral spirits. After two reviews of the dispute, the Review Committee issued a finding in favor of the Hawaiians' claim on these grounds.[3] This, however, led to an even greater threat of dispute, as the museum filed suit against the Native Hawaiian claimants and the DOI in federal district court, asserting constitutional violation of due process and takings rights. Hui Mālama and the OHA counterclaimed on the grounds that the obligation for NAGPRA-mandated consultation had not been fulfilled by the museum.[4] This dispute was thus situated to become one of the first major tests of the law. But before this could transpire, the parties settled out of court, the Hawaiians taking control of the object and agreeing to make a "donation" to the museum.[5] Quite apart from the specifics of the dispute, this case had greater implications, carrying the possible burden of testing the problematic takings implications of NAGPRA (i.e., repatriation could trigger property-rights claims on the part of museums).

In any case, the dispute illustrates the kinds of issues that emerge when NAGPRA is implemented, specifically with regard to evidentiary matters. The sides differed about the object at many levels, as we will see, and no matter the intent of the law, neither showed willingness to compromise. In such a context religious language takes on a heightened relevance, as the competition takes place between mutually exclusive maximalist discourses.[6]

The Museum: No Apologies for Typologies

Well before the dispute was finally resolved, museum representatives argued that the figurine was merely secular, not sacred in any capacity. Their position was articulated with reference to an uncomplicated past: a time before the present, now departed and fixed, that should not be impinged upon by counterclaims in the present. In the committee's first review of the dispute, a museum representative asserted flatly: "Our object does not exhibit the characteristics of an ʻaumakua. However, it does exhibit the characteristics of a utilitarian support figure."[7] More specifically, she stated that the object was not war related at all but was a support mechanism used to hold fishing spears. The representative's next move was to cast a threat to the Review Committee: "We believe, as well, that should this Review Committee make a decision that this particular support figure should be repatriated to Hawaiʻi, you will have expanded the NAGPRA guidelines dramatically, and well beyond the intention of the drafters and, indeed, of the Congress. . . . We believe it would open a Pandora's box where literally any object now held by any museum could be repatriated, however inferential or speculative the evidence."[8] This argument, as is readily apparent, runs parallel to the concerns of physical anthropologists with regard to native claims upon culturally unidentified remains, the prime issue being concern with the scope and perceived integrity of claims announced in the present in terms that are not scientifically verifiable or authorized by Western mechanisms.[9]

The next museum representative stated that none of the museum's staff present at the meeting had a background in anthropology. "For that reason," she continued, "the museum has sought the expert advice of a universally-recognized scholar in this type of Hawaiian sculpture, Dr. William Davenport."[10] Already here, in its choice of authorizing claims and strategies, we see the museum's tactic emerging: to represent its position as one based on putatively universal and scientific truths vis-à-vis local and political interests. Developing her position, the representative set up an implicit opposition between kinds of knowledge: "My feeling is—is that what the Board and probably what the National Park Service, overall, needs to consider, is what is the relative weight, in fact, going to be between available, existing, scholarly literature, categories, typologies versus what documentation and data might be provided to us by members of Native Hawaiian organizations and Native American groups over-all."[11] Drawing her comments to a close, she asserted baldly that the museum accepted Davenport's scholarly opinion "that our figure is a support figure that was not used in any ritualistic way."[12]

The next museum representative presented a slide show intended to explicate the museum's contention that the object was not and could not be sacred. Showing a slide of the figure, she appealed to "the physicality of the object itself."[13] On the basis of this "physicality," she asserted that the object could not have been an 'aumakua figure. Specifically, she noted the object's purportedly supportlike characteristics, which, in her view, demonstrate its utilitarian nature. In a nutshell, then, the museum argued as follows: support = utilitarian = nonsacred. This equation, of course, is redolent of long-held and long-analyzed traditions of Western dichotomization.[14]

The representative continued to make her case, listing a variety of characteristics to indicate the object's utilitarian aspect, including a rack appendage and a mount by which it would have been attached to a canoe. From these features she deduced that "it's very, very clearly form-function designed."[15] Following upon this declaration, she sought to defuse assertions that the object resembles other known 'aumakua figures, quoting Davenport: "These support figures have an ingenuity, a composition, charm, and informal treatment that is completely lacking in the better-known religious images."[16] Here we have another expression of a dichotomy: sacred = serious = fixed // secular = playful = malleable. Continuing to develop her categorization, the representative showed numerous slides of figures, classifying them according to their correspondence with the aforementioned characteristics. Half resembled the object in question, and half did not. When she finally concluded, she declared that the viewer had just witnessed the difference between the profane and the sacred. Understandably, it was perhaps difficult for viewers to step back and remind themselves of the constructive process by which this division had been promoted.

Nevertheless, as noted earlier, the Review Committee was unswayed, recommending repatriation. In response the museum returned for the second hearing, in Norman, at the committee's thirteenth meeting. Attorney Gregory Benik led the charge, declaring in his opening comments that "we believe that the issue is one which must in the final analysis be driven by evidence."[17] With that he called his first expert, Adrienne Kaeppler, curator of oceanic ethnol-

ogy at the National Museum of Natural History at the Smithsonian
Institution. Regarding the object's sacredness, Kaeppler stated that
"it appears, of course, to be a spear rest." Continuing, she made the
following general remarks about the nature of 'aumakua figures:
"What I have heard from Hawaiians in the past is that . . . these were
primarily places into which to call the gods. They were a vehicle for
bringing the gods, a place to rest, a resting place for them; that they
were not actually the gods; that they were a place into which you
called the gods."[18] These observations were meant, it would seem,
to show the transitory nature of sacredness in Hawaiian religious
traditions. This sacredness, as Kaeppler presented it, is thus not a
quality of objects themselves but rather a state any object might
obtain should a spirit be called into it. Her assertions were thus cast
in the service of distinguishing between the sacred and its possible
vessels, the conclusions being, first, that no object is therefore inherently sacred and, second, that many objects could in principle suffice
for activating the sacred. On their face these claims appear damaging
to the Hawaiians' case. However, by emphasizing the role of activa-
tion, of ritual activity, Kaeppler preserved for the Hawaiians a point
they could elaborate and turn to their advantage. This would prove
crucial to their case.

Indeed, the museum's attorney seemed to perceive that the testimony of his star witness might come perilously close to backfiring.
To shore up the situation, he pressed Kaeppler to state that the object had never been sacred. Despite his leading questions, however,
Kaeppler only offered more "friendly fire." Responding to his question regarding the object's sacredness, she said: "But in itself, in my
opinion, it is not a sacred figure. But you could call something to it
to make it sacred, just as you could do that to a plain block of wood,
if it is the right kind of wood, on a heiau."[19] The formal vagueness of
her claim thus shifted the burden back to the museum, which would
need to demonstrate that the object had not, in fact, been used in
this way. Such negative claims would prove hard to come by for the
museum's attorney.

Clearly frustrated, Benik called his next presenter, Herb Kāne, a
renowned artist and canoe builder. Introducing Kāne, the attorney
clearly wanted to establish that the museum had the support of
Native Hawaiians. But here again his intentions were subtly foiled:
"Gregory Benik: 'Mr. Kāne, before you go on, are—are you a Native
Hawaiian?' Herb Kāne: 'I'm part Hawaiian, yes. . . . We're all part
Hawaiian these days.'"[20] But Kāne's presentation quickly turned
more favorable to the museum as he characterized the Hawaiians'

claim with this analogy: "It's like they're going after a pickup truck and trying to turn it into a Cadillac."[21] Upon development, however, his position revealed a weakness that the Hawaiians would later capitalize upon, as we will see. Specifically, Kāne argued that the object was no longer needed for religious purposes because formal religion was no longer practiced in Hawai'i.[22]

The next presenter called by the museum was Rubellite Kawena Johnson, scholar-in-residence at the Kawananakoa Foundation and professor emeritus at the University of Hawai'i. Beyond her academic credentials, Johnson described herself as a "Hawaiian religious leader."[23] Furthermore, she directed the committee to her resume, specifically to the fact that she was a founder of the Council of Hawaiian Elders under the OHA. On this basis she had insider (native and religious) authority; outsider (academic) authority; and, significantly, authority with reference to one of the groups opposing the museum, the Office of Hawaiian Affairs.[24] Johnson stated unequivocally: "The object is not needed by religious leaders today, because that object was used as a canoe rest."[25] At this moment the attorney jumped in to direct his witness:

> GREGORY BENIK: Let me just end by giving you a hypothetical. I want you to assume that I have a carved 'aumakua and I call a certain spirit into that 'aumakua. Do you have that in mind?
>
> RUBELLITE JOHNSON: Yes. I'm—I'm listening to you.
>
> GREGORY BENIK: Okay. And let's assume that I lose that carved figure. In your opinion, will I have the—will I be able to call the spirit that I called into my lost 'aumakua into another animate object?
>
> RUBELLITE JOHNSON: Yes. It's—it's possible to carve an entirely new image and to call the spirit into it. The—the wood does not have the spirit.
>   You're—you're always in control of the spiritual source of your 'aumakua. So you can move that spirit into the element which you designate to receive communication with that spirit.
>
> GREGORY BENIK: So in your opinion, it is not necessary for me to have in my possession the lost 'aumakua for me to worship the spirit that is—
>
> RUBELLITE JOHNSON: No. You don't have to have the object, because the spirit is the real thing. The object is not.[26]

At this moment there was a palpable sense in the room that the Hawaiian claimants were doomed. After such a seemingly devastating presentation, in which academic and cultural authorities had rejected claims regarding the object's possible ritual use and sacred status, I wondered how the Hawaiians could possibly respond. I'm sure I wasn't alone in underestimating the compelling power of tradition in action.

Hawaiians: Ancestors before Us

The Native Hawaiian representatives proceeded to deftly describe how the object did indeed fit the law's definition, which reads as follows: "'Sacred objects' shall mean specific ceremonial objects which are needed by traditional Native American religious leaders for the practice of traditional Native American religions by their present day adherents."[27] As we have noted, this idiosyncratic definition of "sacred object" rests on two primary features: demonstration of traditional religious authority and contemporary ritual use. The *Final Rule and Regulations* for the law further complicated this definition with the addition of a critical word, *renewal:* "[sacred objects are those] objects that were devoted to a traditional Native American religious ceremony or ritual and which have religious significance or function in the renewal of such ceremony."[28] Inclusion of this potentially contentious language revealed a yet wider and more densely featured interpretive horizon: emphasis upon renewal suggests that not only the past but also the present and future will be weighed in deliberations regarding purportedly sacred objects. Moreover, this language entails a direct reference to the legislative history, during which various native representatives and legislators explicitly and repeatedly stated a hope that ritual renewal would lead to broad cultural renewal.

Before they addressed the law's definition or anything else, however, the Hawaiian claimants prayed aloud as a group, chanting Hawaiian in a manner that unmistakably conveyed reverence and gravity. Such a moment could be dismissed as empty gesturing; in my view, however, it succinctly encapsulated and foreshadowed the Hawaiians' position. Before speaking even one English word, they made the bedrock assertion that their claims would rest upon: they are religious people, and this was a religious dispute. To establish themselves thus was tantamount to leveraging the highest possible authority, situating themselves within the parameters for authoritative speech established by NAGPRA. Much of the remainder of their presentation would be a sustained project of adding substance, example, and texture to the formal claim firmly established by their public prayer.

The Hawaiians' representation of indigenous authority—what I earlier called "minority-specific authority"—was carried forward by their first representative to speak, Linda Kawai'Ono Delaney of the OHA. Before introducing herself, she addressed the audience in Hawaiian, staking a claim to Hawaiianness and indicating, however subtly, that correct understanding is dependent upon native knowledge, which is most palpably expressed through speech performance. Switching to English, Delaney spoke in a notably religious and cultural key, tacking back and forth from present to past:

> We have traveled 6,000 miles to join you and to assure that the *mana,* or spiritual power, of the *ki'i 'aumakua* . . . will rejoin us.
>
> We are accustomed to long voyages, having sailed tens of thousands of miles to settle and make our homes on the scattered Islands of the Pacific. . . . We are heirs to a civilization which spanned the largest geographic area in human experience. . . .
>
> Now, we stand to reclaim and return to our rightful stewardship; our bones, our ancestors, our Gods, the lands, and the self-determination of the Hawaiian people. . . .
>
> Throughout our existence in the brightest and the darkest days, we have known we were one people. . . . We are of one placenta, sustained by shared genealogy and shared descendants. When we are most vulnerable, we call on the strongest of our ancestors, the *'aumakua.*[29]

With stunning verve Delaney thus trampled both the tidy boundaries of NAGPRA and commonplace notions of tradition and the sacred. Her language recast the terms of the debate altogether, moving it from a narrow discussion concerning the function of one object to an expansive account of Hawaiian religion, history, and sovereignty. Establishing the leading front of what would become an exhaustive assault, Delaney captured the audience's attention with her confident, even bold handling of "tradition." She did not shy away from invoking tradition metaphorically; indeed, she announced strikingly that her people were used to traveling far to settle: her ancestors had sailed the Pacific to settle the islands, and today she had traveled far to settle this matter. Likewise, she invoked bodily terms metaphorically to link contemporary Hawaiians with their ancestors: "We are of one placenta." With such claims Delaney also unapologetically advanced a political agenda. The dispute over the object, she made clear, could not be considered independently from Hawaiian political contexts, for the *ki'i,* the ancestors, and the land are intimately related to the quest for Hawaiian sovereignty.

If the museum's formula equating tradition with fixity was meant to imply that political claims in the present were not relevant to the status of the object—or, more strongly, that political ambitions revealed the insincerity of the religious claims to which they were harnessed—then Delaney's response sought to unbind this formula's hold in the committee's perception of tradition in the present.

The next Hawaiian representative to speak was Lani Ma'a Lapilio, who declared: "The eyes are also an outstanding feature [of this object]. . . . The Hawaiians saw the eyes, the pearl eyes, as all-seeing and all-knowing, enabling the *ki'i la'au* to be able to see—have clear vision of the battlefield. . . . The upraised left hand signifies that the spears are ready for battle, and again, the eyes would reflect the lights to—to blind his enemy."[30] Having described the warrior-god characteristics of the spirit who putatively could be called into the object, Lapilio turned to addressing the limiting terms of NAGPRA. She did so by filling legal definitions with Hawaiian concepts, describing the figure as a "sacred object" used in "consecration ceremonies as the chiefs prepared for battle. And in these ceremonies, the *ki'i 'aumakua* served as a conduit to the gods. And when the *'aumakua* was called upon through prayer and praise, it was the *akua*, or God, who would imbue the spear with *mana*, or life forces and energy."[31]

The testimony of Kunani Nihipali, then *po'o* (head) of Hui Mālama and the next representative to speak, was remarkable in a number of ways. In particular, his opening prayer was a tour de force:

We call upon our ancestors from the sun's rising to the sun's setting. We call upon our ancestors to spin and stand at our back and our front. We call upon our ancestors to stand at the right side of us, for we are your children; safeguard us, that we may grow in the heavens, that we may grow on the earth, that we may flourish in the land of our birth.

Grant us the intelligence. Grant us the understanding. Grant us the avenue of communication. Grant us good energy. Grant us your spiritual guidance and assistance. Be kind to us who are burdened. Pardon our instincts. Pardon our imperfections. Pardon our ceremonial faults. Pardon our weaknesses of the heart. Pardon our unfulfillment of vows. Pardon our speech impediments. Let your anger be appeased by our humility this day. Look upon us with favor. Grant us life in the true Hawaiian sense. Awaken within us the true depth of this work. Allow us to become one in mind, only then will we go forward in strength, in humility, and understanding. We are your children, your descendants.

For that which is above shall be brought down. For that which is below shall be lifted up. Our islands will again be united. Our walls shall once again rise and stand upright.[32]

This prayer is a masterful weaving of ancient sources and contemporary resourcefulness. The first several lines recall the ancient *Pule Hoʻola*, the middle section speaks from and to the predicament of the present, and the last lines spring directly from Kapihe's famous prophecy regarding Kamehameha's ascendancy.[33] Nihipali's words are so moving, in their combined force and economy, that it might not have occurred to the audience that the disputed object had not even been mentioned. Hawaiianness as a value, not the disputed object, was the focus of the prayer. Specifically, Nihipali was giving an account of the religious and political rectitude of Hawaiians. Once established, this cosmological depiction of Hawaiians would be condensed and restated with regard to the disputed object itself. The committee would then be asked to assent to claims about the object on the basis of demonstrated religious authenticity and the credibility this confers.

Nihipali's rhetoric was brilliant: double meanings, metaphors, and inversions are present within his every sentence. Just prior to the section of the prayer quoted above, for example, Nihipali established an affiliation with Native Americans and their ancestors, implicitly adding the moral weight of their histories to his own cause. The manner in which he called upon the Hawaiian ancestors "before us" was likewise ingenious, as this phrase carries a striking double significance: the ancestors are presented as "before us" in the (usual) chronological sense, which serves as a reminder of and homage to their history, but they are also invoked as "before us" in the sense of standing in front of the Hawaiians in the present, as leaders and defenders.[34] Nihipali's prayer also shows homage and deference toward the gods and ancestors: "Grant us the intelligence. . . . Be kind to us who are burdened." We also see here the discourse of humility: "Pardon our instincts. Pardon our imperfections." Among other things this language afforded the Hawaiians a way to preempt any accusations of incomplete knowledge and cultural incompetence that might be leveled by the museum.

Nihipali's next move was to call forth sentiments of affiliation, to call people to a higher level of connection—one including the land and the ancestors, beyond petty factionalism and, most significantly, the non-Hawaiian world. Notably, given how thorny questions of ethnicity have become in the context of contemporary

Hawaiian sovereignty movements, just who is legitimately Hawaiian is not explicitly addressed. Here, instead, the problem of belonging is implicitly resolved: those who care for the ancestors and the land are the true Hawaiians; the ancestors and the land, in turn, will care for them. Obviously, this construction is circular—but this is no mistake of logic; rather, it is representative of much religious language that seeks to depict and authorize social boundaries. The circularity of the position is not a weakness but a strength, hermetically sealing the position from external challenges. Here, then, even ethnicity—Hawaiianness itself—becomes demonstrable through religious appeals that are effectively immune from challenge. Finally, Nihipali's prayer takes an explicit political turn, as apocalyptic images of an unmistakably revolutionary hue are evoked in a staccato fashion: "For that which is above shall be brought down. For that which is below shall be lifted up. Our islands will again be united." For an audience attentive to the symbolic weight of Kamehameha's dynasty, such a closure could not fail to bring up strong emotions and images.

Upon completing his prayer, Nihipali offered an interpretation of it. Most saliently, he collapsed the voice of the prayer, so that the speaker became at once himself, the elders, the ancestral spirits, and finally the gods of the Hawaiian pantheon: "The voices you have heard are the voices of our *kupuna*, our elders. The voices you have heard are the voices of our *'aumakua*, our spiritual guiding. The voices you have heard are the voices of our *akua*, our gods, who speak to us to inspire these thoughts, this *mana*."[35] Directly following this remarkable set of linkages, Nihipali articulated yet another, this one pertaining to his specific authority: "I am *Po'o* of Hui Mālama . . . a title bestowed upon me . . . in a ceremony that took place within the beautiful valleys of *Waipio* on the Island of *Hawai'i*. A major responsibility came with that entitlement, that responsibility to our *'aumakua*, to our *na 'aumakua* and to our *kupunu* [*sic*], a responsibility in part to restore the *mana* of our nation."[36]

Barely allowing the audience to keep up, Nihipali invoked his personal *'aumakua*, Noa:

> I'd like to introduce you to another member of our family this morning, Noa. Noa is not an it. Noa is not a jester. Noa is not a buffoon. . . . Noa represents my personal *'aumakua*. It is an image of how I see our ancestors. Noa serves . . . as a receptacle of this *mana* that has been called to influence and assist in the understanding of what is taking place today. Noa represents our *'aumakua* and has seen and been to

the places we have been in the repatriation efforts these past years. Noa has been instilled and enticed with offerings and prayer, once again, to come to our aid, to respond to our prayers. . . . Noa represents the continuance of *'aumakua* worship and practice. Noa represents a connection to our past, irrespective of the influences the *hewa* have played. The protocol in use today is an extension of yesterday. Noa will be passed on within my *'ohana*, my family, who will continue future deeds and battles like these. For this is what we do today, we battle. We battle for our *ki'i lā'au 'aumakua*.[37]

With this speech Nihipali made a direct personal connection between past and present. In so doing he again wielded the Hawaiians' central metaphor: the dispute is a battle, a battle over the *ki'i* and sovereignty itself. Nihipali made this connection yet more explicit: "What we do understand is that our *iwi*, this *ki'i* in question, represents a sense of place, a sense of our continued struggle for sovereignty. . . . Those *ki'i* will empower ourselves again as a nation of people."[38]

In this claim Nihipali made a crucial segue: he described the *ki'i* (object) as *iwi* (bone). This gave the auditors a more concrete sense that the object was an ancestor; more significantly, it enabled Nihipali implicitly to bring into his presentation the leverage NAGPRA affords with regard to human remains. The more cultural objects can be described in the lexicon of human remains, the more support NAGPRA affords by way of association. That is, if auditors could be persuaded that the *ki'i* was *iwi*—even if metaphorically so—the Hawaiians would have made a strong case that it deserved the deference usually reserved for culturally affiliated human remains: immediate repatriation. Thus ended a remarkable presentation.

The next Hawaiian representative to speak was Edward Halealoha Ayau. Ayau, a member of Hui Mālama, was also participating as administrator of the State Burials Program. Ayau situated himself by way of genealogical authorization and, in doing so, asked for the assistance of his ancestors in the matter at hand: "As I stated earlier, by name, my parents, their parents, 32 generations of my ancestors, as a means of calling upon them for strength, for the intelligence, for knowledge, for righteous understanding, for all the tools that are necessary to engage in—in a situation like this."[39] Having called upon his ancestors, Ayau then made their relevance clear. Continuing to use the metaphor that had by now been well-established, he emphasized the agonistic nature of the dispute: "Although we are—we recognize the comments that was made by—by Dr. Haas about the amicable nature of—of the proceeding, we ask the Committee to also recognize what our responsibilities are, to our people, to our *'aumakua*, our ancestors, and especially for those who will come after us. As far as we are concerned, this is a competition. What is at stake is a *ki'i* that once housed a powerful *'aumakua*."[40] He then shifted from this point to take up where Nihipali had left off, arrestingly asserting the isomorphism of *iwi* and *ki'i*: "For us, this *ki'i* is the same as *iwi*. It's the same as bone. The name that we chose for ourselves, Na Oiwi O Hawai'i Nei, we are the bone of *Hawai'i*. We are *Hawai'i*. In our bones are our spirits. And in the bones of our ancestors are their spirits. The *ki'i* had the same function. It was used to house the spirit of an ancestor."[41]

Ayau then listed specific ancestors connected to the object, establishing genealogical connections relevant under the law. Following this claim, he asserted that the *ki'i* had been removed from a burial cave, thus gaining additional potential purchase under NAGPRA's definition of "associated burial object." Having squarely framed his presentation within the concerns of the law, he related the history of chiefs and ancient Hawaiian warfare to the present case: "The opening chants that we did, included a recitation of *mo'o kū auhau* genealogy, which specific ancestors were called upon. The specific ancestors I called upon were these ruling chiefs from this family. So for me this is very personal matter."[42] Ayau next spoke of the creation and consecration ceremonies related to the *ki'i*, thus adding further detail to the assertion that this was a sacred (i.e., ritually used) object under the law. Developing this position, he deftly transitioned from ancient practices to contemporary ritual:

Consecration of the *ki'i* occurred when the *'aumakua* was called forward and was called to—to dwell in the *ki'i*. The *'aumakua* was then fed. The *ki'i* was fed. And then the *ki'i* was directed to provide the service. The idea is, in Hawaiian thought, just because you die doesn't end your role in the family. For some, it enhanced it.

The next ceremony that was conducted included the consecration of the *ki'i* as a war weapon. . . . Warriors concentrated their weapons to seek *lokahi* between their gods and themselves to assure success in war.

Ongoing ceremonies by living descendants may be conducted to call upon the *'aumakua*, to call the *'aumakua* back. . . . The ongoing significance for this *ki'i*, especially for descendants of these ruling chiefs, is to be able to reactivate them, to ask for the same kind of strength and knowledge needed in modern-day confrontations. . . .

The *'aumakua* that is summoned through use of the *ki'i* could be called upon to help sharpen our minds, our tongues, and the spirit of contemporary Hawaiian warriors.[43]

As we have seen, museum representatives and the authorities they called upon had difficulty accepting a link between the object's past and tradition in the present; Hawaiian representatives, clearly, were notably limber in this respect. In this dispute, as I argue concerning NAGPRA in general, conflict over an object created—or, in this case, called into being—the object's purportedly sacred qualities. Hawaiian minds and tongues were most definitely sharpened in this context; focusing on this object stimulated a clear and forceful, warriorlike articulation of present desires.

At this point Ayau described a most interesting event. Having learned that the object was to be auctioned, the Hawaiians had contacted Sotheby's and asked to perform a ritual in its presence. What probably seemed to Sotheby's an innocuous if odd request was actually a coup de grâce on the part of the Hawaiians: having performed a ritual with the object gave them heavy artillery in the dispute, as this ritual met one condition of the legal definition of "sacred object." Unwittingly, and much to its subsequent chagrin, Sotheby's had thus enabled the Hawaiians to meet a pivotal condition of the law. Now the Hawaiians could declare: we are religious leaders, we performed a necessary religious ritual, ergo the object is sacred. This was the final prong of the Hawaiians' persuasive case: "We asked the museum and Sotheby's for permission to conduct a ceremony. That ceremony was intended to do exactly what I explained, call upon the 'aumakua. What you see here in this picture is . . . 'awa. 'Awa was used in Hawaiian ceremony . . . to entice the 'aumakua. On this side, 'iliahi, sandlewood [sic], again used to entice the 'aumakua to come back."[44]

During the thirteenth Review Committee meeting, in Norman, the Hawaiian claimants continued to make their case for the sacred status of the object. The first "traditional religious leader" called upon to speak was Pualani Kanaka'ole Kanahele. Kanahele offered a stunning response to the museum's effort to present insider/outsider authorities, representing her own authority in expansive terms:

My name is Pualani Kanaka'ole Kanahele, and I am a resident of Hawaii Island. I am pure Hawaiian. I have been raised in a family of people who practiced the culture in many different aspects of the culture. I am, besides, an instructor of Hawaiian language and Hawaiian studies

at the community college, I am also a *kumahula* . . . who has received
this particular tradition from the—my mother's side of the family and
again from her mother's side of the family and again from her uncle's
side of the family, besides a *kumahula* from matrilineal descent. I am
also a practitioner of the fire deity *Pele*. . . . I am a leader in ceremonial
practices to *'aumakua*. And so, that's who I am, thank you. Who are
you, by the way?[45]

After introducing herself, Kanahele reiterated the Hawaiians' position that the figure was a long-venerated *'aumakua* object that had
once been the possession of the famous chief Kahekele (Kahekili)
and was thus linked to his genealogy and his family's guardians,
thunder and lightning. She agreed that the object was a spear support
imbued with *mana* for warfare. Kanahele's testimony became especially engaging, however, as she responded to a question regarding
the object's role in the present:

> We just got the island of Kahoolawe back from the military, but the
> whole thing of these problems of entrance into the land is a war; is
> in our minds, a battle. And so we continue with—we continuously
> battle with those entities who are outside of the culture, who come
> onto our land, buy up our land or use the land for reasons that we're
> not used to, for reasons that we see are desecrating our land. And so
> these are all, to us, battles in our own mind.
>
> And sometimes we handle the battle in court, and sometimes we
> handle the battle in legislative levels. It doesn't matter, they are bat-
> tles. And battles, we will call on the battle *'aumakua*. We will call
> on those war gods that need to help us in those battles. And so I can
> see that as the *ki'i*, and there are still many of us that's connected
> to the *kawela*, or the lightening [sic] and thunder, because we still
> carry those names in our family, and so, genealogically, we're still
> connected, that would use those particular entities to help us in these
> battles to maintain a level of being Hawaiian, a level of connectedness
> to the land, to the air space above us, and to the ocean. That's how we
> view this today.[46]

Committee member Jonathan Haas responded to these claims by asking "how a support for war spears on a war canoe from an object that
dates to the late 18th or early 19th Century continues to have that
same kind of sacredness as defined under the law."[47] Kanahele's rejoinder made explicit the pivotal dynamic of the Hawaiians' position:

Because an object is old and was used in the 1800s or the 1700s does not mean it has lost its usefulness. We need today to reinterpret our—our connection to these particular objects.

That particular *ki'i*, as I was saying earlier, was used a long time ago. However, it still has that same function for us today. And the function is that we're still fighting the battle of maintaining a very high level of being connected to our land. That was something that held the spear. The spear was an implement to—to win wars. The—the—the holding on to the spear was a very necessary part of maintaining the spear.

Now, our implements to winning wars are in another form. Metaphorically, it is still the spear, and it's still holding on to that particular tool which allows us to have a—a sense of freedom for being Hawaiian.[48]

Kanahele's swirling language creates a vortex of sorts wherein spirits, wars, the land, and time itself become vertiginously compressed, held together by the centrifugal force of her metaphors: the object was used in battles; is now embattled; is a warrior in this battle over itself, which is also the ongoing battle of being Hawaiian, a battle over land and political self-determination.

The next person called by Delaney was Lilikalā Kame'eleihiwa. If Pualani Kanaka'ole Kanahele's testimony had staged the battle, this was the siege: "My name is Lilikalā Kame'eleihiwa. I'm an Associate Professor at the Center for Hawaiian Studies at the University of Hawaii in Manoa, but more importantly, I'm a descendant of the—of the (Native Hawaiian name) of (Native Hawaiian name) of Oahu, of (Native Hawaiian name), the (Native Hawaiian name) of (Native Hawaiian name), who was cousin of Kahekele. I call upon the spirits to come into this *ki'i* and that this *ki'i* be returned to us."[49] In one succinct paragraph she thus asserted both minority-specific and majority-inclusive authority. Moreover, she claimed ritual authority through a dramatic speech act, calling the spirits into the *ki'i* in the process of demanding the object's return. In this way she demonstrated new grammatical rules for the sacred and the law: the sacred has a verb quality; it can be activated. What is more, as a verb it has tenses: past, present, and future. Sacred grammar follows this rule: its use is predicated on the combination of right speaker and right audience.[50] Kame'eleihiwa assumed the role of correct speaker and gambled that the force of her claims would persuade the audience to assume their appropriate role:

We must bring back all of those things that are sacred to our ancestors, including our ancestors, including the bones that have been taken from our land, the bones that have been stolen from our land, the bones that have been tested by so-called anthropologists and archaeologists, who are nothing more than grave robbers to us, and all of those sacred objects.

This is a *ki'i* we are talking about. And I have listened patiently, for the last three or four hours, not wanting to interrupt those people, many who do not speak Hawaiian, many who do not practice Native religion as we do here in Hawaii, many who are Christian talking about this *ki'i* . . . as if it was some mere object. . . . This is *ki'i* to us. . . .

So, when I look at all these things that have been said, I find it very disturbing and I call upon the ancestors to be with us. I call upon the ancestors to come back and enter this *ki'i* and bring him home to us.[51]

At this juncture Delaney again took over the Hawaiians' presentation, making a novel appeal that can be read as foreshadowing aspects of the Kawaihae dispute. She observed that Native Hawaiians had participated on both sides of the dispute and expressed remorse about this divisiveness. This unfortunate situation, she said, could be remedied by the power of the *ki'i:*

There is a heavy weight, but it is not something we will try to personalize. Just know that that [the intra-Hawaiian tension] is a part of the harm we are talking about that needs that kind of ritual and ceremonial presence to help us heal. And it is part of what we come to ask once again that you support us in, that we are bone of one bone, blood of one blood, all descendants of *Hāloa.* That practice and belief will carry us, will support us, which is what *haka* means at the deepest level, to support. Look at the figure, look at the *ki'i,* to join heaven and earth to once again be the bridge that we so much need, and for which it once served. We will care for it; it will care for us.[52]

Another speaker called by the claimants was Hannah Kihalani Springer, who identified herself as a member of the OHA's board of trustees and as a religious practitioner. Speaking of herself and three of the other Hawaiians, she said:

This morning, the four of us gathered upon the earth of this land, beneath the sky of this place, and we called forth through traditional

prayers asserting our interdependent relationship with (Native Hawaiian language), the ʻaumakua who come from the place where the sun
rises to the place where the sun sets, from the zenith in the Heaven
and from the horizon about us. We, further, called forth in a manner
taught us by our kuma Hawaii Pua Kanahele using the kalaoʻo kauila
[a piece of wood used as proxy for the disputed object]. . . .

We were instructed that by this focus object we would connect
to that which has been embodied in the past and comes through our
voices again to the kiʻi lāʻau at Rhode Island. We do these things as
practitioners. We do these things today. Where our ancestors were the
practitioners that have provided data for the anthropologists of yesterday and today, it is our practice that provides that information for
those yet to come.[53]

Springer's commentary includes two lynchpins of the Hawaiian presentation: first, she again described ritual use of the object in the
present; and second, she represented herself and others as traditional
religious leaders—as practitioners (i.e., as authorized voices in the
context of NAPGRA). To this end her final claim—that the Hawaiian
representatives would be a resource for future anthropologists—is
astounding in its novelty and is, at least by way of this book, true.

Stranger Kings Have Happened

Returning to our question concerning the status and function of tradition, I would like to conclude by tracking one claim made by Edward
Halealoha Ayau. My point in doing so is to provide an example of
how to read tradition in a way that seeks to understand seemingly
discordant invocations of the past in the present. Building upon his
testimony introduced earlier, Ayau went on to add substance to a
central metaphor of the Hawaiians: this dispute was a battle, and
the kiʻi was a warrior. Specifically, Ayau described the object as a
Kū-style figure: "This kiʻi was carved in what's called the Kū style.
Kū is a war god. Kū in Hawaiian also means 'upright.' It means 'to
stand.' That's what this kiʻi was—was used for. It was used in a Kū
tradition, which is warfare."[54] This identification of the object with
the god Kū leads us into the riches of ancient Hawaiian tradition. It
also confronts us with our central question: is this a traditional use
of tradition?

When Ayau invoked the name of Kū, he was doing so in congruence with preceding claims that the object had been used in warfare
by leading chiefs, for Kū is widely understood to have been the primary

deity in charge of warfare.[55] Two important points offer support for the object's association with Kū. First, sources agree that Kū was the deity pertaining to craftsmen, in particular to the carving of images.[56] Second, Kū was believed by some Hawaiians to imbue warriors and chiefs with the ability to wield their spears expertly in battle.[57]

These observations notwithstanding, two other aspects of Hawaiian tradition make the appeal to Kū seem spurious. First, even if it is granted that the object is an 'aumakua figure, a serious categorical discrepancy must be addressed. Namely, precontact Hawaiian religion recognized two kinds of deities, akua and 'aumakua.[58] The former were understood to be primary deities and the latter minor spirits. Akua formed the basis of the kapu system and were understood to be responsible for all major issues of social and cosmic existence. The latter, most often described as familial spirits (occasionally malevolent and used in sorcery), were also believed to be manifest in various natural phenomena.[59] Not only was Kū one of the four akua, but in another manifestation he was the paramount deity of the Hawaiian cosmos.[60] Thus, in a system that distinguished between major and minor deities, Kū stood at the furthest remove from the relatively minor 'aumakua. Thus, for Hawaiians in the present to link Kū to an 'aumakua vessel would seem to violate the very order of their own tradition.

The second problem with the invocation of Kū is related to the first. The Hawaiian claimants represented themselves as the kanaka (people) and routinely made reference to the 'āina (land) and their tenure upon it as the literal ground of their authority.[61] We might expect this move, given the political nature of the Hawaiians' grievances and the explicit ways in which they linked the return of the object with their project of regaining sovereignty. But given this context, it seems awkward for the Hawaiians to invoke Kū as their champion. Like much of Polynesia, Hawai'i (at least in the time surrounding European contact) was a realm ruled largely by stranger kings who appealed to fierce Kū as their source of power and rule. By way of today's political realities, the power of Kū, then, would seem to rest with an entirely more modern stranger against whom the kanaka must struggle. So it seems strange and incongruent to appeal to Kū as champion of the people in the present. Is it, though?

Both of these problems are cast in a new light if we consider the breakdown of traditional Hawaiian religion in 1819 with the end of Kamehameha's reign and the end of the kapu system. The kapu system was among other things a collective representation of anti-collective interests. It was a mechanism by which things were made "taboo"; in practice this involved a system of distinctions that separated the spheres of the nobility and the *kanaka*, as well as the roles of men and women. Matters changed significantly when traditional religion was largely abandoned after Kamehameha's death, in a time of cultural and economic upheaval. At this time worship of the primary deities (*akua*) effectively ended. Simultaneously, traditional systems of *kanaka* feudalism were breaking down as chiefs became entrenched in European trade and consumption patterns as the primary means of accumulating and displaying *mana*.[62]

'Aumākua worship, however, was not abandoned in 1819. While many of the cultural elite adopted various Christianities, many of the *kanaka* continued to worship familial spirits and other *'aumākua*. In fact, *'aumākua* worship appears to have subsumed elements of *akua* worship and the traditional temple religion. As Valerio Valeri argues, "it is likely that since the cult of *'aumakua* survived the abolition of the traditional, official religion, this notion was used increasingly to describe the deities of the past and their natural manifestations even when they did not traditionally belong to the *'aumakua* class."[63] Thus, as the people were no longer directly subordinate to chiefs, so too the *'aumākua* were not subordinate to the *akua*. Rather, in both cases the formerly inferior incorporated the formerly superior in the face of a new foreign threat (European commerce and Christianity).

In this context, then, some of the apparent tensions in contemporary Hawaiians' appropriation of Kū begin to dissolve. Traditional religion reappears, as it were, through a camera obscura of sorts. Images of Kū the warrior are domesticated by the people in order to fight against a new stranger king: the Haole. Indeed, this sort of appeal to a protective Kū has a recent precedent in the work of George Kanahele, interestingly titled *Kū Kanaka*. Kanahele argues that contemporary emphasis should be placed upon Kū's bravery and the example he sets for his people in "standing tall" for the land.[64] "Kū'e"—resist—is the rallying call for many activists in Hawai'i today. Moreover, attentive visitors to Hawai'i will notice the prevalence of fierce Kū images in street and surf settings, attesting to his attractiveness to those who find themselves at odds with an increasingly non-Hawaiian society.

Linking past and present understandings of Kū, I do not view contemporary appropriations of Kū as spurious. "Tradition" is not left behind at this juncture; rather, tradition is rearticulated in the present as the chief means by which native peoples confront authorities and epistemologies not of their own making or choice. In the case at hand, the choice to invoke Kū was surely motivated by present concerns. But it is not thereby mere artifice. As Peter Nabokov notes: "Uncovering the synthesized nature of indigenous claims does not mean that they are composed of thin air. Study of their components and adhesive compounds identifies cultural processes that can also be upstreamed to identify their presence and consistency over earlier eras."[65] My goal here has been to provide an example drawn from one culture but constituted in different historical periods, showing how religious discourse is always at work and constantly worked upon. To suggest that we distinguish between pure tradition and political invention is tantamount to marking off the past and discounting the present—both acts that ignore the profoundly human and social quality of tradition.

6

RELIGIOUS VOICES AND SOCIAL BORDERS

As I lowered the young girl to her grave, I realized the magnitude of my emotional attachment to her. She is a part of my life. Although our contact was brief, I continue to remember her today, as a person and not as a skull.

—Connie Hart Yellowman, "'Naevahoo'ohtseme'—
We are Going Back Home"

Footprints of Ancestors

IMAGINE YOU are with me as I paint a picture of a scene as it unfolded in the summer of 2004. We are back in the Four Corners region of the Southwest, in the heart of Anasazi country. High on a juniper-covered mesa at an elevation approaching seven thousand feet, we can see the better part of a hundred miles in all directions. Beneath a cobalt sky the scope of our grand view includes, in the distance, southeast Utah and northwest New Mexico, the locations of our two previous encounters with the storied Anasazi—one at the hands of the nonnative miner; the other in the Chaco dispute among the Navajo, the Hopi, and other Puebloan groups regarding cultural affiliation.

Our vantage point is itself another narrative nexus in the many-authored tale of ancient peoples and contemporary identities in the Southwest. A long, dusty drive brought us to the edge of a canyon rim where our Native American guide now assembles us, a group of fifteen or so nonnative tourists and scholars, for an orientation. Wiping his brow with a bandanna, he describes the relationship of his people to the Anasazi, including a cosmographic depiction of the dead in relationship to the living. In a hushed tone he proclaims that we are about to enter "the spirit world," which is often dangerous. To protect us, he says a long prayer in his native language and then performs a simple cleansing ceremony with sage. As he slowly circles the group, we each take a pinch of the herb to bless ourselves. We then hike across the red rock of the canyon rim toward a hewn-wood ladder. Our guide pauses to point out circular depressions in the rock, declaring that the Anasazi handcrafted these to channel precious water into their homesites. He muses about the ingenuity of his ancestors. We descend the ladder and arrive in the cool shadow of a spectacular cliff-side ruin, Ponderosa House. *Monos, matates,* ancient corncobs, and pottery fragments are abundant. Rock art, especially painted hands, bedecks many walls. The rooms of the structure are in excellent shape, partly due to the recent stabilization efforts of the tribe. Our guide leads us through rooms and passageways, taking us down corridors of the past.

But whose past? Our guide is neither Puebloan nor Navajo. He is a Ute Indian, and we are visiting the Ute Mountain Tribal Park, an archaeological preserve on the Ute Mountain Ute Reservation. By most accounts, scientific or indigenous, the Ute have no historical connection to the Anasazi. In the present, however, they manifestly do.

The stories we have listened to and the ritual we engaged in push us to continue refining our understanding of the relationship of traditions, identity, and law. Following upon the previous chapter's analysis of tradition as metaphor and metaphors of tradition, here we take up two contexts in which narratives of tradition invoke religious language to describe group boundaries in several diverse and telling respects. The first is an elaboration of Ute claims upon the Anasazi; the second considers an internal Cheyenne conflict regarding Sand Creek Massacre remains. Exploring these examples, their components unexpected and agonistic, we will continue to puzzle out the larger themes of this book, analyzing the ways several native representatives faced the daunting task of representing their epistemological and moral authority at multiple levels, from the microlocal to the macrocosmic. The bedeviling theoretical and practical question we will face is this: if traditions operate metaphorically through interpreting the past in terms of the present, then what happens when literal demands are placed upon metaphorical truths, when traditional claims must speak to legal code, when symbolic boundaries map incongruently with political ones?

Angry Spirits

Despite the fact that it contains hundreds of "Anasazi" ruins, including many spectacular cliff houses, the Ute Mountain Tribal Park is relatively unknown to tourists of the U.S. Southwest. This is surprising, given its contiguity with Mesa Verde National Park and its proximity to other cultural and tourism sites, such as the Four Corners, Ship Rock, and Chaco Canyon. To understand this situation, one must look to the history of the park and Ute culture. The park itself is part of the Ute Mountain Ute Reservation, which was established in 1895.[1] Utes controlled much of the Colorado high country and the surrounding canyons to the west at the time of white encroachment into their land, which accelerated rapidly in the late nineteenth century. With the influx of miners and ranchers, Utes were pushed onto several reservations in Colorado and Utah.[2] These reservations were within Ute traditional lands, but being limited to them radically disrupted Ute subsistence patterns and cultural life generally. As described earlier, during this period non-Indians newly arrived to the region were "discovering" the ruins and remains of the Anasazi, putting their objects and skeletons on parade at World's Fairs and elsewhere, where they played an iconic role in the narrative construction of a national claim to a uniquely American antiquity.

The Utes' position was tense for two primary reasons. First, many Anasazi remains were on their land, which led to the unwanted presence of non-Utes on the reservation. Second, various accounts suggest that Utes of that time regarded Anasazi remains with fear, manifested through avoidance.[3] Ute myths recorded in the early twentieth century suggest that the Anasazi were imagined as cannibals and sexual predators, representing chaos, danger, and disease.[4] According to Ute accounts, as well as various non-Indian sources, Utes neither inhabited the many dwellings left by the Anasazi nor, apparently, utilized Anasazi pottery or other domestic utility objects.[5] Indeed, metonymically, the ruins were historically considered a well of illness. That is, they contain the dead and the remains of the dead, which, in historical Ute understanding, renders them highly contaminated. Ute soul theory holds that souls linger near the remains of a corpse, becoming potentially malicious upon death. These souls are thought to seek out living souls by infecting people who come into contact with them. Illness—and possibly death—result from contact with these spirits.[6] Traditional Ute mortuary practices thus involved abandoning the dead and burning their possessions so that all sources of possible contagion would be eliminated.[7]

These mortuary practices were not peripheral to daily Ute religious concerns: Ute ritual life was organized around the preservation of health, understood biologically, socially, and cosmologically as a single reality.[8] A primary strategy in seeking health was to constrain ritually the sources of illness in order to keep malicious spirits at bay. The role of ritual leaders was precisely to identify and banish such spirits. Those who came into direct contact with spirits and professed to communicate with them were thought to be powerful indeed, though malevolent. Accusations of witchcraft frequently surrounded people who were suspected of being in contact with the dead or their remains. This reasoning is not merely artifactual: some Utes today continue to speak of the dead and their things as dangerous, though their mortuary practices reflect modern American trends.[9] And further, these anxieties still extend to the Anasazi. When traveling in Ute country, one hears many anecdotes regarding the potential perils of entering ruins or participating in archaeological projects.

Most relevant and challenging for our purposes, nothing in the sources I have consulted suggests that nineteenth-century Utes considered themselves culturally or genealogically related to the Anasazi. In the twentieth century, however, Ute discourse regarding the Anasazi underwent a shift, marked most notably by the opening of the Ute Mountain Tribal Park for tourism in 1971.[10] Though it is much larger than Mesa Verde, the park has not been similarly developed. It has no paved roads or tourist facilities, and a Ute guide must accompany tours. The park does bring in steady income to the tribe, but it could hardly be considered a cash cow.[11] Nonetheless, in the course of developing the park and giving tours, tribal park representatives and guides have undertaken a redescription of Ute perceptions of and relations to the Anasazi and their things. The discourse of fear and the practice of avoidance have been replaced with a discourse of respect and affiliation, made evident through ritual offerings at ruins and generalized references to the ancestors. In fact, in touring the park and speaking with tribal members affiliated with it, I noticed a double narrative at work: at times elements of the older pattern emerge, with emphasis placed on the distance between Utes and the Anasazi; at other times Ute speakers narrate continuities with the Anasazi, continuities that speak most directly of spiritual inheritance and contemporary identity politics in the Southwest.

We need to broaden our scope somewhat in order to appreciate the context of this discursive shift. Namely, it is relevant to note that the economic and symbolic value of the Anasazi has been escalating in recent years throughout the Southwest. As we have seen, along with the Utes, a diversity of Puebloan tribes and the Navajo Nation share an interest in ancestral cultural capital. These groups seek to describe their relationship to the Anasazi in various ways, and nowhere is this clearer than in the context of repatriation disputes. The repatriation battles at Chaco Canyon National Historic Park and Mesa Verde National Park have made this negotiation of relationship especially vivid. Both institutions have contended with more than twenty different claimants from the region, all asserting "cultural affiliation" with the Anasazi. As we have seen, this situation has placed tremendous pressure on the law as these groups explicitly and contentiously challenge one another's rights to claim the Anasazi as ancestors. In this context Utes do not stand to emerge singularly triumphant; they have neither positivist evidence nor a substantial body of oral tradition to support their position vis-à-vis larger and wealthier tribes like the Hopi and the Navajo. But they do stand to gain something rather significant if rulings include Utes' claims to affiliation: a legally recognized anchoring point for claims to their geographical and cultural space that would be far more visible than prevailing histories and attitudes allow. Indeed, with the Mesa Verde repatriation of 2006, this is the situation that appears to be emerging.

Regardless of how NAGPRA affiliation rulings emerge, however, I suspect that some Utes will continue to look to the Anasazi as a resource for the articulation of their identities. An example of this may be found in a recent newspaper article whose headline caught my attention immediately: "Utes See 'Spirits' in Calamities." The accompanying picture showed a representative of the Ute Mountain Ute Tribe with whom I was familiar from NAGPRA-related events. The caption read: "Terry Knight, the spiritual leader of the Ute Mountain Ute Indian tribe, appears in his traditional native garb."[12] Straining to bring the headline and picture into correspondence with my understanding of Ute religion, I was reminded that representations of tradition, like all representations, often entail more and less than meets the eye.

First, Utes do not historically have a single spiritual leader, but multiple specialists who serve religious functions in various capacities (e.g., medicine healers, sweat-lodge specialists, Sun Dance leaders, and peyote Road Men).[13] Moreover, religious authority in any one of these spheres is seldom invested wholly in one person. Pragmatic in addressing their ritual needs, Utes will often consult more than one specialist with regard to a given situation, often leaving the reservation to seek assistance from Navajo and Puebloan specialists. In this context specialists cannot rest on their laurels; they must continually assert and demonstrate their authority and effectiveness in relation to rivals. This dynamic has been well documented with regard to the history of Ute peyotism and the Ute Sun Dance.[14]

Several recent events suggest that the contemporary context has much in common with this history, as Ute leaders routinely juxtapose themselves with others in the tribe who claim positions of authority. Terry Knight's public speaking is particularly revealing in this regard. At a repatriation conference in Denver that focused on Colorado tribes, Knight promoted his vision of Ute spirituality vis-à-vis the presentations of several other Ute leaders, who emphasized a spirit of cooperation with government and museum officials and spoke in the cadenced lexicon of a specifically North American syncretic monotheism, employing phrases such as "One Master," "We have access to the Great Spirit," and "In our Indian Way."[15] These particular phrases come from the presentation of Everett Burch, a member of a long-standing family of Ute leaders and a cultural-preservation officer of the Southern Ute Tribe. Roland McCook Sr., chairman of the Uintah and Ouray Tribe, used similarly inflected language when he spoke, representing a joint utilization and even merging of minority-specific and majority-inclusive rhetoric. Frank Sherwood, of the Denver Indian Singers, had set the tone for this mode of speaking by opening the meeting with a song and a prayer, then speaking about Native American dignity in the context of repatriation, discussing the meaning of citizenship, detailing his career in the U.S. military, and concluding that "we fight for this country." Responding to these presentations, Knight emphasized three themes: first, adherence to traditional religious principles; second, a corresponding rejection of "white" values and particularly those of "Christian archaeologists"; and third, a relationship between Anasazi remains and Ute culture. His words and tone made it clear that he was asserting minority-specific authority, with an eye toward differentiating his position from that of other Ute leaders.

Knight's approach was evident again at another meeting later the same year. This meeting, at the Colorado Springs Fine Arts Center, was held in celebration of the opening of an exhibit on Ute culture.[16]

Various Ute representatives spoke on a range of themes, nearly all of them touching on religion, if in frequently divergent ways that could not be easily reconciled. Knight spoke toward the end of the day, and his presentation, entitled "Ute Leaders of the Past," included a genealogy of Ute leaders and a description of their qualities: dignity, seriousness, and experience. Effectively, if not explicitly, the thrust of Knight's presentation was that he is heir to this tradition of Ute leadership. Consider his opening comments:

> I want to say good morning. Mique Nuche-u burr-ow-won [Hello Utes, my relatives]. I had a lot of stuff to read and talk about, but I didn't know there was going to be a whole group of ten people that they had scheduled. Usually when I talk, I talk about an hour minimum or three or four hours. That's from my old council days. I'll start with the old days: when the people talked they had something to say. They could talk for a good three to four hours easy. They'd talk about a lot of things—they'd talk about personal life and how it should be integrated within the sociological system of the tribe. And, of course, the man was talking—do you hear that ladies? The man was talking. He was a leader—of the family, of the band.[17]

Knight concluded by saying that he was "getting older now, more serious, no more room for joking." This was meant as a pointed jab at fellow presenters, especially Alden Naranjo, whose discussion of Ute creation had utilized Ute humor.

I remembered Knight's presentation when I saw the newspaper article. It is possible that I am overreading here; perhaps the definitive article ("the" spiritual leader) was a mistake on the part of the journalist. Still, whatever the source of the singular imputation, its effect is best understood as a joint authorship/authorization of "Indianness" in a manner that includes native speakers and nonnative auditors (in this case a journalist) in a dialogical relationship. In short, I am suggesting that NAGPRA-related media exposure has further complicated the already vertiginous processes by which images of Indians are created, circulated, apprehended, and reproduced. The expectations of the audience influence the genre, here as elsewhere: the pronouncements that would follow would be bold, and a satisfying attribution of authority seemed a necessary precondition of their articulation.

Indeed, the body of the article, which addressed Ute views of a forest fire then raging at Mesa Verde, was stunning in its novelty. It began by setting up a distinction between modern and traditional

Utes, with the romantic conjecture that real Utes are somehow at a remove from civilization, living at a distance that allows them a window to "the spirits" and a view of time not limited by the present:

> Away from the coin clatter and flashing lights of the Ute Mountain Casino, there are still some native people here who watch and listen for signs from the natural world, signals from another dimension. These traditional Ute Mountain Ute Indians have taken to heart the stories of their fathers, grandmothers and great-grandfathers that explain events in their world. And when they look east from Sleeping Ute Mountain of their reservation at the columns of smoke standing in the hazy sky over Mesa Verde National Park, they see bad signs.[18]

The article continued with a quotation from Terry Knight: "The old spirits that are there are not at rest. Their energy is off-balance, and this causes things to happen in the metaphysical world." More specifically, according to the article, Knight reported that "elders have told him the spirits of the ancient ones who inhabited the area from 500 to 1300 AD are tired of being excavated, analyzed and legislated." Knight added: "There is something happening with that tribe within the ground. These spirits are getting back at people for doing this and doing that."

This retribution, which Knight asserted had been foretold by ancestors, was said to be in direct response to abuses of NAGPRA. As reported by the author, Nancy Lofholm, museums and universities holding human remains from Mesa Verde had returned only a "smattering" of the thousands of remains eligible for repatriation. Knight asked, "How can these spirits not be mad?" Knight vented his frustration with NAGPRA processes, recommending that details of the law be pushed aside in order that the remains be buried "in one huge site with proper ceremony so the spirits can rest." Then, with reference to the fire, Knight made another appeal for the necessity of a ceremony. As Lofholm reported: "Knight said a ceremony should be performed once the ashes have cooled. Or else as his late father, the medicine man Charlie Knight told him, the earth will burn again." As Knight represented the situation, Anasazi spirits were responsible for the fire, Utes communicate with these spirits, and certain Ute leaders are able to ritually manage this relationship.[19]

This was not the first time Knight had expressed such ideas. In 1992 he had made similar claims, if in a more local way. Some houses were to be built near Towaoc, the center of the Ute Mountain Ute Reservation, but the site that had been selected was adjacent to a group of Anasazi ruins. Responding to mounting anxiety concerning this situation, Knight blessed the site. Jim Carrier provided the following account:

> This week he performed special prayers prior to ground-breaking for units being built near an Anasazi ruin. Dressed in jeans and a cowboy shirt, Terry built a fire and burned cedar and herbs near the old kiva wall, a round ceremonial chamber used about AD 1000. "I talked to the old Anasazi spirits and told them we're going to be building some new homes, and not to let the machinery and people disrupt them. I told them families would be living there, I asked them to be more like a guardian force." Had Terry not "balanced" the area, Ute families would have been reluctant to move in, said Gerald Peabody, the housing director. Those who did "most likely would be haunted and not sleep too good."[20]

Parallel to my argument regarding the role of tradition in the dispute over the Hawaiian *ki'i*, much of Knight's professed relationship with Anasazi spirits can be analyzed in terms of the "invention of tradition." This observation, however, is not meant to dismiss the cultural relevance of his position. Were he Kiowa or Arapaho, his relationship to Anasazi spirits would undoubtedly be expressed in different terms. But the novelty of Knight's claims and Ute discourse on the topic more generally—wherein Ute ethnic identity has been recast to include rather than exclude the Anasazi—goes beyond what many models of "tradition" can account for comfortably. In this case the novel expressions have sources beyond Ute "ontology." And yet we surely want to acknowledge that Knight's claims are constitutive of tradition in the making. Analysis of such discourse misses the mark if it reifies tradition in the past-perfect or sees only the agentic, individual aspects of strategic speech. For comparative and theoretical purposes, then, our concern is as much with the category of tradition as it is with the ways Knight's discourse does or does not fit this category.

It seems to me that we might abandon the category or work to liberate it from the assumption that tradition pertains primarily to "content" rather than to habits of mind and action over the long run. Here I am not only appealing to a model of historical structuralism, though I would suggest that Marshall Sahlins's views concerning the cultural organization of modernity are illuminating in this regard.[21] I suggest linking Sahlins's conceptual understanding of tradition in action to a position that views tradition as the manifestation of applied political wisdom and strategy over time.[22] Viewed from this perspective, Knight's narrative can be understood as emerging from a tradition of fierce oratory that informs the way a group positions itself in relation to potentially helpful allies, even if those allies were ancestral foes.[23]

The Enemy Within

A well-documented example of repatriation concerns the "sacred pole" returned from the Peabody Museum to the Omaha Nation.[24] This object, known in Omaha as Umon'hon'ti (Venerable Man), was undoubtedly central to the tribe's religious life before it was conveyed to the museum.[25] A fine documentary film made at the time of the repatriation is instructive with regard to the manner in which long-standing intragroup tensions become manifest when a politically charged and publicly visible religious event occurs.[26] Interviews conducted for the film make clear that Omaha society today is still split in ways hearkening back to a nineteenth-century tribal cleavage that developed as various members of the tribe aligned with or rejected assimilationist interests espoused by the anthropologist Alice Fletcher and her informant and colleague, Francis LaFlesche.[27]

At the time of the repatriation (1989), two distinct visions of history were promoted. Tribal government representatives spoke of Fletcher's role in acquiring the sacred pole for the Peabody as an act of charity, a decisive step in preserving Omaha heritage for the future. But another group of contemporary Omaha tribe members, who identified with "the last of the real spiritual leaders," accused Fletcher of having taken the pole without authority, effectively robbing the Omaha of their central religious object. Most pointedly, they claimed that LaFlesche, who became quite famous as a pioneering Native American anthropologist, was not a member of the Omaha tribe but an impostor from the Ponca tribe.[28] Despite these strong differences, the situation was tentatively resolved, with representatives of each group finally endorsing the repatriation and leading different ceremonies upon its return.[29]

A more recent intragroup dispute is similarly revealing: the Cheyenne dispute that I witnessed at the thirteenth Review Committee meeting, in Norman, Oklahoma, in March 1997, which exposed a rift between tribal-government representatives and self-described traditional religious leaders of the Southern Cheyenne Nation, or Tsistsistas Tribe. The contention centered on the repatriation of human remains from the Smithsonian Institution to the tribe, remains that had heightened significance due to their provenance: they were from the darkest hour of Cheyenne history, the Sand Creek Massacre.

On 29 November 1864 a several-hundred-strong force of militia and volunteer soldiers rode all night from Fort Lyons, south of Denver, to an encampment of Arapaho and Cheyenne people who believed that they were under the protection of the U.S. military—an American flag flew in their tipi circle. When dawn broke, the Indians' worst fears were realized as the soldiers descended, killing approximately two hundred Cheyenne and Arapaho individuals.[30] At the time the U.S. surgeon general was offering a bounty on Indian heads to be used in craniometry studies, so soldiers at Sand Creek severed heads from Indian corpses and shipped them to the Smithsonian.[31] This grim episode marked the end of Cheyenne and Arapaho habitation of their High Plains domain. From that time Cheyenne and Arapaho people have thought of themselves as survivors of Sand Creek, and those who perished there are regarded with profound honor.[32]

Given this history, it is by no means minor when Cheyenne people dispute the right to control the disposition of human remains from the massacre. The conflict I observed unfolded as the three-day Review Committee meeting was drawing to a close. The committee, as usual, opened the floor for public comments. Various speakers came forward, briefly addressing a range of issues, and then Luther Medicine Bird approached the microphone: "I am a Southern Cheyenne Priest of the Sacred Arrows, and I come before you today because our tribe is in serious trouble because of the present representation that is on the board here. For five years, maybe ten years, we have not been getting adequate information. It has been suppressed. The representative that sits on this board, Mr. Hart, does not meet with us nor does he pass on information."[33] "Mr. Hart" referred to Lawrence Hart of the Southern Cheyenne Nation, a Review Committee member who was attending one of his first meetings. A highly visible Cheyenne representative, Hart was a key organizer of the repatriation of Sand Creek ancestors from the Smithsonian.

Medicine Bird continued, somewhat disjointedly. Apparently, Hart had been party to a lawsuit filed in tribal court against Medicine Bird regarding treatment of the Sacred Arrows, the central ritual objects of the Southern Cheyenne, whose possession and use had been hotly contested for centuries.[34] Medicine Bird's point, I surmised, was to illustrate a cleavage in the tribe between the tribal business committee and the "traditional" members of the tribe. The lawsuit had not been heard by the tribal court, on jurisdictional grounds. Medicine Bird continued:

The following year, in 1991, we had a meeting at our great ceremonies, the Sacred Arrow Renewal Worship, our Chiefdom Ceremony, our Traditional Societies and our New Life Lodge. And during this time, there was recommendation by the chiefs, the headsmen, the society people to banish seven men in our tribe for four years; and Mr. Hart was one of these people. And so in the four years to follow, they did not comply to come to our Keeper of our Sacred Arrows or our Arrow Priests to say that they were sorry for their outrageous behavior and personal actions that they took against our sacred arrows. This is why we went to court. So in the four years that they did not comply, these men have been banished forever in our Tsistsistas Southern Cheyenne Tribe.[35]

At the heart of Medicine Bird's complaint was the repatriation of the Sand Creek remains. In his view the repatriation should not have been handled by Hart and his compatriots, as they were not "true" Cheyenne religious leaders.[36] Because the repatriation had not been conducted by the proper authorities, Medicine Bird argued, the event was a sham and a sacrilege. At this point he proposed a startling remedy:

Several years ago, these men, they were appointed by the business committee. They went to the Smithsonian Institute to get 12 skulls—20 skulls. We were not told about this. All the information was suppressed. And they did not contact the Keeper of our Sacred Arrows, our Blue Sky Keeper, our Arrow Priest, our Sun Dance Priest, or our 44 chiefs and headsmen. And so these men, they said they were bringing home the skulls to our people. And these skulls came from—they say the Sand Creek descendants. And these men did not notify the Sand Creek descendants about them burying in this land at Concho, Oklahoma.

So therefore, we are going to ask that these skulls be dug up and taken back to the Smithsonian Institute because we heard that they were not Cheyenne skulls. We don't—we don't have any information to prove that because these individuals have suppressed all this information.[37]

Elaborating, he accused Hart and his sympathizers of being cultural mavericks who had effectively reconstituted Cheyenne religious life outside the proper channels of authority. Particularly egregious was the burial ritual performed for the repatriated remains: "When these skulls were buried, we don't know where they got this reburial ceremony from because we certainly don't do that in our tribe, our Cheyenne Tribe. We don't have that kind of reburial ceremony. So therefore, we're going to ask that these skulls be dug up and brought back to the Smithsonian, because our main body was left out."[38]

Before anyone had a chance to process this, another self-described Tsistsistas traditionalist approached the microphone, introducing himself as James Mann and offering support for Medicine Bird's account of the situation. Specifically, he accused the Cheyenne and Arapaho business committee of usurping traditional religious authority for personal gain. This, he said, had resulted in a dangerous situation. Speaking of a Sun Dance held by the business committee, he said: "And when—when I learned about this sun dance that we have—we I learned about this sun dance that was being placed at Concho, Oklahoma, the basis of our—both of our tribes' complex— I guess it would be—we had—me and my grandmother had gone over there and took part of one ceremony, but later that summer my life was put in danger because of that; my participation, and I nearly lost my foot over that."[39]

Mann's account is by no means anomalous; there are a variety of examples of similar power struggles that took place at other Sun Dance events throughout the Great Plains and Rocky Mountain regions.[40] More recently, in the summer of 2006, a major conflict erupted at a Cheyenne Sun Dance at Concho, Oklahoma, over who held the authority to conduct the dance. The dance arbor was destroyed and numerous vehicles damaged in the ensuing violence.[41] Precisely because these events are so symbolically laden and invested with such tremendous amounts of cultural energy, they become sites of explicit competition and status differentiation, even while the symbolism of the Sun Dance is focused on group unity and sacrifice on behalf of the group.[42] For all that they condense, then, such ritual moments become the sites of boundary negotiations. Here we see an internally constructed boundary marked bodily by a ritual inversion: in Mann's view, rather than promoting health and well-being, the dance resulted in bodily danger—he had been harmed by Sun Dance power, evidence that the ritual was improper.

At this time the chair of the Review Committee interrupted Mann, asking him to conclude his comments as the meeting was going over its allotted time. Closing, Mann turned to a discussion of "truth": "I was taught to respect my Cheyenne ways and to respect the truth. The truth is the truth, and one may win with the truth or one may lose with the truth. But the truth is always there. The white man is taught to win at all costs. No matter what happens, the white man must win, that—that's where the phrase 'It doesn't matter how the game is played, as long as you win.' And right now, to me, the Tsistsistas ceremonial people, all they have is the truth and they abide by that. Thank you."[43] In Mann's view the "real" Cheyenne people possess the truth, and it defines them. Moreover, the Cheyenne people possess truth over and against the competitiveness and duplicity of "the white man." More specifically, only religiously marked—properly ceremonial—Cheyenne people have access to the truth, not imposters.

The point of Mann's reflection on "truth" was implicit. An ethnic division of the most clear-cut type was brought home: he and his sympathizers are the "real" Cheyenne; Hart and the business committee are "white." This reveals two significant aspects of ethnic discourse: first, it concretely illustrates the congruence of ethnic and moral language; and second, it shows that the telescoping retraction of ethnic boundaries does not necessarily stop at the tribal border but can operate even inside it. Moreover, in doing so, such discourse does not lose its oppositional quality in relation to the dominant culture; rather, most jarringly, the opposition between "the people" and "the enemy" is internalized.

Narrative Remains Contested

I hope to have demonstrated that repatriation processes cannot be understood as guided simply by literal "facts." No matter how struggles over the past emerge and shift, what remains constant is the fact that these disputes entail narrative enunciations of tradition. And these narratives express and construct group boundaries in metaphorical ways that run counter to literalist expectations regarding the nature of social groups and cultural affiliation. However, against those who would argue that metaphorical reckonings of tradition and group boundaries are fictions and fabrications, I would insist that ethnic identities and the social and geographical spaces marked out by them are always metaphorically constituted. Indeed, human social life always unfolds metaphorically insofar as our medium—our human condition—is change. Yet, in the face of this, we seek out and embrace resemblance—change as continuity. Literalists mistake resemblance for sameness. When laws like NAGPRA are interpreted as demanding sameness, then the appearance of legal certitude comes at the cost of human reality.

Rejecting literalism of this sort, I propose a simple analogy saved for a rainy day: in a basic sense narratives of identity are umbrellas that expand or contract to create a privileged and protected space for those covered by them. One possible approach is to extend the ethnic umbrella, the boundaries of the possessors of "truth," to include all other Native Americans in relation to non-Indians. This approach, evident throughout the legislative history of NAGPRA, is frequently seen in national press statements by Indians concerning the law. I suggest that this approach is utilized when the broad validity and language of the law are being contested and is usually registered in terms of native "truth" versus science, and native collectivism versus Western private-property interests. However, when specific implementation of the law is at issue, we often find a collapsing of affiliations and far less pan-Indian rhetoric—as at the intertribal level in the Ute case and the intratribal level in the Cheyenne case. In each case religious discourse was the principal means utilized to articulate boundaries. Furthermore, in each case the religious language employed was markedly oppositional. Our analysis would have proceeded differently had we opted to perceive Cheyenne voices as univocal and Ute manifestations of tradition as unchanging.

To extend our observations from these case studies, as repatriation disputes emerge and erupt in the future, we should not be surprised to see alliances and social boundaries redrawn and fought over. In the process we should expect to see the articulation of emergent and occasionally insurgent narratives. One might argue that I have selected my case studies to emphasize conflict and narrative expansiveness and that, for this reason, my more general claims do not hold. My response is, first, to acknowledge that I have selected cases for reasons of particular narrative interest and, second, to stress that my choices nonetheless do not represent anomalous situations. It is true that many hundreds of repatriations have proceeded smoothly, with evident benefits to numerous communities. Without wanting to detract deserved attention from these political successes, my analytical point here is to suggest that repatriation narratives cut many ways, as is readily evident if we read past and through simplified accounts.

Let me provide an example to support my position. Russell Thornton has written movingly about the Sand Creek repatriations: "Remains from some of the Cheyenne massacred at Sand Creek were obtained by the Army Medical Museum and later transferred to the Smithsonian; in 1993, they were repatriated to the Southern Cheyenne. Tears were shed; words were spoken about how, at last, the people were being brought home and some of the pain of the Sand Creek Massacre could be eased."[44] My intention is not to belittle or dismiss Thornton's account, for I think his view is in some measure accurate. However, it is worth noting the tension existing between Thornton's account and the conflict at the Review Committee meeting. If Cheyenne people shed tears at the reburial, then, as we saw in the bitter dispute between Hart and Medicine Bird, some of them also shed metaphorical blood in the struggles that ensued thereafter. An honest and critical understanding of social processes such as repatriation demands that scholars never assume that any-thing—including bones, grudges, or pride—is easily buried. Indeed, as the Kawaihae conflict shows, even things buried are not necessarily thereby put to rest.

7

DEAD RECKONING AND
LIVING TRADITION
SOURCES OF POWER AND AUTHORITY IN
THE DIVIDED PRESENT

The purpose today is to conduct a status conference and the reason—please be seated—the reason we're doing this on a regular basis in this case is because, of course, there is a lot of public interest in this matter from all segments of the community, including, of course, and primarily, the Hawaiian community.

[This conference is] for the purpose of accounting for them [the Kawaihae objects] and making sure those objects are where they are supposed to be.

Because there are numbers of individuals in this community who doubt the veracity and truth of Hui Malama and its representatives. You've all heard them. They don't believe what Hui Malama says. They believe that Hui Malama has got them stashed someplace else or has done something else with them. They don't know.

—Federal Judge David Ezra

REPATRIATION conflicts in Hawai'i intensified in late 2005, as the Kawaihae (Forbes Cave) dispute—which involves fourteen Native Hawaiian organizations and the Bishop Museum—escalated in dramatic and decisive ways, culminating in a watershed moment. On 27 December federal judge David Ezra found Hui Mālama representative Edward Halealoha Ayau in contempt of court for refusing to disclose the location of the contested objects. After giving him a final chance to reveal the objects' whereabouts, Judge Ezra ordered Ayau to a federal detention center in Honolulu. For the first time under NAGPRA, a native person was incarcerated in the context of the law. All eyes were on Judge Ezra and Edward Ayau as the Hawaiian public and repatriation experts alike watched this cultural spectacle for hints of what would transpire when two stubborn forces—law and tradition—clashed head-on.

A tentative answer came on 5 January 2006, when Judge Ezra proposed that the contending Native Hawaiian organizations engage in traditional Hawaiian dispute resolution. The principal groups agreed, and to facilitate the process, Judge Ezra changed Ayau's status to limited house arrest, allowing him to participate in the meetings. The dispute-resolution process, known as ho'oponopono, included members of four groups: Hui Mālama; the Bishop Museum; and two groups that had recently brought suit against the first two, the Royal Hawaiian Academy of Traditional Arts and Na Lei Ali'i Kawananakoa. Ho'oponopono—"making right"—is a process of communal soul searching and grievance bearing guided by putatively neutral cultural authorities in the service of reaching mutually agreed-upon solutions to a crisis.[1] The process in this case was conducted behind closed doors, the judge issuing a standing gag order for everyone involved in the dispute. All parties went on record declaring their good-faith participation, and Judge Ezra said that he would end Ayau's confinement if ho'oponopono produced resolution. He also made it clear that he would resume pursuing legal channels and incarcerate Ayau once again if the process failed.

By late April 2006 newspapers were reporting that ho'oponopono had indeed failed, several parties calling the process "a farce."[2] Maintaining his gag order, Judge Ezra indicated that the legal process would continue. Meanwhile, both sides further amplified their respective positions. Complicating matters, the Bishop Museum filed a cross-claim against Hui Mālama, accusing it of breaching its contract with the museum when it refused to return the "loan" of the Kawaihae objects.[3] By the summer of 2006, parties across the Kawaihae spectrum were being deposed for a complicated series of hearings.

The judge's incarceration order, his subsequent request for the disputants to engage in ho'oponopono, the failure of this process, and the subsequent intensification of legal battles have churned the undercurrents of contemporary Hawaiian tradition. Daily letters to the editor published in Hawaiian newspapers attest to the cultural turbidity of these muddied waters. Still, while some observers lament this mucked-up state of affairs, I see in it the rich primordia of lived tradition. If NAGPRA was meant to restore tradition, then it has done so in spades. A law designed to undo the damage of dispossession is catalyzing the creation and rediscovery of communal identities and ritual practices, if in dramatically contested ways.

This context of religious crisis has the potential to shape Hawaiian religion in considerable and lasting ways. What makes the Hawaiian case particularly notable is its specificity. Far more than generalized references to or displays of Hawaiianness, repatriation disputes invoke and evoke tradition in detail (e.g., in the form of genealogies, prayers, and ritual protocol). Moreover, these examples of tradition in action are contested and negotiated in practice. No one can assert traditional claims without having them vetted—often quite publicly. Indeed, news articles that include quotations regarding Hawaiian religion are frequently rebutted in the next day's letters to the editor, which are in turn supported or rejected by subsequent letters. In this manner Hawaiian tradition in the present is being shaped—one might even say edited—by peer review and public opinion. In a seeming paradox contesting claims to tradition are resulting in a peculiar and spirited democratization of it.

Surrounding Kawaihae in particular, two predominant lines of argumentation have emerged that can best be understood in the context of a specific example. Take the word *moepū*. Is *moepū* a "traditional" word, or is it a recent invention?[4] Some argue that it means "grave goods" or "funerary objects" and that much ancestral Hawaiian religion was focused on burial rites and, in recognition of their sanctity, burial rights. In this view objects containing *mana* were placed with the dead and are *kapu*—sacred and inviolable. Disturbing such objects defiles the violator and the *iwi kūpuna*. Proponents of this position insist that virtually all objects found in lava-tube caves (such as those near Kawaihae) are *moepū* and are therefore funerary objects under NAGPRA and should be reburied, regardless of their rarity or economic value. Another camp, however, insists that this sense of the word *moepū* has been invented for political purposes—namely, to keep certain repatriation organizations in business. It insists that objects like those from Kawaihae are not funerary objects at all. Instead, they are important and potent cultural objects that should be regarded as the cultural property of all Hawaiians, not as the private property of the dead. Contrary to the *moepū* argument, this position asserts that such objects were secreted in caves during the fall of traditional Hawaiian religion in 1819. Vigilante groups, this camp says, were pillaging homes and temples in order to collect and destroy all vestiges of Hawaiian religion. Seeing their way of life pass before them, and having witnessed the preserving capacity of European museums, sage elders hid objects so that future generations of Hawaiians could learn about their past. Some advocates of this position argue that spirits have henceforth guarded these objects and now control their revelation. In this perspective nonnative archaeologists served as vehicles of these spirits, used to bring forth these physical manifestations of Hawaiian tradition at historically important moments. Museum presentation, they argue, is the best expression of the spirits' wishes.

In the context of Kawaihae, Hui Mālama represents the former position, the two groups that have brought suit against Hui Mālama the latter. To advance their respective positions, whether to the media, in Review Committee meetings, or in courtrooms, both sides have marshaled a wide variety of claims. The maximal claim from each side is that it has received direct revelation from ancestral spirits regarding the truth of its position. At a this-worldly level, each side presents claims as to the nature of traditional knowledge and training behind its views, reciting genealogies that link it to Kawaihae by way of kinship and residence. Further, each side has asserted class-based claims to substantiate its authority, insisting that its proponents speak as *ali'i* (nobility), a status that confers speech rights and that renders their *mana'o* (opinions, views) consequential. Perhaps most tellingly, all parties to the dispute have at one time or another described direct connections to Kamehameha I. As noted earlier (see chapter 2), the Kohala region of the Big Island was Kamehameha's home; it is also the site of Kawaihae.

As the example of *moepū* illustrates, the Kawaihae disputants have invoked a suggestive array of claims to advance their positions. From class status in this world to spiritual access beyond it, the power to define and claim the objects and, by extension, the power to be the prevailing voice and arm of tradition are at stake. The task of this chapter is to add detail to this saga and tell the related and unexpected story of the Bishop Museum's claim to native identity.

Bishop's Move

In the summer of 2004, I sat down with members of Hui Mālama, representatives of the Bishop Museum, a former employee of the Bishop Museum, an OHA representative, and several National Park Service employees around a conference-room table. A palpable tension pervaded the room as we listened by phone to the proceedings of the twenty-sixth NAGPRA Review Committee meeting, which was being conducted by teleconference from a number of designated sites across the country. This was a key meeting for Hawaiian repatriation issues because both the Bishop Museum's newly proposed Native Hawaiian organization (NHO) status and the ongoing Kawaihae affair were becoming increasingly volatile. Both issues pitted the Bishop Museum and allied groups against Hui Mālama and its sympathizers in what was rapidly turning into a showdown over repatriation law and cultural politics in Hawai'i. At the meeting Hui Mālama succeeded in getting both issues on the agenda for the subsequent Review Committee meeting in Washington, D.C. The stage was thus set for a battle royale.

Both fronts in this conflict have entailed various side skirmishes, involving a range of other participants with varying degrees of affiliation with the principal antagonists. Given all of the players and factors embroiled in this setting, it is easy to lose sight of the basic issue that configures the conflict: what groups are able to advance persuasive claims regarding their authority to control the disposition of objects covered by NAGPRA? Technicalities, legalese, and innuendo abound, but the struggle has been as classic as it is basic. Who speaks for what objects? On what grounds? With what degree of receptivity from various audiences?

The Bishop Museum's claim to NHO status, set forth in the museum's "Interim and Proposed Final Guidance Policy" (GP), is not historically separable in any neat way from the festering Kawaihae dispute.[5] Whereas Kawaihae represents Hui Mālama's maximal attempt to extend its authority, the Bishop Museum's NHO claim served as a rejoinder, designed to project its authority by way of a new status that could deflect and even undermine repatriation claims from groups like Hui Mālama.

The Bishop Museum's GP was the result of a leadership change at the museum. Donald Duckworth had been president when the Bishop Museum made its now infamous "loan" of the Kawaihae objects to Hui Mālama in 2000. When William Brown became president of the museum in 2001, he began to implement repatriation policy changes. According to the former vice president for cultural studies at the museum, Guy Kaulukukui, Brown began an assessment of NAGPRA and cultural affiliation in January 2004. At the same time the Bishop Museum placed a freeze on repatriations. According to Kaulukukui, this move was meant to stem the tide of objects being transferred into the hands of Hui Mālama.[6]

Brown asked Kaulukukui to sign off on this policy, but he refused and was subsequently fired. Brown's assessment of NAGPRA continued, resulting in publication of the GP on 30 June 2004. This document begins with a quotation from Patience Namaka Bacon, a Bishop Museum staffer since 1939: "I remember when I started working at Bishop Museum and the old Hawaiians came and brought their grandchildren. They saw the wooden images, feather capes, kapa, and much more. They wept with joy to see that some things remained from the old days, and they thanked the ali'i for having kept them."[7] These opening sentences thus announce the Bishop Museum's roots in class—*ali'i*—and royalty, leading back to "High Chiefess Pauahi Bishop," Princess Ruth Ke'elikolani, and Queen Emma.[8] After this announcement of secular authority, the document constructs the museum's religious and cultural status:

> A reporter attending the event [the opening of the museum] wrote: "Many aged Hawaiians recognized among the large collection idols which their ancestors reverenced with fear and awe. The god of Kamehameha I, and a god of rain attracted a large share of their attention."
>
> More than a century later, the Bishop Museum remains a steward of these treasures. Ku ka'ilimoku, Kamehameha's war god, still looks fiercely on those who stand before it, and some tremble. This past year, when the Pleiades rose and Makahiki began, the wooden image of Lono was dressed as in days gone by and turned in the Museum vestibule as the trade winds filled its kapa sails. This image is the last of its kind: none other remains from the days when the ancestors lived in the old ways. Bishop Museum keeps the old for those who live now and who will live later.[9]

The document then moves immediately to a "legal analysis" of the Bishop Museum's responsibilities under federal law with regard to its "dual role as a steward of Native Hawaiian culture as well as a museum with repatriation responsibilities defined by the Act."[10] Through this assertion of its dual role, the Bishop Museum advanced its principal rebuttal to Hui Mālama. Its reaffirmation of its curatorial and preservation mission was not problematic; its assertion of stewardship over Native Hawaiian culture, however, provoked intense reactions. The remainder of the document goes on to support this claim, casting it in ways designed to satisfy NAGPRA definitions. Indeed, to this end the GP turns to the NAGPRA definition of a Native Hawaiian organization. Recall that this definition reads as follows: "any organization which—(A) serves and represents the interests of Native Hawaiians, (B) has as a primary and stated purpose the provision of services to Native Hawaiians, and (C) has expertise in Native Hawaiian Affairs, and shall include the Office of Hawaiian Affairs and Hui Malama I Na Kupuna O Hawai'i Nei."[11] After reproducing this definition, the GP asserts that "to be an NHO as defined by NAGPRA does not require traditional history or native membership."[12] In reaching this conclusion, the Bishop Museum played upon the intersection of NAGPRA and several legal decisions in Hawai'i that challenged race-based privileges.

Other features of the Bishop Museum's GP document also merit attention. It describes how the museum's Articles of Incorporation were amended in 2003 to state "that the purposes of the Corporation shall include 'as a primary purpose providing services to and in general serving and representing interests of Native Hawaiians.'" The document then recounts the museum's role in various Hawaiian cultural projects and revivals. It moves quickly from stating the museum's association with Hawaiian culture to asserting "cultural affiliation" with Native Hawaiian tradition as defined by NAGPRA.[13] In an interesting twist the document extends the category of "cultural affiliation" in Hawai'i to render it coextensive with NHO status, with the conclusion that "as a NHO, Bishop Museum is culturally affiliated with all Native Hawaiian items." Yet more pointedly, the document then asserts "*close* cultural affiliation" with objects in its collections (emphasis added).[14]

These assertions alone would have been plenty to initiate a cultural battle, but the Bishop Museum went for a full assault, purporting that it has no associated burial objects for which lineal descendants have been ascertained and no sacred objects or objects of cultural patrimony. To dispatch with possible claims on objects of cultural patrimony, the GP simply states that all such objects could have been alienated by ruling chiefs and therefore do not meet the criterion of inalienability demanded by the statute.[15] Sacred objects are dismissed with similar efficiency on the grounds that, even if an object the museum holds is apparently sacred, "other objects may be used in present day religious practices."[16] The GP ends with an overarching caveat: even if the museum did have objects that fit either of these categories, it would nonetheless have clear right of possession, and taking said objects would constitute a violation of the Fifth Amendment.[17]

Response to the museum's GP was swift, the respondents including, most pointedly, Guy Kaulukukui. He immediately notified the NPS of the GP, characterizing it as trivializing NAGPRA. Kaulukukui authored two position papers that detailed a stinging rebuttal, one that could only have been produced by a former museum insider.[18] Kaulukukui wrote that the GP "violates the spirit and intent of NAGPRA by providing the museum with an absolute monopoly over repatriation processes."[19] In particular, Kaulukukui emphasized the conflict of interest that would ensue if the GP were enacted. Namely, the museum would be in the position of being a claimant as an NHO, while simultaneously assessing claims as a museum. As Kaulukukui pointed out, this would constitute a radical short-circuiting of the processes contemplated by the drafters of NAGPRA. Edward Ayau and others have echoed this point.[20]

In addressing the GP's position on sacred objects and cultural patrimony, Kaulukukui's comments were similarly barbed. According to Kaulukukui, the Bishop Museum's guidelines enacted "a veiled attempt to close the books on NAGPRA repatriations by trying to convince Native Hawaiians that it has completed its obligations to them under the Act. In reality, the museum's responsibilities under NAGPRA will increase over time as Native Hawaiians continue to renew traditional religious practices and make claims for the sacred objects that are associated with these activities."[21] Kaulukukui then categorically listed various objects held by the museum that could be claimed as sacred objects. In particular, he pointed to the museum's famous Lono image used in Makahiki ceremonies, which, as he observed, are experiencing a contemporary revival in Hawai'i.[22] He provided fewer specific examples of potential objects of cultural patrimony, but he did advance several scenarios regarding transfers of such objects, casting doubt on the museum's claim that it has none.

Turning to the right of possession, with particular reference to unassociated funerary objects, Kaulukukui provided two examples intended to refute the museum's claims. One involved a *niho palaoa* (pendant) from Moloka'i found in 1937 on a beach strewn with bones. (Actualizing Kaulukukui's point, Hui Mālama has indeed made a repatriation claim upon this object, creating an ongoing controversy.) The other example pertained to two *ki'i* taken from a burial cave on Maui in the 1960s. It is certainly conceivable that an NHO could make claims upon these objects as sacred and as funerary items.

Beyond Kaulukukui's potent criticism, the museum's GP generated press throughout the summer. According to the *Honolulu Star-Bulletin*, Lurline McGregor, who had worked on drafting NAGPRA as a member of Senator Daniel Inouye's staff, commented: "I am appalled the museum would consider itself a native Hawaiian organization when it is clearly not. The museum was not contemplated as a recipient of repatriated items."[23] On 8 August the *Honolulu Advertiser* ran dueling opinion pieces on the topic. Representing the museum's position was an excerpt from the GP. Resisting was a piece written by Edward Ayau and signed by twenty-three prominent Native Hawaiian activists, cultural leaders, and scholars. Referring to Senator Inouye's concern over the issue, Ayau wrote that "amendments to NAGPRA that would prohibit Bishop Museum from qualifying as a claimant are being considered."[24] "All of this," Ayau continued, "points to a need for a leadership change. We insist that the board of directors repeal the interim guidance, remove Brown and undertake efforts to identify a qualified Native Hawaiian to serve as the new director of Bishop Museum."[25]

Only three days after this exchange, another major story broke. Once again the Bishop Museum and Hui Mālama were in the news together, this time with regard to the alleged trafficking of artifacts that the Bishop Museum and the Peabody Essex Museum had repatriated to Hui Mālama in 1997 for reburial in Kanupa Cave. According to the *Star-Bulletin*, Brown commented, "This is a critical moment to remember the great significance of Hawaiian cultural heritage and to reflect on what stewardship that heritage genuinely requires."[26] On 12 August Hui Mālama responded with a news release, declaring support for federal efforts to investigate the situation. The release also replied to suggestions that Hui Mālama was responsible for the trafficking or, at a minimum, had acted irresponsibly by not taking precautionary measures to ensure that the objects would be safe.

Pertinent here are the parallels with Kawaihae surrounding such issues of "stewardship." Both contexts—Kanupa Cave and Kawaihae—involve priceless collections reburied by Hui Mālama in the Kohala region of the Big Island; both also involve sealing off cave entrances. It is clear why the Bishop Museum would cast the removal of artifacts as a morality tale of relevance to its GP and to the Kawaihae dispute. But the Bishop Museum was not alone in drawing parallels and making conclusions regarding repatriation in general. La'akea Suganuma, head of the Royal Hawaiian Academy of Traditional Arts, which has been firmly counterposed to Hui Mālama in the Kawaihae matter, was quoted in the *Star-Bulletin* as saying of Hui Mālama: "These people are the self-appointed guardians or kahu of the caves. They cannot be absolved, by tradition, of their responsibility to guard the caves. . . . In the old days, if something happened to a cave, the perpetrator was taken to task, but so was the kahu that was sworn to protect the cave. . . . Hui Malama took the responsibility and failed. They might escape the laws of man but not the laws of tradition and the spiritual world."[27] After a protracted investigation, a man apparently unrelated to Hui Mālama or any other repatriation group pleaded guilty in the matter in 2006.[28]

It is hard to imagine that matters could have been any more intense on the eve of the twenty-seventh NAGPRA Review Committee meeting, in Washington, D.C. Indeed, the atmosphere at this meeting was electric. Adding to the frenzied aspect of the Hawaiian disputes, it was timed to coincide with the opening of the National Museum of the American Indian, an event directly connected to the history of repatriation processes. Thousands of Native American representatives were thus in town, and many packed the Review Committee meeting, including numerous Native Hawaiians.

When the committee turned to the Bishop Museum's GP, it became abundantly clear that the various Native Hawaiian contingents had traveled thousands of miles to demonstrate their convictions. When the floor was opened for comment, Guy Kaulukukui spoke first by phone, summarizing his position papers described above.[29] I followed, challenging the GP on the basis of my research on the legislative history of NAGPRA. A representative of the OHA, Lance Foster, then provided an ambivalent assessment of the GP. Hui Mālama and its various supporters followed, beginning with Kehu Abad, a Native Hawaiian with a Ph.D. in archaeology and ethnohistory. She emphasized that NAGPRA's definition of cultural affiliation builds upon the concept of shared group identity, arguing that the Bishop Museum cannot be construed as having shared group identity with the Native Hawaiian community. Then, wearing a large red sash and carrying herself with a grave demeanor, the next speaker, Lilikalā Kameʻeleihiwa, approached the microphone. She cited her academic credentials and declared that she represented one hundred generations of Hawaiian history and had connections to four of the Hawaiian islands, then urged the Review Committee to "err on the side of justice."[30] Kameʻeleihiwa then read a letter from her colleague Jonathan Osorio, who described the GP as offensive and argued that it "asserts a strange devaluation of current Native Hawaiian organizations to justify itself."[31]

Just when it appeared that Native Hawaiians would be univocal in renouncing the GP, however, Van Horn Diamond came forward to support the museum. He was draped in a red cloak very similar to Kameʻeleihiwa's, which he claimed signified his elected status and his years of service to his ʻohana. He first read a letter from Hailama Farden, president of an influential NHO, Hale O Na Aliʻi O Hawaiʻi.

Farden wrote that his group "is the only Hawaiian organization that has written burial protocols dating back to the time of the high ali'i."[32] Having made this claim, his letter announced support for the Bishop Museum and the GP. After reading the letter, Diamond presented testimony on behalf of his own NHO, stating "that it would be refreshing and beneficial to have the Bishop Museum as a Native Hawaiian Organization." He closed by saying, "What is there to fear?"[33]

William Brown of the Bishop Museum then took questions from the Review Committee, its members posing pointed queries and expressing general skepticism regarding the GP. They voiced concern with conflicts of interest that would attend the museum's NHO status, particularly with regard to adjudication of the disposition of objects in the museum's collection. Questions regarding NAGPRA's intent were also raised. In this context Garrick Bailey expressed "his strong feelings that Bishop Museum cannot be defined as a Native Hawaiian organization."[34] While the committee elected to defer action on the GP in lieu of a pending congressional hearing on the matter, a majority of its members weighed in with comments indicating clear resistance to the museum's position.[35]

Although the Review Committee had made its view apparent, the matter took a turn several days later when the Department of the Interior issued a legal analysis of the GP, which asserted that museum status and NHO status are not necessarily mutually exclusive under the law.[36] Nonetheless, Senator Inouye continued to apply pressure against the museum. The SSCIA reportedly began redrafting NAGPRA's NHO definition to render it more stringent.[37] By early October the museum was reconsidering its position. According to a *Star-Bulletin* editorial, "The museum, confronted with awesome political artillery, appears prepared to raise the white flag, but the spoils at stake are immense."[38]

On 7 October 2004 the Bishop Museum rescinded its claim to NHO status in its "Final Guidance."[39] This document acknowledged community concerns over possible conflicts of interest but rebutted all other challenges to the GP, including challenges to its claim that the museum has no sacred objects or objects of cultural patrimony. In response to the museum's decision, news media representatives interviewed the members of various NHOs, who once again revealed their divisiveness. Ayau called the GP "a gross waste of everyone's time," whereas Richard Paglinawan offered support for the museum on the basis of his role as a religious practitioner, stating, with reference to the museum's Lono staff, "We don't need the original in our practice, but we do need access to the original to study and make our own."[40] His sentiment echoes the key division between disputants in the Kawaihae case, to which Hawaiians' attention once again turned.

Ancestral Intentions

The Bishop Museum's GP had put the repatriation community on edge in the summer of 2004, particularly with regard to questions of the authority to claim and speak for objects and ancestors. Without exception, all of the people I interviewed about the GP, including ten directly involved in the Kawaihae dispute, immediately stated their bases of authority. Not surprisingly, they usually did so contrastively, their own credentials counterposed to those of others, which were represented as categorically inferior or fraudulent. Direct revelation from ancestors and spirits, mastery of tradition, histories of residence, histories of religious and social action, and genealogies— always elite and usually royal—were elaborated in detail. Returning to Hawai'i in the summer of 2006, I found much the same dynamic in place, though I also noted a stronger emphasis on local authority and, on the Big Island, fairly widespread resistance to "people from O'ahu" controlling the process.

All such distinctions were drawn in the service of marking affinity with contested sites, objects, and remains. Proximity—by blood, place, and spirit—defines and confers *kuleana,* religious and moral responsibility. Several people with whom I spoke asserted Hui Mālama's *kuleana* with reference to Kawaihae, pointing to the *hui*'s repatriation record, its proficiency with ritual protocol, and the status of its *kumus* (teachers). Others rejected Hui Mālama's claim to *kuleana* outright. Its members were described as "Western," grant-hungry imposters who did not have geographical connections to Kawaihae and whose tactics were "czarlike" and in "the warrior mode." They were accused of silencing '*ohana* (family) claims and of bullying other NHOs. After the Kanupa Cave story broke, they were also accused of being thieves and traitors. Hui Mālama responded by underscoring its history of successful repatriations and characterizing the opposing groups' members as "Christians" who were, willfully or not, beholden to a colonized mentality in general and to the Bishop Museum in particular.

The aforementioned twenty-seventh Review Committee meeting was an early stage in this battle. Under serious attack from numerous angles, Hui Mālama came out full force. Group members opened

with a chanted prayer; then *hui* members Hoʻoipo Pa and Kunani
Nihipali asked the Review Committee to vacate its 2003 finding
that recommended restarting repatriation processes. Edward Ayau's
presentation began with a chanted prayer, referred to in his written
testimony as a *Pule ʻOkia*.[41] According to Mary Kawena Pukui and
Samuel Elbert, *ʻokia* means to "cut, sever, or finish."[42] It was in this
prayer that Ayau invoked the names of Laʻakea Suganuma, William
Brown, and Van Horn Diamond, commanding them to "e ʻoki" (stop
your actions).[43] The tone, intensity, and emotion of Ayau's prayer
were such that the gravity of Hui Mālama's position could not be
mistaken. After his prayer Ayau recited his claim to *kuleana*, his
standing to speak and act. Here, as in much Native Hawaiian discourse, responsibility and authority were represented as coextensive.
Ayau summarized his genealogy, taking it back to Kamehameha, and,
in doing so, asserted his geographical and royal link to Kawaihae. He
then cited the authority of his teachers, including cultural and legal
experts. Ayau followed this with an account of Hawaiian religion
and *kuleana*, with particular attention to *iwi* and *moepū*.[44] Building
on this general discussion, he detailed Hui Mālama's litany of successful repatriations. Challenging assertions of Hui Mālama's bullying tactics, Ayau described the group's experiences working with
many other NHOs.

After this exhaustive accounting of Hui Mālama's *kuleana*, Ayau
presented a legal analysis of the Review Committee's previous
Kawaihae finding, asking for it to be vacated. He insisted that the
committee had overstepped its legal mandate in a number of ways,
especially in recommending the reopening of a repatriation matter
that Hui Mālama claimed was finished. After summarizing other
grievances with the committee, Ayau turned to a detailed history of
the Kawaihae objects. Ayau closed his presentation with a quotation
attributed to Queen Liliʻuokalani:

> I cannot turn back the time for political change, but there is still time
> to save your heritage. You must remember never to cease to act be-
> cause you fear you may fail. The way to lose any earthly kingdom is
> to be inflexible, intolerant, and prejudicial. Another way is to be too
> flexible, tolerant of too many wrongs without judgment at all. It is a
> razor's edge. It is the width of a blade of pili grass. To gain the kingdom
> of heaven is to hear what is not said, to see what cannot be seen, and
> to know the unknowable—that is aloha. All things in the world are
> two; in heaven there is but one.[45]

Hui Mālama's presentation was supported by Lilikalā Kameʻeleihiwa and Jonathan Osorio. It was firmly challenged by Van Horn Diamond, who acknowledged William Brown's openness to resolving the matter. The strongest response to Hui Mālama came from Laʻakea Suganuma, who had been largely responsible for bringing the dispute to the Review Committee's attention in 2003. He opened by returning Ayau's words "tenfold" and accused Hui Mālama of lacking *aloha*.[46] He then declared that the ancestors and their desire for the objects to be displayed in museums were guiding the entire dispute.

After these presentations the members of the Review Committee were visibly flustered. Ultimately, they decided formally to reconsider the case at a future meeting, which they stipulated should take place in Hawaiʻi so as to encourage and enable as much community involvement as possible. In order to facilitate logistical matters regarding this proposed meeting, the Review Committee held a teleconference on 2 November 2004, then settled on a March 2005 date for its Hawaiʻi meeting. During the teleconference Review Committee member Vincas Steponaitis called the Bishop Museum's loan to Hui Mālama "a sham" that "pre-empted a good-faith process in which all claimants had a say." Always present and prepared, Ayau continued to resist the Review Committee's position, declaring that the issue "should be decided in a court of competent jurisdiction."[47]

Ayau also asked the Review Committee to consider the repatriation status of objects held by the Bishop Museum at the upcoming 2005 meeting in Hawaiʻi. Hui Mālama had requested the repatriation of objects from Molokaʻi in an apparent attempt to test the museum's assertion that it does not hold sacred objects, objects of cultural patrimony, or funerary objects. Museum officials responded by accepting the standing of other NHOs to make claims upon the objects, including the Royal Hawaiian Academy of Traditional Arts, headed by Suganuma. The museum also recognized another group as an NHO in this context, a group now central to the Kawaihae dispute—Na Lei Aliʻi Kawananakoa, headed by a wealthy heiress of the Campbell Estate, Abigail Kawananakoa. According to a 7 December 2004 editorial in the *Star-Bulletin*, Kawananakoa "traces her ancestry to King Kalakaua, has the cultural and financial wherewithal to wage such a battle against Hui Malama I Na Kupuna ʻO Hawaiʻi Nei, and threatens to do so." Ayau was quoted in the same editorial, saying Kawananakoa "reeks of someone who does not live within Hawaiian tradition."[48]

On 8 December the SSCIA held a meeting at the East-West Center of the University of Hawai'i. Originally slated principally to address possible amendments to NAGPRA in light of the Bishop Museum's GP, the meeting now shifted to address NHO status generally. Hui Mālama was once again on and under attack. Numerous groups presented testimony that asked for a tightening of the NHO definition so as to emphasize the role of family claims. Several groups asked for Hui Mālama to be stricken from the definition. Anti–Hui Mālama rhetoric included characterizations of them as "Pontius Pilate," as "a band of lepers" (a reference to Ayau's residence on Moloka'i, which housed an infamous leper colony), and as "kidnappers."[49] Suganuma, who was on hand, called Hui Mālama's motivation "financial rather than cultural."[50] With his testimony, and that of Melvin Kalihiki, discussion then turned specifically to Kawaihae. Suganuma said:

> To me, it is not a question of showing the artifacts or displaying the artifacts. It is a matter of truly respecting the wishes of the ancestors, because nothing can be discovered without their permission. On a higher level of understanding, they made the decision for their descendants that these things be there. Otherwise, they would not have been there. So it is not a matter of our deciding to show these things. It is a matter of their deciding that they should be shown. It is also a matter of Hawaiian is a state of being.[51]

Suganuma's now-staunch ally Abigail Kawananakoa also weighed in with testimony on Kawaihae:

> Under NAGPRA, certain favored groups and individuals have been treated as if they were the legitimate representatives of the Hawaiian people. Their treatment has been as if they are the leadership of recognized tribal nations. However, under Hawaiian culture and society these individuals and organizations would have no rights of ownership. Indeed, their involvement would be contrary to the core values of Hawaiian traditions. The result of NAGPRA has been to allow those without legitimate standing to take possession of priceless Hawaiian treasures.[52]

This view was echoed by Cy Kamuela Harris: "These sacred objects were meant to be found and shared for all the people of Hawaii to cherish and admire at the very least, not buried in a cave or being sold on the black market; their security always in question. The system cannot allow one organization to make a decision of this magnitude, ever."[53]

In this contentious setting Senator Inouye and Edward Ayau engaged in a telling exchange:

SENATOR INOUYE. In your testimony, you suggest amending the definition of Native Hawaiian organization, making a claim under NAGPRA to have as a primary purpose the practice of Native Hawaiian cultural values.

In your view, how would a Federal agency or museum distinguish among several Native Hawaiian organization claimants, each holding to and practicing a different set of Native Hawaiian cultural values?

MR. AYAU. Well, are you asking me how the agency itself distinguishes?

Senator Inouye. No; they are all claiming that they are practicing Native Hawaiian cultural values, practices, and protocols. They may differ from yours.

MR. AYAU. Right, but I would say, from the museum or Federal agency perspective, as long as they satisfy that condition, then you go on to the next one, to see if they satisfy them, as well. Then if they do, then you accord them Native Hawaiian status.

SENATOR INOUYE. Well, obviously, these questions point out the complexity of the problem before us, and it will take a lot of work, and some collaboration. Otherwise we will not get anywhere.[54]

Several months later the Review Committee held its scheduled meeting in Honolulu. On the eve of the meeting, Hui Mālama was in the press again as Isabella Abbott, chairwoman of the Bishop Museum's collection committee and herself a Native Hawaiian, called its actions the result of "ambition gone wild."[55] Hui Mālama supporters responded with equally strong language. Lilikalā Kameʻeleihiwa, for example, said: "For Hawaiians who say that, ask them if they are Christian or not. That's where the divide is. It is a religious one."[56] Once the meeting started, matters did not settle down. Hui Mālama even engaged in a tactic it has since used several times: having children testify on its behalf.[57]

The cultural drama continued unabated for several days. A snapshot from the *Star-Bulletin* captured the milieu: "Dressed in a long black ceremonial gown, EliRayna Adams of the Daughters and Sons of Hawaiian Warriors sat before a microphone yesterday afternoon to testify before a federal committee that is in Honolulu this week to rule on several disputes over treasured Hawaiian artifacts. 'Today we withdraw our support from Hui Malama,' said Adams, who is kuhina nui of the royal order, 'and we would like to be recognized as a native Hawaiian organization in our own right.'"[58] The Review Committee showed signs of frustration. Vincas Steponaitis castigated both the Bishop Museum and Hui Mālama: "The flaws in this repatriation case are so egregious I have never seen anything like it and hope never to see it again."[59] Other committee members concurred, agreeing that the repatriation process should be restarted, thus once again upholding its 2003 finding.

Hui Mālama refused to abide by this finding and therefore made no effort to return the artifacts or disclose their precise location. The next several months were the calm before the storm. Then, on 9 August 2005, Ne Lei Aliʻi Kawananakoa and the Royal Hawaiian Academy of Traditional Arts filed a suit in federal district court against the Bishop Museum and Hui Mālama over Kawaihae, seeking a court injunction requiring Hui Mālama to return the objects. The Bishop Museum was included in the suit on the technical grounds of its role in the "loan" to Hui Mālama. By now, however, it was clear that the Bishop Museum under William Brown supported restarting the repatriation process and was working with, not against, Kawananakoa and Suganuma to this end. Hui Mālama promptly asked the court to deny the requested injunction, asserting that neither of the filing groups had standing to request such an order. However, on 2 September district court judge David Ezra ordered Hui Mālama to return the objects to the museum. Hui Mālama immediately refused the order and announced plans to appeal the decision.

On 9 September Hui Mālama asked the U.S. Ninth Circuit Court of Appeals to postpone enforcement of Ezra's ruling on First Amendment grounds.[60] "There is no safe manner by which to carry out the District Court's order as it would place . . . members of Hui Mālama in real physical and spiritual danger," it claimed.[61] Several days later Hui Mālama asserted that opening the cave would cause its collapse.[62] Hui Mālama then held a forum at the University of Hawaiʻi to discuss its position. "This is a wake-up call to take care of our ancestors," Ayau told the audience.[63] The next day representatives of Na Lei Aliʻi Kawananakoa and the Royal Hawaiian Academy of Traditional Arts offered to retrieve the objects for Hui Mālama. The attorney for Hui Mālama, Alan Murakami, replied, "That's like saying, 'I don't have to push my baby off a cliff but I can get someone else to do it, and it's not going to affect me.'"[64]

The news media continued to report on developing issues on a near-daily basis. Abigail Kawananakoa moved increasingly into the spotlight. Her principal claim to authority continued to be her connection to royalty. Speaking to a *Star-Bulletin* reporter, she "questioned the source of Hui Malama's burial practices, saying, 'The ability to receive instructions from the ancient kupuna is mana (authority or power),' and 'such mana rests solely with the alii (aristocratic class).' Referring to Hui Malama members as commoners, or 'makaainana,' and noting that Kawaihae was an alii burial site, Kawananakoa said, 'At no time was the commoner allowed to participate at any stage of the rituals concerning the burial of an aristocrat.'"[65] The next day Hui Mālama supporter Mehanaokala Hind circulated an email in the Native Hawaiian activist community that attacked Kawananakoa's claims to *kuleana* by way of *ali'i* status. She wrote:

> Hawaiian Alii were not feudal figureheads of their people and instead were the champions of the people lest they be replaced. In the Hawaiian language we have words like naau alii and opu alii which defines the character and integrity of the Alii as being generous and pono. We also have wise sayings that call the land the Alii and man the servant of the land. Our history teaches us that you were not only born an Alii, but in order to maintain that status, the people and the Gods needed to agree that you were deserving of that kuleana. This is where Ms. Abigail has failed. . . . Ms. Abigail is an Alii in terms of white America, simply, an aristocrat. The mana of her royal ancestors does not reside within her.[66]

On 20 September the Ninth Circuit Court of Appeals suspended Judge Ezra's order until it could hear arguments on the matter.[67]

In mid-November 2005 the Review Committee convened for its thirtieth meeting in Albuquerque, New Mexico. Ayau was on hand to address the committee "with a heavy heart."[68] Regarding Kawaihae, he reiterated Hui Mālama's position that the Review Committee has repeatedly overstepped its authority in recommending that the repatriation process be restarted. Once again he asked for this position to be vacated. As an alternative Ayau asked the Review Committee to recommend Native Hawaiian traditional dispute resolution, ho'oponopono. Next Ayau brought to the committee's attention the fact that the Bishop Museum had recently withdrawn seven Notices of Intent to Repatriate. Ayau asked the committee to ask Brown the reason for these actions. His presentation led to another round of Review Committee discussions, during which it became clear that its finding regarding Kawaihae at the Honolulu meeting had not been adequately conveyed to the relevant parties or to the public. The committee clarified its position in the following terms:

> Mr. Monroe stated that in Honolulu the Review Committee reached the following decision regarding the Kawaihae Caves matter. One, the Review Committee reaffirmed the St. Paul [2003] decision that the Bishop Museum's repatriation of these materials was flawed and incomplete; two, the Review Committee instructed the national NAGPRA staff to convey to all parties involved in this matter three additional points. The first point was that the Review Committee's decision and finding in Honolulu in no way implies or requires that the Kawaihae materials be removed from their present location; two, that the Review Committee strongly encourages all parties, particularly and specifically Native Hawaiians who are involved in the dispute, to use traditional or other methods to resolve their differences; and three, that the Review Committee asserted that its decision should in no way be interpreted to mean or support a potential claim by the Bishop Museum that it has a right of ownership or control of these objects.[69]

Although this restatement did not represent an out-and-out victory for Hui Mālama, it did recast important issues, especially concerning the physical removal of the objects and the committee's desire to see the parties engage in alternative dispute resolution.

While Hui Mālama was making some headway with the Review Committee, it was becoming clearer by the day that it was losing ground in the courts. In late November the appeals court dismissed Hui Mālama's claim regarding the danger of opening the cave.[70] On 6 December the court questioned Hui Mālama about the location and status of the objects. Judge Stephen Trott told Hui Mālama's attorney, "The case to me has every appearance of your side trying to hijack the process."[71] Trott's anxiety was a harbinger of the following day's court ruling, which upheld Ezra's injunction.[72] The court gave Hui Mālama sixteen days to execute the order. Hui Mālama immediately issued press releases proclaiming its intent to continue challenging the order, citing the Review Committee's finding that the objects need not necessarily be removed for the evaluation process to move forward.[73] The same day the *Honolulu Advertiser* published a piece entitled "Moepu Are Not for Our Eyes to See," by columnist Lee Cataluna, who explicitly supported Hui Mālama and implied that contesting groups had succumbed to "Western values": "Who is Hui Malama to decide where moepu rest? It can be argued that Hui Malama did not decide, but only acted on the decision of the ancestors."[74]

On 20 December 2005 Ayau said he would defy the court's order. "Our responsibility is not to Judge Ezra, it's to the kupuna," Ayau told the *Honolulu Advertiser*. Ezra responded by threatening to find Hui Mālama in contempt, saying, "This is a court of law, this is not a cat and mouse game."[75] On 22 December Hui Mālama supporters sent out an Internet call for all cultural practitioners to support the group.[76] On the same day Hui Mālama supporters began organizing protests of the court's impending action. Supporters and detractors of Hui Mālama bombarded Hawaiian newspapers with letters.

Forestalling action over the Christmas holiday, on 23 December Judge Ezra requested that Hui Mālama members appear before him on 27 December to explain their noncompliance with his order.[77] On 26 December groups opposed to Hui Mālama held a press conference, engaging in a blistering attack on Hui Mālama's reputation: "This is not a cultural issue. It is a legal struggle. . . . This is a fight between Hawaiians resulting from Hui Malama's mistaken attitude that it has the authority to make decisions for all Hawaiians and then shove it down our throats."[78] In a dramatic riposte Hui Mālama supporters began gathering outside the courtroom the next day. "For us, it's like arguing in federal court over objects in the Sistine Chapel," exclaimed one Hui Mālama supporter.[79]

One newspaper account described the subsequent scene as follows: "Dressed all in black with his hair cascading over his shoulders framing his tattooed cheek, Edward Halealoha Ayau left a federal courtroom yesterday flanked by U.S. marshals. He was sentenced to 'an indeterminate amount of time' in prison for violating a court order to identify specific locations within Big Island caves where he buried 83 native Hawaiian artifacts. 'Mr. Ayau, you have backed this court into a corner and forced its hand,' said U.S. District Judge David Ezra, adding, 'I didn't want to do this.'"[80] Ayau's arrest was the culmination of a frenzied court session attended by more than one hundred Hui Mālama supporters. Judge Ezra had to halt the proceedings several times when members of the audience began chanting and otherwise disturbed the court. One Hui Mālama supporter persisted in chanting after being warned and was sentenced to five days in jail. Other Hui Mālama members and supporters cursed Abigail Kawananakoa before parading out of the hearing. Still others sang "mournful songs."[81] Responding to the setting, La'akea Suganuma was quoted as saying that Ayau "wants to be a martyr. But he has an agenda, and there is more than appears on the surface."[82] In his comments Judge Ezra said, "Hui Malama does not have a corner on the Native Hawaiian religion," and declared that Ayau would be imprisoned until he complied with the court's order.[83]

Upon Ayau's incarceration matters immediately shifted from federal court to the court of public opinion. Already on 27 December letters were flying. Cy Kamuela Harris wrote the *Honolulu Advertiser*, declaring, "Moepu is a word created by Hui Malama, along with a list of other words they use in their mumbo-jumbo, so-called rituals."[84] On 28 December the *Advertiser* opined that Ayau's arrest, while viewed as heroic by some, was "really the culmination of a tragic mistake."[85] That same day the paper ran a letter from Hui Mālama defending its conception of *moepū*.[86] Two letters in the *Star-Bulletin* captured the controversy in a nutshell. One declared, "Ayau is a victim of religious persecution."[87] The other stated, "Hui's disrespect invites criticism."[88] The former beseeched the community to "pray that our descendants don't only know us through a museum display." The latter characterized Hui Mālama as "wolves in sheeps [*sic*] clothing." On 30 December *Advertiser* columnist Lee Cataluna weighed in again with another outspoken defense of Hui Mālama, imploring readers to "respect the kupuna."[89]

The new year was ushered in by juxtaposed commentaries in the *Advertiser*. Signed by members of three NHOs involved in Kawaihae, one argued strenuously for respecting the sanctity of *moepū* and defended Ayau's stance: "Prevent the second desecration. Repatriation is complete. Free Eddie Halealoha Ayau."[90] The other, written by Nanette Naiona Napoleon, was entitled, "Defiant Hui Leader Is No Hero."[91] She attacked those who viewed Ayau's actions as those of a noble martyr and took exception to a catchphrase that had recently begun to circulate: "Eddie Would Go." This is a reference to Eddie Aikau, a legendary Hawaiian surfer and activist who perished while attempting to save boat mates when the famous voyaging canoe *Hokule'a* capsized in 1978. "Eddie Would Go" is now an iconic slogan captured on bumper stickers and posters throughout the islands, signifying boldness and commitment. Rejecting the imputation of these qualities to Ayau, Napoleon wrote that he "is nothing more than a bully with a law degree and a zealot's heart. . . . It has always been the Hui Malama way or the highway." She added that, upon Ezra's ruling, she had heard "someone shout out to the kupuna in the spirit world to 'descend, descend' to harm 'those evil people' who stand against them." The *Star-Bulletin* followed on 2 January with an editorial opinion declaring that "Hui Malama's unyielding tactics are hurtful to Hawaiians."[92]

For weeks the pendulum thus swung back and forth. Indeed, the day after the *Star-Bulletin* challenged Ayau, it published a letter declaring that he "walks in the path of Jesus."[93] Subsequent letters in this mode likened Ayau to Gandhi, Martin Luther King, and Thoreau; one described him as a prisoner of war.[94] Other letters affirmed the anti-*moepū* position, reveling in how the ancestors had supposedly preserved the culture for future display.[95] Jonathan Osorio weighed in with a sharply worded letter that supported Ayau, took the court and the Bishop Museum to task, and supported a view of the objects as *moepū*.[96] Meanwhile, Hui Mālama supporters were holding a vigil and staging protests outside of the federal detention center in Honolulu where Ayau was held.

Perhaps this charged atmosphere and consideration of the Review Committee's restated position persuaded Judge Ezra to shift his approach to Kawaihae, because on 5 January 2006 he asked the parties to the dispute to consider engaging in *ho'oponopono:* "The whole idea is to take the matter out of the courtroom and into the hands of Hawaiians."[97] Ezra proposed moving forward on a dual track of *ho'oponopono* and legal proceedings. Representatives of Hui Mālama and the Royal Hawaiian Academy of Traditional Arts welcomed the proposal.[98] The *Advertiser* supported Ezra's new position in an editorial on 7 January: "In the midst of a temperate Hawaiian winter, the Forbes burial cave conflict has generated unseasonal heat. Anything to break the fever might be just what the doctor ordered."[99] The *Star-Bulletin* chimed in with its own editorial to the same effect.[100] Lee Cataluna followed with another column, writing: "What would be the right word to describe this new turn in the story? Enlightened? Hopeful? Historic?"[101] She noted, however, the intensity of *ho'oponopono:* "It will take a great deal of fortitude to commit to that action, the right thing and the hard thing at the same time."

On 9 January attorneys for the disputants agreed to explore alternative dispute resolution by way of *ho'oponopono*.[102] Ayau broke his media silence, calling this development promising: "Having said this, as long as I am ordered to disclose how we conducted the Kawaihae reburial, I am compelled to decline, respectfully."[103] In a letter to the *Advertiser*, he wrote: "I am not a hero. But I am hard-headed, as we all should be. Whenever faced with the need to be 'onipa'a [steadfast] regarding fundamental values, I practice from wa kahiko [ancient times]."[104] Ayau's reaction to the prospect of *ho'oponopono* comes across as notably ambivalent—he embraced the idea in principle but expressed rigidity with reference to the core issue to which it would apply.

On 13 January Judge Ezra selected two engineering firms to determine the safety of reopening the cave.[105] On 17 January Ezra ordered the release of Ayau so that he could participate in hoʻoponopono.[106] The judge appointed two Native Hawaiian authorities to mediate the process: Nainoa Thompson, who was very active in the revival of Polynesian navigation in Hawaiʻi, and Earl Kawaa, an educator.[107] Ezra gave the parties a tentative date of 24 February 2006 to reach a solution.[108] That date came and went, and, as I noted earlier, by April 2006 it was clear that the process had failed.

Because of Judge Ezra's gag order, little was reported on Kawaihae throughout the summer of 2006. Then, in early September, the *Star-Bulletin* reported that, with Ezra's consent, representatives of the Bishop Museum had entered Kawaihae Caves and retrieved the objects. This settled the question of whether or not Hui Mālama had reburied the objects. It also settled the question of whether or not Judge Ezra and the Bishop Museum would be willing to reopen the cave. For our purposes, however, it is important to recognize this event not as the end of the dispute but as yet another catalyst for the enunciation of tradition in action. For example, Hui Mālama member Charlie Maxwell told the *Star-Bulletin*'s reporter that "someone will pay spiritually."[109] The *Honolulu Advertiser* quoted Jon Osorio as saying, "Those who believe they were moepu (funerary objects) are going to be outraged and will be devoted to getting them reinterred."[110] Only weeks later a major earthquake shook the Big Island, hitting the immediate area of Kawaihae the hardest, leading to a new wave of speculation about the actions of ancestors' spirits in the present.

Then, in early December 2006, a pivotal moment in the dispute came when Judge Ezra approved a settlement stipulating that the Bishop Museum and Hui Mālama were to share the $330,000 cost of retrieving the objects. The agreement also released Ayau from home confinement.[111] While resolving the lawsuit filed by Na Lei Aliʻi Kawananakoa and the Royal Hawaiian Academy of Traditional Arts, and the counterclaim filed by the Bishop Museum against Hui Mālama, the settlement does not address the future disposition of the objects. As Gordon Pang reported in the *Honolulu Advertiser*, "What ultimately happens to the objects remains up in the air."[112] With aspects of the dispute settled and others undecided, rhetorical struggles between the parties remain entrenched. Ayau continues to defend Hui Mālama's fidelity to the ancestors, while Abigail

Kawananakoa has reflected on the settlement in equally charged terms: "This is a turning point in saving the authentic history of the Hawaiian people. . . . We are just beginning."[113]

Speaking Up, Shouting Down, Leveling Out

Yet another factor was introduced into this tempest in May 2006 when Volcanoes National Park announced that it had categorized objects in its collection from Forbes Cave as being unassociated funerary objects and therefore open to repatriation pending the park's review of claims.[114] By July 2006 sixteen claimants had come forward, including the fourteen Kawaihae claimants. Thus another chapter in the Kawaihae saga is now unfolding. However, while these objects are from the same site, the conditions of their possible repatriation are considerably different. Unlike the Bishop Museum, Volcanoes National Park has communicated with as many claimants as possible while still retaining possession of the objects.[115] This has allowed the process to move forward in a manner more in line with NAGPRA prescriptions. How the park will weigh the religious arguments of various claimants is difficult to foresee.

What is clear is that people affiliated with a range of parties view this as a potential fresh start for repatriation in Hawai'i. It might be said that Native Hawaiian activists were fast-forwarded into narrative and material control of their pasts by Honokahua (the Ritz-Carlton site on Maui) and related events. Responding, they quickly searched for their voices—often to productive ends—and the loudest ones garnered the most attention. Since then many more voices have emerged. Sometimes these voices speak in unison; oftentimes they shout one another down, as in the Kawaihae dispute. This in no way discounts these voices; rather, it illustrates their commitment. Perhaps the Volcanoes repatriation will lead to a moment when cooler heads will prevail and listening will play as important a role as speaking. Antagonisms might be sustained, consensus might emerge, or there might be agreements to disagree. Whatever the case, tradition will be at work.

It would be satisfying to wrap up my analysis of Kawaihae and related matters with a historical conclusion. However, as is clear by now, I work in an unfolding present, in the context of stories that appear far from any lasting resolution. But even if a crisp historical conclusion were available, it would draw the reader's eye, I am afraid, away from the significance of the cases we have followed, away from what matters in the analysis of lived tradition generally.

It might draw attention away from utterances and actions, away from perceiving how these are unfailingly contextual, frequently oppositional, strongly marked, religiously coded, socially indexed, and politically engaged. And, I would add, astoundingly creative and patently human. To lose sight of these realities in favor of tidy representations is, in my view, tantamount to abandoning the study of lived religion in favor of a tour through a wax museum.

8

REPATRIATION, TRADITION, AND THE STUDY OF RELIGION

This is because myth is *speech stolen and restored.* Only, speech which is restored is no longer quite that which was stolen: when it was brought back, it was not put exactly in its place.

—Roland Barthes, *Mythologies*

Tradition and the Law

HAVING DEVOTED considerable attention to the claims and actions of various Native Hawaiian organizations, the media, the NAGPRA Review Committee, and the courts, it is appropriate here to summarize the core argument of this book by way of the Kawaihae conflict. To do so, I propose a deceptively simple formulation: "tradition" is not found in objects in a cave; rather, tradition is located in the contemporary dispute surrounding the objects. This is not to say that tradition is coextensive with the position of one party, which at some future time—whether through the channels of Western law or some other mechanism—will be revealed to be the legitimate heir of Native Hawaiian religion. Such a view is predicated on understanding tradition as a thing or as a traceable linkage of connections between the now and then. Certainly, tradition in this literalist understanding has its relevance, which may be more or less adequately charted and studied by empirical means. However, leaning on this approach to tradition involves serious potential for misunderstanding and misrepresentation if care is not taken to appreciate and analyze ways in which even the most objective linkages to the past always and everywhere entail interpretation, a process that is never simple and is always subjective.

As I have argued, tradition is better viewed as a discursive strategy —narrative when announced, combative when challenged, metaphorical when analyzed—and as lived practice, which imparts meaning, power, and enrichment to human lives and community visions. In the Kawaihae case and in the other contexts we have considered, tradition is the sum total of disputes, performances, and postures that together amount to a process by which communities seek to define themselves, along external and internal lines, through speech and actions in the present that make reference to ideals, expectations, and practices in terms of narrated pasts. The lessons of Kawaihae, Anasazi country, Sand Creek, Congress, and the courts are not just for Hawaiians, Native Americans, legislators, and judges; indeed, perhaps the clearest lesson of all regarding the dynamics of tradition is for scholars of religion.

Even were it revealed that some of the disputants in the Kawaihae case have falsely construed their genealogies, have trafficked in relics, or are beholden to a museum, my approach to tradition in this context would not change. Nor do the manifestly political elements of Cheyenne conflicts or Ute claims upon Anasazi ancestors cause me to doubt my approach. To the contrary, in such cases the politics of everyday life do not cut against the grain of tradition but run with it. This is a tough conclusion to swallow for those who prefer tradition in distilled, purified forms. Regarding Kawaihae, for example, one might ask whether some of the claimants have factually stronger connections to Native Hawaiian heritage than others. Or, on a related note, whether we might agree that some disputants have nobler intentions than others. In answering such questions, I would reiterate my position that tradition is not located only in factual content or moral fidelity. Rather, tradition takes form as and through intentions and desires rendered operative by metaphorical elaborations of select and valorized components of the narrated past in the service of the present. Thus, how Eddie Halealoha Ayau will react to the opening of Kawaihae Cave is not in itself a barometer of tradition, though his arguments supporting his actions will be—so long as he continues to refer to ancestral desires, genealogies, and other ways of speaking forth the past in the present.

Beyond Kawaihae and the Hawaiian context, I would like to play out a few concluding points regarding Native American invocations of tradition and the sacred. More than Hawaiians, Native Americans have developed a dual inflection for announcing their claims. I have analyzed this strategy according to a model of minority-specific and majority-inclusive claims. Why have Native Hawaiians been less apt to follow this pattern? First, regardless of their views on federal recognition, Native Hawaiians generally share a strong sentiment of cultural independence from the U.S. government. In Hawai'i, for historical and geographical reasons, indigenous and "American" identities are far less cross-fertilized than they are on the mainland, so appealing to images of citizenship and soldierly tropes would have fewer positive resonances (and indeed, potentially negative ones) than for Indians. Second, Native Hawaiians' principal interlocutors have been representatives of Native Hawaiian organizations and the Native Hawaiian public generally. Thus, in many ways their struggles have been over authority within the native community, so appeals to external modes of legitimation would serve potentially negative functions: adversaries could recast such claims as evidence of the "colonized" status of a person or group. As we have seen, Native Hawaiian disputes are almost always largely concerned with the micropolitics of minority-specific claims.

For Native Americans, however, I hope to have shown how pivotal their double inflection of identity claims has been. Exploring this context yields insights regarding the ways identity claims function in other settings. Specifically, I would emphasize the correspondence we have tracked between Native Americans' layered subjectivities and layered discursive resources. They speak in a range of ways according to their perception of their audience and their sense of which aspects of their experiences and heritage will best reach a specific audience for a particular purpose. This lesson about articulations of tradition intersects with current work in the theory of politics and representation. Describing what he has called "the representation of an impossibility," Ernesto Laclau has recently written the following: "One of the many consequences of the increasing fragmentation of contemporary societies is that communitarian values—contextualized in so far as we are always dealing with specific communities—are supplemented by discourses of rights (such as, for instance, the rights of peoples or cultural minorities to self-determination) which are asserted as valid independently of any context. Are these two movements—assertion of universal rights and assertion of communitarian specificity—ultimately compatible?"[1]

Responding to this crisis, Native Americans have announced their identities in defiance of the narrative suppositions of Western law, speaking forth identity claims outside the normative confines of "linear" and "literal" expectations.[2] In this context they have become, to borrow a phrase from Marcel Detienne, "masters of truth" through their ability to link rhetorical means to cultural and political ends.[3] With regard to Indian land claims, anthropologist James Collins has recently framed this issue in terms that recall Laclau's postulation of the impossible:

> Modern liberal society, based on propertied individualism and an associated political sphere of citizens, is confronted by Indians' counterclaims to the lands of the New World, which recall violence and expropriation, rather than contract and legal appropriation; by Indians' heterogeneous political subjectivities, which combine individual and collective statuses; and by Indians' cultural politics, which crosscut the public and private. In these clashes and challenges we find a familiar dilemma faced by contemporary social thought and political action: How to understand and negotiate ostensibly universal and avowedly specific traditions, identities, and rights.[4]

Collins's discussion of "heterogeneous political subjectivities" underscores one of our central conclusions: the degree to which Native American representatives have been successful in the context of NAGPRA is largely due to their insistence on inhabiting—and exercising the speech potency of—multiple social identities.

From multiple positionalities Indians have cast their voices in a remarkable diversity of ways. Precisely by way of exercising communicative stratification, Native American representatives have outvoiced their opponents, who typically speak in a single voice, according to Western paradigms concerning the status of the individual.[5] Speaking from multiple subject positions has allowed Native American representatives to construct themselves as insiders as well as outsiders to the American nation-state, which has enabled them to voice grievances in ways that make clear demands upon institutions of the hegemonic bloc without alienating audiences who support the institutions but sympathize with repatriation efforts. Native American representatives have accomplished this insofar as they have been able, as Gerald Sider puts it, "to situate themselves historically across, rather than impossibly against, the breaks that power imposes."[6] In a sense the representational "impossibility" that Laclau alerts us to is countered by the possibilities of Native Americans' history and present: they convert "liabilities" of identity fragmentation into discursive vitality in the legal arena.

Analysis and Law

The perspectives on tradition and religious discourse I emphasize stand in tension with categorical expectations of the law wherein nonfalsifiable claims, and competing ones at that, are asked to serve as evidence. As I see it, NAGPRA sets up the condition of possibility for an effulgence of religious expression that it cannot begin to contain, channel, or otherwise manage in predictable ways. Religious testimony under the law has at times served the role legislators anticipated, tipping the balance of "preponderance of evidence" in favor of native claims. At other times it has played a far greater role in advancing native claims than was forecast, persuading audiences of claims in ways that eclipse consideration of other forms of evidence. At still other times religious discourse in a traditional key has hindered native efforts, particularly when nonnative audiences have been confronted by competing and conflicting religious assertions, as in the Kawaihae and Sand Creek disputes. This range of reactions to religious speech is a result of a disjuncture between expectations regarding tradition as a concept—usually imagined in rigid ways—and the realities of tradition in action.

While it is beyond my training and role to recommend changes to the law and its implementation, I would reiterate a point I have made several times in various ways: tradition in action—lived, necessarily political, and often contentious—should not be dismissed by legal audiences on the grounds that it is ideologically fueled and occasionally opportunistic. So long as tradition and religion are asked to perform evidentiary roles, none of the actors or actions that constitutes this drama should be left out. I am not arguing that all claims to tradition deserve equal treatment, but they do deserve equal consideration. The Review Committee seems to strive for this position, which, as it has seen, leaves us far from mechanical implementation of NAGPRA. To his credit Judge David Ezra appears to have adopted a similar stance in recommending *ho'oponopono*. While promoting a dynamic and democratic view of tradition renders implementation of laws like NAGPRA problematic, this is nonetheless a principled and realistic approach to social processes that are defined by actions, lives, and interests, not by categories, conventions, and caricatures.

As a caution to those who would rush to judgment with regard to the sorts of conflicts we have considered—and here I am particularly concerned with courts and other legal audiences—I would insist that narrative constructions emergent in these and other cases should not be viewed as somehow inherently less valid than apparently unproblematic cultural claims.[7] Multiple narratives of identity and conflicting claims to authority do not cut against the "truth" of a culture; they constitute it. Of the many things we might say about "culture," it bears emphasizing here that it is an analytic term describing a domain of contestation over resources (both material and symbolic) within a framework of largely shared values and histories defined and constructed against those understood to be "other." And we want to note, as Jonathan Z. Smith reminds us, that others include near-others—those close enough to one's own group to make boundary distinctions matter.[8] But whether announced with reference to "others" near or far, narratives of identity give expression to and often cut across internal and external boundaries of "culture." The stories we have followed speak to this view of cultural life as a vibrant and occasionally contentious process.

But this leaves a serious issue to worry about. How should scholars address perceived abuses of repatriation rhetoric and abuses of religious discourse in general, particularly if one accepts my argument against "authenticity" as a political and analytical construct? I do not foresee how courts will wade through these issues as NAGPRA begins to be tested, though indications are that they will raise constitutional concerns, particularly with reference to religious claims and the establishment clause of the First Amendment. As indigenous religious claims face judicial scrutiny, it is reasonable to assume that their authenticity will be questioned. I hope that courts will nonetheless embrace a narrative view of religion in order to see the ways most repatriation stories convey sincere desires in response to harsh histories. But this is certainly expecting too much, for the chains of "authenticity" are binding to all involved, at least as legal reifications and expectations of identity are currently configured. Loosening the seemingly impossible bonds of authenticity might begin with a shift in attention toward accountability. After all, repatriation laws have been put into place for this reason: to hold states and institutions accountable for their treatment of indigenous peoples' material heritage. Scholars and the media can help keep attention focused upon accountability, but I think courts will be most effectively persuaded, and hostile publics most effectively disarmed, when they see native representatives emphasize accountability not only to their communities but within them as well.

As with all situations of potential conflict, a basic sense of fairness can go a long way here. A language for describing and modeling fairness needs to be developed in the repatriation context, preferably with recourse to dialogical frameworks that are more democratic in spirit than current contests over authenticity allow. For my part, I can extrapolate from my analyses to speak to matters of fairness in the repatriation context, however tentatively. Here my claims are weak, not strong. They amount to concerns over cultural bullying (from inside and out), the dangers of wounded pride, and the way authority constructed in repatriation contexts is put to use elsewhere and vice versa. In the cases we have considered, I cannot say that any party strikes me as being guilty of these charges in a strong sense, though a number of the primary speakers may give me momentary pause. None of my anxiety at this level, however, causes me to believe that repatriation policies and politics are somehow not worth the effort people invest in them.

Sacred Claims and the Study of Religion

If I have relatively little to say about how legal audiences and disputants might best resolve the complexities NAGPRA puts into play, I have more to say about what the study of repatriation processes can yield for the study of religion generally and for the study of native traditions specifically. If readers are persuaded that repatriation under NAGPRA entails considerable religious negotiations, and that such discourse is shaped and reshaped by shifting contexts and strategies, then I hope readers are open to the conclusion that the study of native peoples and their traditions ought to be likewise rooted in commitments to analyzing religious claims as phenomena of this world, of the entrenched, real-time present—whenever that present may be. Only then, in my view, can analysis proceed to explore the possibilities and perils of religious language and traditions in a principled and consistent manner that is neither beholden to political fashions nor bereft of the ability to situate the stakes of religious struggles in ways that do not merely parrot religious claims or, conversely, ignore them and the worlds of meaning they entail and reveal.

In the course of my research for this book, I reached this analytical position as a result of tracking a wide range of disputes, paying close attention to the religious language and performances that gave them life. I agree with *New York Times* writer Edward Rothstein when he opines, "The effects [of NAGPRA] have been profound, not because of the loss of objects, but because the law enforced a way of thinking about them" (i.e., as the narrative property of Native Americans). I do not, however, share his conclusion that the situation has "diminished the stature of independent scholarship and scientific inquiry" and that "investigations of the Indian past are now characterized by the desire not to fully explore but to fully appease."[9] Certainly, Rothstein's position holds true in some cases. In this book, however, I have deliberately resisted the trajectory he points to. NAGPRA has, to be sure, put into place a new wave of essentializations and romanticizations of native traditions, but it has also provoked novel incarnations of tradition in action, as well as analyses of these that make a contribution to scholarship and public understanding through illuminating how religion and identity claims are constructed, advanced, embraced, and challenged.

With this study of repatriation processes, I hope to have added to the weight of analytical guidelines espoused by a number of scholars working in a variety of fields and contexts by rendering their significance clear through specific and contemporary case studies. The lessons I have learned include the following. First and foremost, one must be open to the living present. In my experience focusing upon the present enables one to apprehend processes of tradition in the making that become exceptionally hard to discern once a tradition becomes ascendant or, alternatively, forgotten or denied. Whether in the field or in an archive, one should look not merely to objects or objectifications (texts, prophets, rituals, etc.) but to that for which they stand in specific contexts and the subject positions to which they are harnessed in particular struggles. When attending to subjects and subjectivities, one should not assume these are configured monolithically; instead, they should be viewed as drawing upon multiple repertoires that may be spoken, enacted, and enlivened at a range of levels. Said another way, one should not seek religious truths as a function of stable identities but conceive of religious claims as bridges and boundaries employed in the articulation and crafting of identities. This approach requires a recalibration of perception, as one is no longer straining to hear the one "true voice" of tradition but instead must be attuned to a cacophony of voices. And when the "true voice" of tradition is abandoned as the subject of analysis, so too must quests for authenticity also be abandoned. In place of these reifications, one should seek to discern and describe processes of authentication and authorization. Once I began to engage the study of repatriation processes in these terms, I quickly became dissatisfied with literal accounts of the meaning of tradition and struggled to locate and interpret the metaphorical content and mechanisms of tradition as process. This enabled me to see and appreciate the broad scope of human possibilities contained in and conveyed by sacred claims.

NOTES

Introduction: Sacred Claims and Religious Acts

1. Public Law (PL hereafter) 101-601 (25 U.S.C. 3001). On NAGPRA generally see, e.g., Fine-Dare, *Grave Injustice*; Bray, *Future of the Past*; Gulliford, *Sacred Objects*; Mihesuah, *Repatriation Reader*; D. Thomas, *Skull Wars*; McKeown and Hutt, "In the Smaller Scope"; Pensley, "*Native American Graves Protection.*"

2. For the purposes of NAGPRA, Native Hawaiians and Native Alaskans are categorized as Native Americans, which is a convention followed in this book.

3. NAGPRA has instigated all manner of conflicts in its short career. Some of the more intractable issues pertain, e.g., to the categorical relation of "cultural affiliation" and "culturally unidentified remains," the disposition of ancient remains, and the status of so-called unrecognized tribes under the law. On persistent dilemmas in the implementation of NAGPRA, see Fine-Dare, "Anthropological Suspicion."

4. NAGPRA mandated the creation of a seven-member review committee to mediate disputes under the law. Three members are nominated by Native American groups, three by museum and archaeological groups. These members jointly nominate a seventh. The committee meets several times a year, issuing nonbinding findings that may be used as evidence in legal proceedings.

5. Three other groups were involved as claimants at this point: the Hawai'i Island Burial Council, the Department of Hawaiian Homelands, and the Office of Hawaiian Affairs. The degree to which they consented to the reburial remains unclear and contested. See, e.g., Hawai'i Island Burial Council Minutes, Thursday, 17 Nov. 2005; Burl Burlingame, "Claimant Groups Worked Together on 'Forbes Cave' Artifacts," *Honolulu Star-Bulletin*, 26 Apr. 2000, http://starbulletin.com/2000/04/26/news/story5.html.

6. Author's transcript, twenty-seventh Review Committee meeting (2004).

7. Regarding *'ānai* curses, see Pukui, Haertig, and Lee, *Nānā I Ke Kumu*, 31.

8. On the *kā'ai*, see Rose, *Reconciling the Past*.

9. The Anasazi, also known as Ancestral Puebloans (among other designations), inhabited the Four Corners region of the Southwest from at least

300 BCE until the thirteenth century. I opt to use the designation "Anasazi" here, as this is the usage of the people I am describing. On the Anasazi/ Ancestral Puebloans generally, see Cordell and Gummerman, *Dynamics of Southwest Prehistory*.

10. On this theme generally see Pearce, *Savagism and Civilization*.
11. On historical exploration see Chapin, *Land of the Cliff Dwellers*; McNitt, *Richard Wetherill*. For a classic literary fashioning of discovery, see Cather, *Professor's House*. On this theme with reference to the "New World" generally, see Greenblatt, *Marvelous Possessions*.
12. On this theme generally, with an interesting eye to the present, see Stuart, *Anasazi America*.
13. D. Smith, *Mesa Verde National Park*, 35.
14. See, e.g., the Antiquities Act of 1906 and the Archaeological Resources Protection Act of 1979.
15. A classic manifesto of this era is *Custer Died for Your Sins*, by the late Indian scholar Vine Deloria Jr.
16. See Vecsey, *Handbook*; Harjo, "American Indian Religious Freedom Act."
17. *Employment Div. v. Smith*; *Lyng v. Northwest Cemetery Protective Assoc.* On *Smith* see H. Smith and Snake, *One Nation under God*; on *Lyng* see B. Brown, *Religion, Law*.
18. S. F. Harding, *Book of Jerry Falwell*.

1. Subjects, Stories, and Strategies

1. See, e.g., Clifford and Marcus, *Writing Culture*; Stocking, *Observers Observed*.
2. Notable exceptions include Karen McCarthy Brown's classic, *Mama Lola*; P. Johnson, *Secrets, Gossip, and Gods*; Orsi, *Between Heaven and Earth*.
3. Alexie, *Business of Fancydancing*, 48. Alexie has been writing about cultural possession, dispossession, and repossession in striking ways for a number of years. For a more hopeful account of pawn shops and sacred objects, see his "What You Pawn I Will Redeem."
4. Vizenor, *Manifest Manners*.
5. On indigenous representation in literary and political contexts, see Allen, *Blood Narrative*.
6. "Indigenous" as a concept and category has recently aroused much critical debate, especially in anthropological circles. At issue are the ways an analytically dubious designation is mobilized in political contexts. See, e.g., Guenther et al., "Concept of Indigeniety"; Niezen, *Origins of Indigenism*.
7. See, e.g., Fforde, Hubert, and Turnbull, *Dead and Their Possessions*; Barkan and Bush, *Claiming the Stones*.
8. For good discussions of various components and configurations of American Indian identities, see Gonzales, "(Re)articulation"; Garroutte, *Real Indians*.
9. Barkan, "Amending Historical Injustices." More generally, see Appadurai, *Social Life of Things*; Bond and Gilliam, *Social Construction*.

10. For a related perspective on the relationship of narrative to NAGPRA, particularly with reference to scientific "myths," see C. Dumont, "Politics of Scientific Objections."
11. See M. Brown, *Who Owns Native Culture?*
12. Exceptions include, in varying degrees, Flynn and Laderman, "Purgatory"; M. Brown, *Who Owns Native Culture?*; Fine-Dare, *Grave Injustice*; Ridington and Hastings, *Blessing.*
13. On the crisis of American jurisprudence in relationship to religious freedom, see W. Sullivan, *Impossibility of Religious Freedom.*
14. On this important theme see Warren and Jackson, *Indigenous Movements*; Butler, Laclau, and Žižek, *Identity and Hegemony.*
15. On this line of analysis, see Povinelli, *Cunning of Recognition.*
16. PL 101-601, Sec. 2.
17. Scholars of religion have published several essays on repatriation issues. These include Grimes, "Desecration of the Dead"; Weaver, "Indian Presence"; Grim, "Honoring the Ancestral Bones."
18. On analysis of religion in this key, see Lincoln, "Theses on Method."
19. Fforde, "Collection, Repatriation and Identity," 32.
20. On the problem of "authenticity," see, e.g., McCutcheon, *Discipline of Religion*; Gable and Handler, "After Authenticity."
21. For a recent framing of issues related to religion, metaphor, and tropes, see Tweed, "Marking Religion's Boundaries."
22. Handler and Linnekin, "Tradition, Genuine or Spurious?"
23. On this theme see Engler and Grieve, *Historicizing "Tradition."*
24. Burke, *Rhetoric of Religion.*
25. Regarding Native American political and legal resurgence, see Cornell, *Return of the Native*; Murray, *Forked Tongues*; Nagel, *American Indian Ethnic Renewal.*
26. Goodrich, "Antirrhesis."
27. Fitzpatrick, *Mythology of Modern Law.*
28. On the rhetorical conditions of religious and political authority, see Lincoln, *Authority.*

2. Islands of Practice, Discourses of Permanence

1. Exceptions include Moriwake, "Critical Excavations"; Petrich, "Litigating NAGPRA in Hawai'i."
2. On secretism see P. Johnson, *Secrets, Gossip, and Gods.*
3. A textual example of this passion is Nihipali, "Stone by Stone."
4. See Silva, *Aloha Betrayed.*
5. On land and sustenance issues see, e.g., Blackford, "Environmental Justice"; on open-ocean sailing see Harden, *Voices of Wisdom*; on hula see E. Buck, *Paradise Remade*; on ho'oponopono and Makahiki see G. Johnson, "Incarcerated Tradition"; on literature see Ho'omanawanui, "Ha, Mana, Leo," and Kelly, "Hawaiian Literature and Resistance."

6. B. Miller, *Invisible Indigenes;* Wilkinson, *Blood Struggle.*
7. The exclusion of non–federally recognized tribes is a major shortcoming of NAGPRA that is addressed in chapter 4.
8. On Native American identification see Garroutte, *Real Indians.*
9. For an argument against federal recognition for Native Hawaiians, see D. Kanahele, "Clandestine Manipulation toward Genocide."
10. As will become clear, much of the Hawaiian material considered in this book pertains directly to Hui Mālama, defined in NAGPRA as "the non-profit, Native Hawaiian organization incorporated under the laws of the State of Hawai'i by that name on April 17, 1989, for the purpose of providing guidance and expertise in decisions dealing with Native Hawaiian cultural issues, particularly burial issues." See PL 101-601, Sec. 2 (6).
11. Building upon this proposition, this chapter attempts to supplement the existing literature concerning uses of the past in the present. See Appadurai, "Past"; Bloch, *Ritual, History and Power;* Gathercole and Lowenthal, *Politics of the Past.* Hobsbawm and Ranger, *Invention of Tradition;* Lincoln, *Discourse and the Construction of Society.* Of relevance to Hawaiian examples, see Friedman, *Cultural Identity;* Linnekin, "Defining Tradition."
12. On Hawaiian mortuary practice see, e.g., Kirch, *Feathered Gods and Fishhooks;* Kamakau, *Ka Po'e Kahiko.* An excellent discussion of Hawaiian mortuary customs is found in the archaeological report concerning the Honokahua project: Donham, *Data Recovery Excavations.* See also Ayau, "Honor Thy Ancestor's Possessions."
13. On this theme see, e.g., Valeri, *Kingship and Sacrifice;* Friesen, *Ancestors;* K. Young, *Rethinking.*
14. I do not have the space here to address the vast literature concerning *mana* and *kapu.* For a helpful discussion of this literature, see Shore, "Mana and Tapu." Especially germane is Shore's description of *mana* moving between the realms of *ao* (earth) and *pō* (the realm of the gods, eternity) (147). Another source that is directly pertinent to our discussion is Valeri, *Kingship and Sacrifice,* 99–105. Valeri describes *mana* as life-giving power in speech and, in this context, as a discourse of authority. This is particularly salient to our discussion, especially when contemporary reinterment practices are considered. On the concept of *'aumākua,* see Valeri, *Kingship and Sacrifice;* Pukui, Haertig, and Lee, *Nānā I Ke Kumu,* 35. The concept of *'aumākua* is central to Hawaiian repatriation claims.
15. On this idea see Charlot, *Hawaiian Poetry,* 2–3; Donham, *Data Recovery Excavations,* 20–37.
16. U.S. Senate, Select Committee on Indian Affairs (SSCIA hereafter), Oversight Hearing 103-189 (1993), written statement of Hui Mālama I Nā Kūpuna 'O Hawai'i Nei (108).
17. For a detailed description of the project, see Donham, *Data Recovery Excavations.*

18. The following is based on an interview I conducted with Dana Naone Hall, Wailuku, Maui, 14 July 2003.

19. See Hall's poem "Ka Mo'olelo o Ke Alanui" in her edited volume *Mālama.*

20. Qtd. in Hawaii State Historic Preservation Division, "Na Iwi Kūpuna."

21. The following is based on the author's notes, taken during the 29 June 2006 meeting of the Maui-Lanai Islands Burial Council.

22. Ayau and Tengan, "Ka Huak'i O Na 'Oiwi," 173.

23. P. Kanahele, "Rhythms from the Past," 158.

24. Pukui, Haertig, and Lee, *Nānā I Ke Kumu,* 155. Cf. Pukui and Elbert, *Hawaiian Dictionary,* 257.

25. Pukui, Haertig, and Lee, *Nānā I Ke Kumu,* 155.

26. For an interesting comparative example of prophecies in stone, see Geertz, *Invention of Prophecy.*

27. The repatriation also involved a local group from Moloka'i, Hui Malama O Mo'omomi. For the Bishop Museum's federal notice of intent to repatriate the object, see *Federal Register* 64, no. 68 (9 Apr. 1999): 17410.

28. For a discussion of the political aspects of Hawaiian prophecy generally, see Friedman, *Cultural Identity,* 129. Examples of Hawaiian political prophecy are located in Kalakaua, *Legends and Myths,* 353–67. See Kamakau, *Ka Po'e Kahiko,* 7 and esp. 96, for a description of Kekiopilo, prophet of Kupihea, who Kamakau claims prophesied the coming of white men.

29. On colonial and missionary history in Hawai'i, see, e.g., Daws, *Shoal of Time.*

30. See Osorio, *Dismembering Lahui;* Kame'eleihiwa, *Native Land.* For a comparison of Native Hawaiian and Native American land dispossession, see Parker, *Native American Estate.* On the Dawes Act see, e.g., Niezen, *Spirit Wars,* 176–77.

31. Cooke, *Mo'olelo O Molokai,* 106. However, the archaeologist who helped Cooke remove a section of the stone described the footprints as made by human pecking. See Stokes, "Notes on Hawaiian Petroglyphs," 31–42. In more recent years archaeologists have concurred with Stokes's view.

32. Contrary to media reports and the Bishop Museum's press release, repatriation of the stone was thorny. In fact, as part of a general tightening of its repatriation policies and practices, the Bishop Museum eventually rescinded its repatriation of the objects, asserting that they do not meet the definition of cultural patrimony under the law (*Federal Register* 68, no. 212 [3 Nov. 2003]: 62319–20). Hui Mālama rejected this position and asked the Review Committee to consider the issue, which it did at a meeting on 13–15 Mar. 2005. The committee concluded that the dispute was beyond its purview, but it recognized the cultural significance of the Kalaina Wāwae and asserted its view that the current location of them is appropriate (*Federal Register* 70, no. 104 [1 June 2005]: 31513–14).

33. More than half of Moloka'i's seven-thousand-person population is native or part native.

34. Cooke, *Moʻolelo O Molokai*, 96.
35. Dana Naone Hall, telephone interview with the author, 20 July 2006.
36. Most Native Hawaiians with whom I have spoken refer to the dispute simply by using the name "Kawaihae," which is the usage I adopt throughout
this book. In media accounts and federal sources, it is most often referred
to as the Forbes Cave controversy.
37. Roger Rose, a former Bishop Museum anthropologist, has argued for this
connection in several contexts. See, e.g., Gordon Pang, "For Museum or the
Cave," *Honolulu Advertiser*, 21 May 2006, http://www.honoluluadvertiser
.com.
38. For an account of this, see Review Committee, Minutes of the Twenty-fifth
Meeting (2003).
39. Review Committee, Minutes of the Twenty-fifth Meeting (2003).
40. Review Committee, Minutes of the Twenty-fifth Meeting (2003), 7.
41. Review Committee, "Native American Graves Protection" (2003).
42. Rita Beamish, "Artifacts Suspended in Cultural Tension: Native Hawaiians
Vie with Museum," *Washington Post*, 1 June 2003. Ayau reiterated his position to me during an interview (Molokai, 13 July 2003).
43. Kunani Nihipali, "Seeking the Rightful Home for Bones, Burial Items,"
Honolulu Advertiser, 25 May 2003, http://www.honoluluadvertiser.com.
44. Consider the criticism of Hui Mālama offered by Herb Kawainui Kāne, a
native artist and activist, with reference to an object sealed in Forbes Cave:
"I don't want to get into one of these pseudo-spiritual descriptions that
Hui Malama has been so guilty of, but I will say that the *kiʻi* was a work of
art that was very powerful. . . . I think hiding it away is a great loss to all
Hawaiians." Qtd. in Whitney, "Showdown in Honolulu."
45. Ayau and Tengan, "Ka Huakʻi O Na ʻOiwi," 186.
46. See J. Z. Smith, *Relating Religion.*

3. Writing the Law, Speaking the Sacred

1. SSCIA, Hearing 100-90 (1987), 1.
2. SSCIA, Hearing 100-90 (1987), 2.
3. SSCIA, Hearing 100-90 (1987), 2–3.
4. SSCIA, Hearing 100-90 (1987), 34.
5. SSCIA, Hearing 100-90 (1987), 54.
6. See SSCIA, Hearing 100-90 (1987), 207–8.
7. See, e.g., the continued opposition of the Smithsonian Institution, as expressed by Undersecretary Dean Anderson. See SSCIA, Hearing 100-931
(1988), 46.
8. SSCIA, Hearing 100-931 (1988), 53.
9. SSCIA, Hearing 100-931 (1988), 62.
10. SSCIA, Hearing 100-931 (1988), 122–23.
11. This document is the so-called Bieder Report (*Brief Historical Survey*), prepared by Robert Bieder for NARF (1989).

12. U.S. Senate, Report 100-601 (1988), 7.

13. SSCIA, Hearing 101-952 (1990), 31.

14. SSCIA, Hearing 101-952 (1990), 33.

15. In this context it should be noted that the *Heard Report* states that "after a tremendous amount of discussion . . . the human rights principle applies even there [to so-called unaffiliated remains]." See SSCIA, Hearing 101-952 (1990), 31.

16. SSCIA, Hearing 101-952 (1990), 42.

17. SSCIA, Hearing 101-952 (1990), 52.

18. SSCIA, Hearing 101-952 (1990), 56.

19. In this respect human rights discourse can be viewed as a form of ritualized speech, the primary characteristic of which is the way it limits possible responses. On this topic see Bloch, *Ritual, History and Power.*

20. SSCIA, Hearing 101-952 (1990), 563.

21. The three bills were H.R. 1381, the Native American Burial Site Preservation Act of 1989; H.R. 1646, the Native American Grave and Burial Protection Act; and H.R. 5237, the Native American Graves Protection and Repatriation Act.

22. U.S. House, Interior and Insular Affairs Committee (HIIAC hereafter), Hearing 101-62 (1990), 145–46.

23. HIIAC, Hearing 101-62 (1990), 235; see also Sotheby's written testimony (246).

24. HIIAC, Hearing 101-62 (1990), 237.

25. U.S. Senate, Senate Report 101-473 (1990), 8.

26. U.S. Senate, Senate Report 101-473 (1990), 9.

27. U.S. House, House Report 101-877 (1990), 14.

28. For reports concerning the debate and passage of NAGPRA, see *Congressional Record* (*CR* hereafter), House, 26 Oct. 1990, 10985–91; *CR*, Senate, 22–26 Oct. 1990, 18245–46.

29. Concerning the relationship of authority and tradition, see, e.g., Bell, *Ritual Theory*; Bourdieu, *Field of Cultural Production*; Ortner, "On Key Symbols."

30. Edward Lone Fight, e.g., opened his testimony regarding S. 1980 in this manner (SSCIA, Hearing 101-952 [1990], 49). I have witnessed this practice at many NAGPRA-related events and have come to expect it when native speakers address a nonnative audience in an academic or political context.

31. See, e.g., the testimony of Norbert Hill (SSCIA, Hearing 101-952 [1990], 56).

32. Such cultural performances have been taken a step further in the history of NAGPRA implementation. Claimants on several occasions have enacted rituals during Review Committee meetings as a way to instantiate their claims upon "sacred objects" in real time. See, e.g., chap. 6.

33. SSCIA, Hearing 100-90 (1987), 28–31.

34. HIIAC, Hearing 101-62 (1990), 123–24.

35. HIIAC, Hearing 101-62 (1990), 110.

36. SSCIA, Hearing 100-90 (1987), 236.
37. See, e.g., the story told by Edward Kanahele in his testimony concerning the NAGPRA bills (SSCIA, Hearing 101-952 [1990], 400).
38. SSCIA, Hearing 100-90 (1987), 28.
39. See extensive NARF testimony throughout legislative history, particularly HIIAC, Hearing 101-62 (1990).
40. SSCIA, Hearing 101-952 (1990), 380; see also the testimony of Chief Wallulatum of the Wasco Tribe (SSCIA, Hearing 100-931 [1988], 36).
41. SSCIA, Hearing 101-952 (1990), 545.
42. SSCIA, Hearing 100-90 (1987), 86–87.
43. SSCIA, Hearing 100-90 (1987), 40.
44. SSCIA, Hearing 101-952 (1990), 217.
45. HIIAC, Hearing 101-62 (1990), 102.
46. Herzfeld, *Cultural Intimacy*, 43.
47. Evans-Pritchard, *Nuer*; Barth, *Ethnic Groups and Boundaries.*

4. Tense Negotiations

1. On this history see also Trope and Echo-Hawk, *Native American Graves Protection*; McKeown and Hutt, "In the Smaller Scope"; Rose, Green, and Green, "NAGPRA Is Forever."
2. SSCIA, Hearing 100-90 (1987), 24. Of additional note here is the fact that affiliation is posited with regard to an individual tribe. This assumption and the subsequent reaction to it have informed much of the debate over cultural affiliation to the present.
3. SSCIA, Hearing 100-90 (1987), 54.
4. SSCIA, Hearing 100-90 (1987), 60.
5. SSCIA, Hearing 100-90 (1987), 61.
6. SSCIA, Hearing 100-90 (1987), 68.
7. SSCIA, Hearing 100-90 (1987), 135.
8. SSCIA, Hearing 100-931 (1988), 224.
9. See U.S. Senate, Report 100-601 (1988). The report includes NARF's expanded evidentiary language and, most significant, NARF's position that museums and federal agencies have no property interests in Native American human remains.
10. SSCIA, Hearing 101-952 (1990).
11. SSCIA, Hearing 101-952 (1990), 62.
12. SSCIA, Hearing 101-952 (1990), 531.
13. SSCIA, Hearing 101-952 (1990), 531.
14. The panel did state that it would encourage compromises between Native American and scientific communities regarding the prospect of future research. See "Report of the Panel."
15. SSCIA, Hearing 101-952 (1990), 367.
16. SSCIA, Hearing 101-952 (1990), 416.
17. SSCIA, Hearing 101-952 (1990), 268.

18. HIIAC, Hearing 101-62 (1990), 15.

19. HIIAC, Hearing 101-62 (1990), 137.

20. HIIAC, Hearing 101-62 (1990), 165.

21. HIIAC, Hearing 101-62 (1990), 304.

22. U.S. Senate, Senate Report 101-473 (1990), 8–9.

23. U.S. House, House Report 101-877 (1990), 16.

24. The Review Committee was established by Sec. 8 of NAGPRA.

25. The first Review Committee was composed of the following members: Rachel Craig, Jonathan Haas, Dan Monroe, Tessie Naranjo, Martin Sullivan, William Tall Bull, and Phillip L. Walker.

26. Review Committee, Minutes of the First Meeting (1992), 9.

27. Review Committee, Minutes of the Second Meeting (1992), 9.

28. Review Committee, Minutes of the Fourth Meeting (1993), 5.

29. Review Committee, Minutes of the Fourth Meeting (1993), 8. On Hui Mālama's testimony in the Hearst dispute, see also SSCIA, Oversight Hearing 103-189 (1993), 108–12.

30. U.S. Department of the Interior (DOI hereafter), National Park Service (NPS hereafter), "Finding Regarding Human Remains" (1993).

31. DOI, Office of the Secretary, Proposed Rules (1993), 31132.

32. Review Committee, Minutes of the Fifth Meeting (1993), 20.

33. Review Committee, Minutes of the Sixth Meeting (1994), 13.

34. Review Committee, Minutes of the Sixth Meeting (1994), 13.

35. Review Committee, Minutes of the Seventh Meeting (1994), 15.

36. Review Committee, "Draft Recommendations" (1995), 32163.

37. NAGPRA is limited to federally recognized Indian tribes. On problems facing nonrecognized tribes, see B. Miller, *Invisible Indigenes*. Many tribes and groups are not federally recognized or have had their recognized status terminated. These have become increasingly vocal in recent years. On the whole the Review Committee has been sympathetic to their position, supporting repatriation to them if and when recognized tribes work with nonrecognized groups in making their claims.

38. Review Committee, Minutes of the Ninth Meeting (1995), 11.

39. Review Committee, Minutes of the Tenth Meeting (1995), 13–14.

40. DOI, *Native American Graves Protection* (1995).

41. SSCIA, Oversight Hearing 104-399 (1995), 236.

42. SSCIA, Oversight Hearing 104-399 (1995), 114.

43. On Kennewick Man, also referred to as the "Ancient One," see D. Thomas, *Skull Wars*; Chatters, *Ancient Encounters*.

44. Review Committee, Minutes of the Eleventh Meeting (1996), 7.

45. The second embodiment of the Review Committee included the following members: James Bradley, Lawrence Hart, Vera Metcalf, Armand Minthorn, Tessie Naranjo, John O'Shea, and Martin Sullivan.

46. Review Committee, Minutes of the Fifteenth Meeting (1998), 12.

47. Review Committee, Minutes of the Fifteenth Meeting (1998), 13.

48. Review Committee, Minutes of the Sixteenth Meeting (1998), 14.

49. U.S. Senate, Oversight Hearing . . . 101-601 (1999), 44.

50. U.S. Senate, Oversight Hearing . . . 101-601 (1999), 162.

51. U.S. Senate, Oversight Hearing . . . 101-601 (1999), 77.

52. Review Committee, Minutes of the Seventeenth Meeting (1999), 11.

53. It is relevant to note, however, that "geographical affiliation" was the Hopi's primary form of evidence advanced in the aforementioned Carlsbad claim.

54. For an extended account of Hopi and Zuni cultural affiliation to Southwestern sites, see Dongoske et al., "Archaeological Cultures."

55. See Clemmer, *Roads in the Sky.*

56. Review Committee, Minutes of the Eighteenth Meeting (1999), 7.

57. Review Committee, Minutes of the Eighteenth Meeting (1999), 15.

58. Review Committee, Minutes of the Nineteenth Meeting (2000).

59. Review Committee, Minutes of the Twentieth Meeting (2000), 34.

60. Review Committee, Minutes of the Twenty-first Meeting (2001), 33.

61. Review Committee, Minutes of the Twenty-second Meeting (2001), 15–21.

62. Review Committee, Minutes of the Twenty-second Meeting (2001), 26.

63. *Bonnichsen et al. v. the United States,* 217F Supp. 2d, 116 (2002).

64. PL 101-601, Sec. 2 (9).

65. Review Committee, Minutes of the Twenty-fourth Meeting (2002), 12.

66. *Bonnichsen et al. v. the United States,* 357F Supp. 3d, 962 at 977 (2004); Review Committee, Minutes of the Twenty-sixth Meeting (2004), 20–21.

67. Review Committee, Minutes of the Twenty-sixth Meeting (2004), 21.

68. The new committee members at this meeting were Willie Jones; Dan Monroe, who had served on the first Review Committee; Lee Staples; and Vincas Steponaitis.

69. Review Committee, Minutes of the Twenty-seventh Meeting (2004), 18.

70. Review Committee, Minutes of the Twenty-seventh Meeting (2004), 19.

71. Review Committee, Minutes of the Twenty-seventh Meeting (2004), 20.

72. U.S. Senate, S. 2843 (2004). Senator Campbell's amendment came in response to an SSCIA hearing held on 14 July 2004 (Oversight Hearing . . . 101-601 [2004]). At this meeting several speakers, including Walter Echo-Hawk of NARF, identified the verb-tense problem with Jelderks's opinion and asked for legislative remedy.

73. The new amendment was Sec. 108 of S. 536 (2005).

74. U.S. Senate, Oversight Hearing . . . 101-601 (2005), Hoffman's testimony (4).

75. U.S. Senate, Oversight Hearing . . . 101-601 (2005), Bender's testimony (5).

76. U.S. Senate, Oversight Hearing . . . 101-601 (2005), Kintigh's testimony (2).

77. U.S. Senate, Oversight Hearing . . . 101-601 (2005), Barran's testimony (9).

78. U.S. Senate, Oversight Hearing . . . 101-601 (2005), Barran's testimony (20).

79. U.S. Senate, Oversight Hearing . . . 101-601 (2005), Barran's testimony (15).

80. In the meantime, however, some hopeful signs and successes may be celebrated. For example, aspects of the Southwest conflict were resolved as of early 2006, the Hopi Tribe leading a massive repatriation from Mesa Verde on behalf of all claimants.

5. Ancestors before Us

1. Dodd, *Polynesian Art.* For a photograph of this object, see p. 235.
2. The museum was attempting to sell the object—valued at a minimum of two hundred thousand dollars—because it claimed to have inadequate security to protect such an expensive object and because it needed to raise funds for general upkeep of the museum's collection. See Gregory Smith, "It's Up to U.S. to Put Spear Rest Issue to Rest," *Providence Journal-Bulletin,* 30 May 1996.
3. See Review Committee, "NAGPRA Review Committee Advisory Findings" (1997).
4. For a detailed analysis of this legal history, see Moriwake, "Critical Excavations."
5. Museum of Natural History, "Summary"; Susan Kreifels, "Hawaiian Spear Rest Expected Home," *Honolulu Star-Bulletin,* 19 Mar. 1998, http://starbulletin.com/98/03/19/news/story5.html.
6. Legal scholar Isaac Moriwake has written a penetrating legal and discursive analysis of the dispute that highlights the narrative differences between the museum's and the Hawaiians' accounts of the object. I agree with the broad strokes of his analysis. Building on Moriwake's insights, my aim is to seek out the specific religious components and ramifications of these narratives. See Moriwake, "Critical Excavations."
7. Review Committee, Official Transcript of the Twelfth Meeting (1996), 65.
8. Review Committee, Official Transcript of the Twelfth Meeting (1996), 68.
9. In November 2006 the Field Museum of Chicago invoked similar language in response to the repatriation requests of the White Mountain Apache Tribe during the thirty-third meeting of the Review Committee.
10. Review Committee, Official Transcript of the Twelfth Meeting (1996), 70.
11. Review Committee, Official Transcript of the Twelfth Meeting (1996), 76.
12. Review Committee, Official Transcript of the Twelfth Meeting (1996), 78.
13. Review Committee, Official Transcript of the Twelfth Meeting (1996), 79.
14. Such dichotomies misrepresent Hawaiian epistemologies and practices. Many objects in the past and present might well be characterized as usefully sacred, including ʻawa bowls, funerary baskets, and the personal objects of chiefs. On this theme generally see P. Buck, *Arts and Crafts;* Malo, *Hawaiian Antiquities.*
15. Review Committee, Official Transcript of the Twelfth Meeting (1996), 81.
16. Review Committee, Official Transcript of the Twelfth Meeting (1996), 83.
17. Review Committee, Official Transcript of the Thirteenth Meeting (1997), 10.
18. Review Committee, Official Transcript of the Thirteenth Meeting (1997), 32.
19. Review Committee, Official Transcript of the Thirteenth Meeting (1997), 34.

20. Review Committee, Official Transcript of the Thirteenth Meeting (1997), 43.
21. Review Committee, Official Transcript of the Thirteenth Meeting (1997), 45.
22. This argument is frequently made in other legal and cultural contexts in Hawaii, though not usually by Native Hawaiians themselves. See, e.g., P. Sullivan, "Customary Revolutions."
23. Review Committee, Official Transcript of the Thirteenth Meeting (1997), 62.
24. This dispute, and the fractures within the Native Hawaiian community that it illustrated, foreshadow current internal strife between Native Hawaiian groups as seen, e.g., in the Kawaihae dispute.
25. Review Committee, Official Transcript of the Thirteenth Meeting (1997), 70.
26. Review Committee, Official Transcript of the Thirteenth Meeting (1997), 77.
27. PL 101-601, Sec. 2.
28. DOI, *Native American Graves Protection* (1995).
29. Review Committee, Official Transcript of the Twelfth Meeting (1996), 33–35.
30. Review Committee, Official Transcript of the Twelfth Meeting (1996), 38.
31. Review Committee, Official Transcript of the Twelfth Meeting (1996), 38–39.
32. Review Committee, Official Transcript of the Twelfth Meeting (1996), 42–43.
33. Malo, *Hawaiian Antiquities*, 11 n. 5, 115 n. 4 (notes by Emerson).
34. On ancestors as "before" in Hawaiian tradition, see Kameʻeleihiwa, *Native Land*, 22–23.
35. Review Committee, Official Transcript of the Twelfth Meeting (1996), 44.
36. Review Committee, Official Transcript of the Twelfth Meeting (1996), 45.
37. Review Committee, Official Transcript of the Twelfth Meeting (1996), 45.
38. Review Committee, Official Transcript of the Twelfth Meeting (1996), 47.
39. Review Committee, Official Transcript of the Twelfth Meeting (1996), 47.
40. Review Committee, Official Transcript of the Twelfth Meeting (1996), 47.
41. Review Committee, Official Transcript of the Twelfth Meeting (1996), 48.
42. Review Committee, Official Transcript of the Twelfth Meeting (1996), 49–50.
43. Review Committee, Official Transcript of the Twelfth Meeting (1996), 51–52.
44. Review Committee, Official Transcript of the Twelfth Meeting (1996), 53.
45. Review Committee, Official Transcript of the Thirteenth Meeting (1997), 95.
46. Review Committee, Official Transcript of the Thirteenth Meeting (1997), 101–2.
47. Review Committee, Official Transcript of the Thirteenth Meeting (1997), 103.

48. Review Committee, Official Transcript of the Thirteenth Meeting (1997), 104–5.

49. Review Committee, Official Transcript of the Thirteenth Meeting (1997), 113. Names are not transcribed in the transcript.

50. This point follows Lincoln, *Authority*.

51. Review Committee, Official Transcript of the Thirteenth Meeting (1997), 114–15.

52. Review Committee, Official Transcript of the Thirteenth Meeting (1997), 133–34.

53. Review Committee, Official Transcript of the Thirteenth Meeting (1997), 139.

54. Review Committee, Official Transcript of the Twelfth Meeting (1996), 48–49. For an extended account of the object's Kū characteristics, see Hui Mālama's Web site at http://www.huimalamainakupuna.org/kii.html.

55. Cox and Davenport, *Hawaiian Sculpture*; G. Kanahele, *Kū Kanaka*; Malo, *Hawaiian Antiquities*; Valeri, *Kingship and Sacrifice*.

56. P. Buck, *Arts and Crafts*, 465; Malo, *Hawaiian Antiquities*, 82.

57. K. Young, *Rethinking*, 78.

58. Cox and Davenport, *Hawaiian Sculpture*; Valeri, *Kingship and Sacrifice*.

59. Valeri, *Kingship and Sacrifice*, 23–29.

60. Valeri, *Kingship and Sacrifice*, 13.

61. At the same time a number of Native Hawaiian representatives provided genealogies linking themselves to the object and the traditions in question. These genealogies are uniformly lineages of the *ali'i*, the nobility. The way class issues function in contemporary Native Hawaiian cultural disputes is explored in detail in chapter 7.

62. Sahlins, *Islands of History*; Merry, *Colonizing Hawai'i*, 45.

63. Valeri, *Kingship and Sacrifice*, 29; also see G. Kanahele, *Kū Kanaka*, 81.

64. G. Kanahele, *Kū Kanaka*, 91.

65. Nabokov, *Forest of Time*, 234.

6. Religious Voices and Social Borders

1. R. Young, *Ute Indians of Colorado*, 18.

2. Jorgensen, *Sun Dance Religion*; R. Young, *Ute Indians of Colorado*.

3. The explorer Frederick Chapin, among others, recorded accounts of Ute avoidance of Anasazi ruins in his book *Land of the Cliff Dwellers* (131).

4. A reliable and representative collection of Ute myths is A. Smith, *Ute Tales*.

5. Stewart, "Culture Elements Distribution List," 262.

6. Park, *Shamanism*.

7. Reagan, "Collection of Ancient Artifacts."

8. Hultkrantz, "Mythology and Religious Concepts."

9. See Wood, *When the Buffalo Free*.

10. R. Young, *Ute Indians of Colorado*, 195.

11. On the day that I most recently visited the park, Saturday, 9 Aug. 2004, it had fewer than twenty visitors.

12. Nancy Lofholm, "Utes See 'Spirits' in Calamities," *Denver Post*, 28 July 2000. "Traditional native garb" means that he was attired in a typical Western shirt; wearing his hair in long braids; and brandishing a beaded feather fan and a gourd rattle—ritual paraphernalia of peyote religion, a practice first introduced to the Utes in 1910. On Ute peyote religion see Opler, "Character and History."

13. In fairness to Knight, he has served in a number of religious capacities at one time or another. On the history of the Knight family and Terry Knight's role in religious life on the Ute Mountain Ute Reservation, see R. Young, *Ute Indians of Colorado*; Carrier, *West of the Divide*.

14. The classic study of the Ute Sun Dance is Jorgensen, *Sun Dance Religion*. Also see Wood, *When the Buffalo Free*; Opler, "Integration."

15. The meeting, at which I was a presenter (on the panel "Consultation and the New Partnership Ecology"), was the 2000 symposium of the Colorado Council of Professional Archaeologists (University of Colorado, Denver, 18 Mar. 2000). The symposium, which concerned the regional implementation of NAGPRA, was notable for its inclusion of Native American representatives, who were given equal time with other presenters.

16. Ute Indian Symposium (Colorado Springs Fine Arts Center, 6 Oct. 2000).

17. Wroth, *Ute Indian*, 21.

18. Lofholm, "Utes See 'Spirits.'"

19. It should be noted that Knight did not imply an exclusive relationship with the Anasazi. In fact, the article concludes with Knight saying: "I would encourage the Pueblo tribes after the fire to do a ceremony. They need to get things back in harmony."

20. Carrier, *West of the Divide*, 113.

21. Sahlins, "Cosmologies of Capitalism" and "Goodbye to *Tristes Tropes*."

22. Cf. Friedman, *Cultural Identity*.

23. In a developing situation we soon may see the Ute, Paiute, and Shoshone tribes advance claims upon recently discovered and extremely ancient remains from the Freemont period. See Mindy Sink, "Tribe Members Express Concern over Handling of Ruins," *New York Times*, 4 July 2004.

24. This repatriation occurred before NAPGRA passed but largely followed the act in spirit. Under NAGPRA the item would clearly be considered both an "object of cultural patrimony" and a "sacred object." The Omaha tribe has been notably active in the legal and political arenas over the past century, and this experience helped propel their repatriation claims. On Omaha legal history see Scherer, *Imperfect Victories*.

25. The story of the repatriation of the Sacred Pole is told by the anthropologist Robin Ridington in his articles "Omaha Survival" and "A Sacred Object as Text," as well as in his book with Dennis Hastings, *Blessing for a Long Time*.

26. See *Return of the Sacred Pole.*
27. Fletcher and LaFlesche, *Omaha Tribe,* 217. Infamously, Fletcher's work among the Omaha prompted her to petition Congress for legislation that would allow Native Americans to gain individual title to their land holdings. Her argument was that private-property ownership would expedite the assimilation of Indians into mainstream American culture. Her petition led to a movement that eventuated in the Dawes Act of 1887, which in hindsight is considered one of the bleakest turns in federal/Indian relations, as the ultimate result was an overwhelming loss of land from Indian control. See, e.g., Wilkinson, *Blood Struggle.*
28. On problems in Omaha kinship, with specific reference to multiple lines of reckoning relationship and the relationship of the Ponca to the Omaha, see Barnes, *Two Crows Denies It.*
29. For accounts of other intratribal repatriation disputes, see, e.g., Harding, "Justifying Repatriation," regarding Cree bundles; Berman, "Beyond the Museum," regarding a Kiowa shield; and Review Committee, Minutes of the Twenty-second Meeting (2001), regarding Oneida wampum.
30. Hoig, *Sand Creek Massacre.*
31. Fine-Dare, *Grave Injustice,* 33; D. Thomas, *Skull Wars,* 53.
32. Ortiz, *From Sand Creek.* In many years Cheyenne and Arapaho representatives stage a memorial run from the site of the massacre to Denver, where a commemorative powwow is held. On 9–10 June 2001 the annual Arapaho Memorial Powwow was held at the University of Colorado. Arapaho representatives spoke of the event as a homecoming, variously declaring their ancestral claims upon the Boulder area. The most poignant claim—and the one that capped several speakers' presentations—was the assertion that the area is home to many ancestral graves and, as a result, is still deemed sacred by the Arapaho.
33. Review Committee, Official Transcript of the Thirteenth Meeting (1997), 232.
34. For more on the Sacred Arrows, see Berthrong, *Southern Cheyennes;* Stands in Timber and Liberty, *Cheyenne Memories.*
35. Review Committee, Official Transcript of the Thirteenth Meeting (1997), 234.
36. On the relationship of the business community to religious leaders in repatriation contexts, see Fowler, *Tribal Sovereignty.*
37. Review Committee, Official Transcript of the Thirteenth Meeting (1997), 234–36.
38. Review Committee, Official Transcript of the Thirteenth Meeting (1997), 236.
39. Review Committee, Official Transcript of the Thirteenth Meeting (1997), 243–44.
40. See, e.g., Lincoln, "Lakota Sun Dance"; Wood, *When the Buffalo Free.* Wood's account in particular resembles the Cheyenne situation; she describes how several different influential men sought to represent themselves as the

correct and most powerful Sun Dance leaders. One man made an explicit effort to conduct the dance in "traditional" style, while another introduced a variety of novel elements in his effort to demonstrate ritual mastery. Also resonating with the Cheyenne example, various dancers and attendees at the Ute dance claimed that illness and curses resulted from abuses of power at the ceremony.

41. Judy Gibbs Robinson, "Religious Ceremony Dispute Erupts at Tribal Encampment," *Oklahoman,* 10 June 2006, http://newsok.com.
42. See Walker, *Lakota Belief and Ritual;* Jorgensen, *Sun Dance Religion.*
43. Review Committee, Official Transcript of the Thirteenth Meeting (1997), 244–45.
44. Thornton, "Who Owns Our Past?" 23; see also Yellowman, "'Naevahoo-'ohtseme,'" written by Lawrence Hart's daughter. While devoted to the Sand Creek repatriation, Yellowman's article does not address the conflict I have described.

7. Dead Reckoning and Living Tradition

1. Pukui, Haertig, and Lee, *Nānā I Ke Kumu,* 60–70.
2. Sally Apgar, "Judge Orders Disputed Cave Artifacts Retrieved," *Honolulu Star-Bulletin,* 29 Apr. 2006, http://starbulletin.com/2006/04/29/news/story06.html.
3. Gordon Pang, "Museum Fights Hui Malama in Court," *Honolulu Advertiser,* 16 June 2006, http://www.honoluluadvertiser.com.
4. In their *Hawaiian Dictionary* Pukui and Elbert define *moepū* not as a noun but as a verb, *ho'omoepū:* "to place artifacts with the dead" (250).
5. On the GP sce Losch, "Hawaiian Issues," 206–7.
6. Guy Kaulukukui, interview with the author, Honolulu, 31 July 2004.
7. Bishop Museum, "Interim and Proposed Final Guidance" (GP hereafter) 1.
8. Bishop Museum, GP, 1.
9. Bishop Museum, GP, 1.
10. Bishop Museum, GP, 1–2.
11. PL 101-601.
12. Bishop Museum, GP, 2.
13. Bishop Museum, GP, 3.
14. Bishop Museum, GP, 3.
15. Bishop Museum, GP, 5.
16. Bishop Museum, GP, 5.
17. Bishop Museum, GP, 5. The arguments the museum marshaled recall those advanced by the Roger Williams Museum (see chap. 6) and those made more recently by the Chicago Field Museum in response to repatriation requests made by the White Mountain Apache Tribe. See Review Committee, Minutes of the Thirty-third Meeting (2006).
18. Letter and position papers on file with author.
19. Kaulukukui, "Bishop Museum," 2.

20. See, e.g., Vicki Viotti, "Bishop Museum Prepared to Contest Claims to Artifacts," *Honolulu Advertiser*, 1 July 2004, http://www.honoluluadvertiser.com.

21. Kaulukukui, "Sacred Objects," 1.

22. Kaulukukui, "Sacred Objects," 2.

23. Sally Apgar, "Reclaiming History: Hawaiian Groups Decry the Bishop Museum's New 'Native' Status," *Honolulu Star-Bulletin*, 2 Aug. 2004, http://starbulletin.com/2004/08/02/news/story5.html.

24. Edward Ayau, "Museum Policy Further Threatens Artifacts," *Honolulu Advertiser*, 8 Aug. 2004, http://www.honoluluadvertiser.com.

25. Ayau, "Museum Policy."

26. Sally Apgar, "Artifacts' Sale Investigated," *Honolulu Star-Bulletin*, 11 Aug. 2004, http://starbulletin.com/2004/08/11/news/story1.html.

27. Sally Apgar, "State Secures Entrance to Big Island Burial Cave," *Honolulu Star-Bulletin*, 27 Aug. 2004, http://starbulletin.com/2004/08/27/news/story3.html.

28. Nelson Daranciang, "Guilty Plea in Artifact Theft," *Honolulu Star-Bulletin*, 27 May 2006, http://starbulletin.com/2006/05/27/news/story05.html.

29. Summaries of all testimony described in this paragraph may be found in Review Committee, Minutes of the Twenty-seventh Meeting (2004), 25–27.

30. Review Committee, Minutes of the Twenty-seventh Meeting (2004), 27.

31. Review Committee, Minutes of the Twenty-seventh Meeting (2004), 27.

32. Review Committee, Minutes of the Twenty-seventh Meeting (2004), 28.

33. Review Committee, Minutes of the Twenty-seventh Meeting (2004), 28.

34. Review Committee, Minutes of the Twenty-seventh Meeting (2004), 31.

35. Review Committee, Minutes of the Twenty-seventh Meeting (2004), 31.

36. Sally Apgar, "Museum Rethinks Artifact Proposal," *Honolulu Star-Bulletin*, 3 Oct. 2004, http://starbulletin.com/2004/10/03/news/story1.html.

37. Vicki Viotti, "Native Burials Law to Undergo Revisions," *Honolulu Advertiser*, 5 Oct. 2004, http://www.honoluluadvertiser.com.

38. *Honolulu Star-Bulletin*, "Compromise Should Protect Museum and Hawaiian Sanctity," *Honolulu Star-Bulletin*, 6 Oct. 2004, http://starbulletin.com/2004/10/06/editorial/editorials.html.

39. Bishop Museum, "Final Guidance."

40. Sally Apgar, "Museum Votes against 'Native' Status," *Honolulu Star-Bulletin*, 8 Oct. 2004. http://starbulletin.com/2004/10/08/news/story4.html.

41. Ayau, "Testimony," 18 Sept. 2004, 1.

42. Pukui and Elbert, *Hawaiian Dictionary*, 281.

43. Author's transcript, twenty-seventh Review Committee meeting (2004).

44. Ayau, "Testimony," 18 Sept. 2004, 1.

45. Ayau, "Testimony," 18 Sept. 2004, 7.

46. Author's transcript, twenty-seventh Review Committee meeting (2004).

47. Sally Apgar, "Federal Panel to Revisit Artifacts Dispute," *Honolulu Star-Bulletin*, 3 Nov. 2004, http://starbulletin.com/2004/11/03/news/story11.html.

48. *Honolulu Star-Bulletin,* "Hawaiians Should Avoid Court Battle Concerning Artifacts," *Honolulu Star-Bulletin,* 7 Dec. 2004, http://starbulletin.com/2004/12/07/editorial/editorials.html.

49. SSCIA, Oversight Hearing 108-768, 16, 89, 91.

50. SSCIA, Oversight Hearing 108-768, 19.

51. SSCIA, Oversight Hearing 108-768, 29.

52. SSCIA, Oversight Hearing 108-768, 80.

53. SSCIA, Oversight Hearing 108-768, 22.

54. SSCIA, Oversight Hearing 108-768, 10.

55. Vicki Viotti, "Meetings to Discuss Burial Artifacts," *Honolulu Advertiser,* 13 Mar. 2005, http://www.honoluluadvertiser.com.

56. Viotti, "Meetings to Discuss."

57. Three children, ages fourteen to sixteen, testified. See Review Committee, Minutes of the Twenty-ninth Meeting (2005), 9–10.

58. Sally Apgar, "Battle Lines of Belief Drawn in Artifact War." *Honolulu Star-Bulletin,* 15 Mar. 2005, http://starbulletin.com/2005/03/15/news/story3.html.

59. Sally Apgar, "Burial Return Plan Is Flawed" *Honolulu Star-Bulletin,* 16 Mar. 2005, http://starbulletin.com/2005/03/16/news/story1.html.

60. Ken Kobayashi, "Hui Malama Wants Court to Rule on Its Appeal before Acting," *Honolulu Advertiser,* 9 Sept. 2005, http://the.honoluluadvertiser.com.

61. Sally Apgar, "Group Challenges Court Order on Artifacts," *Honolulu Star-Bulletin,* 9 Sept. 2005, http://starbulletin.com/2005/09/09/news/story1.html.

62. Gordon Pang, "Reopening Artifact Cave May Cause Collapse, Mason Says," *Honolulu Advertiser,* 14 Sept. 2005, http://www.honoluluadvertiser.com.

63. Sally Apgar, "Hui Malama Says Complying with Ruling Is Not an Option," *Honolulu Star-Bulletin,* 14 Sept. 2005, http://starbulletin.com/2005/09/14/news/story3.html.

64. Gordon Pang, "Artifacts Dispute Resolution Elusive," *Honolulu Advertiser,* 15 Sept. 2005, http://www.honoluluadvertiser.com.

65. Sally Apgar, "Showdown over Artifacts Unearths Spiritual Divide," *Honolulu Star-Bulletin,* 19 Sept. 2005, http://starbulletin.com/2005/09/19/news/index1.html.

66. Hind, "Manao."

67. Leila Fujimori, "Court Halts Removal of Hawaiian Items," *Honolulu Star-Bulletin,* 21 Sept. 2005, http://starbulletin.com/2005/09/21/news/story5.html.

68. Ayau, "Testimony," 16 Nov. 2005, 1.

69. Review Committee, Minutes of the Thirtieth Meeting (2005), 16–17.

70. Alexandre Da Silva, "Group's Assertion of Cave-in Dismissed," *Honolulu Star-Bulletin,* 27 Nov. 2005, http://starbulletin.com/2005/11/27/news/story05.html.

71. Sally Apgar, "Appeals Court Pushes for Info on Hawaiian Artifacts," *Honolulu Star-Bulletin,* 7 Dec. 2005, http://starbulletin.com/2005/12/07/news/story04.html.

72. U.S. Court of Appeals for the Ninth District, "Memorandum."

73. Gordon Pang and James Gosner, "Group Spurns Ruling on Hawaiian Arti-facts," *Honolulu Advertiser*, 13 Dec. 2005, http://www.honoluluadvertiser.com.

74. Lee Cataluna, "Moepu Are Not for Our Eyes to See," *Honolulu Advertiser*, 13 Dec. 2005, http://www.honoluluadvertiser.com.

75. Gordon Pang, "Hui Malama Leader Vows to Defy Judge," *Honolulu Advertiser*, 21 Dec. 2005, http://www.honoluluadvertiser.com.

76. Hind, "Kakoo for Hui Malama."

77. Gordon Pang, "Hui Malama Gets New Court Date," *Honolulu Advertiser*, 23 Dec. 2005, http://www.honoluluadvertiser.com.

78. Lynda Arakawa, "Groups Blast Hui Malama," *Honolulu Advertiser*, 27 Dec. 2005, http://www.honoluluadvertiser.com.

79. Linda Coble, "Crowd Gathers in Support of Hui Malama," *KHON2*, 27 Dec. 2005, http://www.khon.com.

80. Sally Apgar, "Hui Malama Leader in Jail for 'Indeterminate Amount of Time,'" *Honolulu Star-Bulletin*, 28 Dec. 2005, http://starbulletin.com/2005/12/28/news/story01.html.

81. Apgar, "Hui Malama Leader."

82. Apgar, "Hui Malama Leader."

83. Gordon Pang, "Group Defies Artifacts Order," *Honolulu Advertiser*, 28 Dec. 2005, http://www.honoluluadvertiser.com.

84. Cy Harris, "Hui Malama Does Not Own Moepu; They Belong to All," *Honolulu Advertiser*, 27 Dec. 2005, http://www.honoluluadvertiser.com.

85. *Honolulu Advertiser*, "Artifacts Opponents Must Seek Solution," *Honolulu Advertiser*, 28 Dec. 2005, http://www.honoluluadvertiser.com.

86. Edward Ayau et al., "Moepu: Archaeologist Wrong on Funerary Objects," *Honolulu Advertiser*, 28 Dec. 2005, http://www.honoluluadvertiser.com.

87. Laura Manuel-Arrighi, "Ayau Is a Victim of Religious Persecution," *Honolulu Star-Bulletin*, 29 Dec. 2005, http://starbulletin.com/2005/12/29/editorial/letters.html.

88. Hoku Taroc, "Hui's Disrespect Invites Criticism," *Honolulu Star-Bulletin*, 29 Dec. 2005, http://starbulletin.com/2005/12/29/editorial/letters.html.

89. Lee Cataluna, "Group Key in Fight for Repatriation," *Honolulu Advertiser*, 30 Dec. 2005, http://www.honoluluadvertiser.com.

90. Nation of Hawai'i et al., "Why Eddie Ayau Must Be Released," *Honolulu Advertiser*, 1 Jan. 2006, http://www.honoluluadvertiser.com.

91. Nanette Napoleon, "Defiant Hui Leader Is No Hero," *Honolulu Advertiser*, 1 Jan. 2006, http://www.honoluluadvertiser.com.

92. *Honolulu Star-Bulletin*, "Hui Malama's Unyielding Tactics Are Hurtful to Hawaiians," *Honolulu Star-Bulletin*, 2 Jan. 2006, http://starbulletin.com/2006/01/02/editorial/editorial01.html.

93. Richard Kinney, "Hui Malama Leader Walks Righteous Path," *Honolulu Star-Bulletin*, 3 Jan. 2006, http://starbulletin.com/2006/01/03/editorial/letters.html.

94. See, e.g., Myles De Coito, "Hui Malama Leader a Prisoner of War," *Honolulu Star-Bulletin*, 5 Jan. 2006, http://starbulletin.com/2006/01/05/editorial/letters.html.

95. See, e.g., John Wright, "Forbes Cave: Perhaps Artifacts Meant to Be Found," *Honolulu Advertiser*, 4 Jan. 2006, http://www.honoluluadvertiser.com.

96. Jonathan Osorio, "Cave Moepu: Judge Ezra vs. Hawaiian Beliefs," *Honolulu Advertiser*, 5 Jan. 2006, http://www.honoluluadvertiser.com.

97. Gordon Pang, "Artifacts Litigants Consider Old Ways," *Honolulu Advertiser*, 6 Jan. 2006, http://www.honoluluadvertiser.com.

98. Sally Apgar, "Judge Says Hawaiians Must Settle Artifact Fight," *Honolulu Star-Bulletin*, 6 Jan. 2006, http://starbulletin.com/2006/01/06/news/story02.html.

99. *Honolulu Advertiser*, "Cooldown Is Needed in Forbes Burial Case," *Honolulu Advertiser*, 7 Jan. 2006, http://www.honoluluadvedrtiser.com.

100. *Honolulu Star-Bulletin*, "Hawaiian Groups."

101. Lee Cataluna, "Major Shift in Resolving Dispute over Artifacts," *Honolulu Advertiser*, 8 Jan. 2006, http://www.honoluluadvertiser.com.

102. Gordon Pang, "Parties in Artifacts Suit Agree to Try Mediation," *Honolulu Advertiser*, 10 Jan. 2006, http://www.honoluluadvertiser.com.

103. Gordon Pang, "Hui Leader Calls Mediation Promising," *Honolulu Advertiser*, 12 Jan. 2006, http://www.honoluluadvertiser.com.

104. Edward Ayau, "Hui Malama: No to Ho'oponopono if It Means Exposing Burial," *Honolulu Advertiser*, 12 Jan. 2006, http://www.honoluluadvertiser.com.

105. Alexandre Da Silva, "Engineers to Advise on Artifact Retrieval," *Honolulu Star-Bulletin*, 14 Jan. 2006, http://starbulletin.com/2006/01/14/news/story08.html.

106. U.S. District Court of Hawaii, Status Conference.

107. Debra Barayuga, "Ayau Out of Prison as Groups Agree to Start Mediation," *Honolulu Star-Bulletin*, 18 Jan. 2006, http://starbulletin.com/2006/01/18/news/story07.html.

108. Gordon Pang, "Judge Sets Ayau Free to Participate in Talks," *Honolulu Advertiser*, 18 Jan. 2006, http://www.honoluluadvertiser.com.

109. Gary Kubota, "Reburied Cave Items Finally Back at Museum," *Honolulu Star-Bulletin*, 8 Sept. 2006, http://starbulletin.com/2006/09/08/news/story02.html.

110. Gordon Pang, "Hawaiians React to Artifact Reports," *Honolulu Advertiser*, 9 Sept. 2006, http://www.honoluluadvertiser.com.

111. Debra Barayuga, "Hui Malama–Bishop Museum Pact Has Them Sharing Artifact Retrieval Costs," *Honolulu Star-Bulletin*, 9 Dec. 2006, http://starbulletin.com/2006/12/09/news/story08.html.

112. Gordon Pang, "Retrieval of Artifacts Settled," *Honolulu Advertiser*, 8 Dec. 2006, http://www.honoluluadvertiser.com.

113. Pang, "Retrieval of Artifacts Settled."

114. Gordon Pang, "Park Releases Hawaiian Relics," *Honolulu Advertiser*, 23 May 2006, http://www.honoluluadvertiser.com.
115. I am grateful to the following for taking the time to discuss the park's situation with me: Cynthia Orlando, park superintendent; Laura Carter Schuster, branch chief of cultural resources for the park; and Keola Awong. This section relies on my conversations with them on 11 July 2006.

8. Repatriation, Tradition, and the Study of Religion

1. Laclau, "Identity and Hegemony," 7.
2. This paragraph and the following are drawn from G. Johnson, "Facing Down the Representation."
3. Detienne, *Masters of Truth*.
4. Collins, *Understanding Tolowa Histories*, 199.
5. On communicative stratification see Feldman, *Formations of Violence*. For a discussion of rhetorical diversification in the context of Native American protest movements, see Lake, "Enacting Red Power," and "Between Myth and History." On the ideology of individualism, see, e.g., L. Dumont, *Essays on Individualism*.
6. Sider, *Lumbee Indian Histories*, 284. For more on ideological analyses applied to Native American contexts, see Sider, "When Parrots Learn"; Dombrowski, *Against Culture*. For a good discussion of related matters from the point of view of rhetorical studies, see Morris and Wanderer, "Native American Rhetoric."
7. This paragraph and the two following rely upon G. Johnson, "Narrative Remains."
8. J. Z. Smith, *Relating Religion*.
9. Edward Rothstein, "Protection for Indian Patrimony That Leads to a Paradox," *New York Times*, 29 Mar. 2006, http://www.nytimes.com/2006/03/29/arts/artsspecial/29rothstein.html.

BIBLIOGRAPHY

Alexie, Sherman. *The Business of Fancy Dancing.* Brooklyn: Hanging Loose Press, 1992.

———. "What You Pawn I Will Redeem." In *Ten Little Indians,* 175–200. New York: Grove Press, 2003.

Allen, Chadwick. *Blood Narrative: Indigenous Identity in American Indian and Maori Literary and Activists Texts.* Durham and London: Duke University Press, 2002.

American Indian Religious Freedom Act. Public Law 95-341 (42 U.S.C. 1996), 1978.

Antiquities Act of 1906 (16 U.S.C. 431-33), 1906.

Appadurai, Arjun. "The Past as a Scarce Resource." *Man* 16 (1981): 201–19.

———, ed. *The Social Life of Things: Commodities in Cultural Perspective.* New York: Cambridge University Press, 1986.

Archaeological Resources Protection Act of 1979. Public Law 96-95 (16 U.S.C. 470), 1979.

Arizona State Law Journal. "Symposium: *The Native American Graves Protection and Repatriation Act of 1990* and State Repatriation-Related Legislation." *Arizona State Law Journal* 24, no. 1 (1992): 1–562.

Ayau, Edward. "Honor Thy Ancestor's Possessions." *Public Archaeology* 4 (2005): 193–97.

———. "Testimony of Edward Halealoha Ayau, Esq., Hui Malama I Na Kupuna O Hawai'i Nei, Before the Native American Graves Protection and Repatriation Act Review Committee." 18 September 2004. Copy on file with author.

———. "Testimony of Edward Halealoha Ayau, Esq., Hui Malama I Na Kupuna O Hawai'i Nei, Before the Native American Graves Protection and Repatriation Act Review Committee." 16 November 2005. Copy on file with author.

Ayau, Edward, and Ty Tengan. "Ka Huaka'i O Na 'Oiwi: The Journey Home." In Fforde, Hubert, and Turnbull, *The Dead and Their Possessions,* 171–89.

Barkan, Elazar. "Amending Historical Injustices: The Restitution of Cultural Property—An Overview." In *Claiming the Stones, Naming the Bones: Cultural Property and the Negotiation of National and Ethnic Identity,* ed. Elazar Barkan and Ronald Bush, 16–46. Los Angeles: Getty Research Institute, 2002.

Barkan, Elazar, and Ronald Bush, eds. *Claiming the Stones, Naming the Bones: Cultural Property and the Negotiation of National and Ethnic Identity*. Los Angeles: Getty Research Institute, 2002.

Barnes, R. H. *Two Crows Denies It: A History of Controversy in Omaha Sociology*. Lincoln and London: University of Nebraska Press, 1984.

Barth, Frederik, ed. *Ethnic Groups and Boundaries: The Social Organization of Cultural Difference*. Boston: Little, Brown, 1969.

Barthes, Roland. *Mythologies*. Trans. Annette Lavers. New York: Hill and Wang, 1972.

Bell, Catherine. *Ritual Theory, Ritual Practice*. New York and Oxford: Oxford University Press, 1992.

Berman, Tressa. "Beyond the Museum: The Politics of Representation in Asserting Rights to Cultural Property." *Museum Anthropology* 21, no.3 (1998): 19–27.

Berthrong, Donald. *The Southern Cheyennes*. Norman and London: University of Oklahoma Press, 1969.

Bieder, Robert. *A Brief Historical Survey of the Expropriation of American Indian Remains*. Boulder: Native American Rights Fund, 1989.

Bishop Museum. "Final Guidance: *Native American Graves Protection and Repatriation Act*." 7 October 2004. http://www.bishopmuseum.org/Final_NAGPRA_Guidelines.html.

———. "Interim and Proposed Final Guidance: *Native American Graves Protection and Repatriation Act*." 30 June 2004. Copy on file with author.

Blackford, Mansel. "Environmental Justice, Native Rights, Tourism, and Opposition to Military Control: The Case of Kahoʻolawe." *Journal of American History* 91, no. 2 (2004): 544–71.

Bloch, Maurice. *Ritual, History and Power: Selected Papers in Anthropology*. London and Atlantic Highlands, NJ: Athlone Press, 1989.

Bond, George, and Angela Gilliam, eds. *Social Construction of the Past: Representation as Power*. New York and London: Routledge, 1994.

Bourdieu, Pierre. *The Field of Cultural Production: Essays on Art and Literature*. Ed. Randal Johnson. New York: Columbia University Press, 1993.

Bray, Tamara, ed. *The Future of the Past: Archaeologists, Native Americans, and Repatriation*. New York and London: Garland Publishing, 2001.

Brown, Brian. *Religion, Law, and the Land: Native Americans and the Judicial Interpretation of Sacred Land*. Westport and London: Greenwood Press, 1999.

Brown, Karen McCarthy. *Mama Lola: A Vodou Priestess in Brooklyn*. Updated ed. Berkeley, Los Angeles, and London: University of California Press, 2001.

Brown, Michael. *Who Owns Native Culture?* Cambridge and London: Harvard University Press, 2003.

Brugge, David. "Navajo Religion and the Anasazi Connection." NHP Museum Archive, University of New Mexico, Albuquerque, 1998.

Buck, Elizabeth. *Paradise Remade: The Politics of Culture and History in Hawaiʻi*. Philadelphia: Temple University Press, 1993.

Buck, Peter. *Arts and Crafts of Hawaii*. Special publication no. 45. Honolulu: Bernice P. Bishop Museum, 1957.

Burke, Kenneth. *The Rhetoric of Religion: Studies in Logology*. Berkeley, Los Angeles, and London: University of California Press, 1961.

Butler, Judith, Ernesto Laclau, and Slavoj Žižek. *Contingency, Hegemony, Universality: Contemporary Dialogues on the Left*. London and New York: Verso, 2000.

Carrier, James. *West of the Divide: Voices from a Ranch and a Reservation*. Golden: Fulcrum Publishing, 1992.

Cather, Willa. *The Professor's House*. New York: Alfred A. Knopf, Inc., 1925.

Chapin, Frederick. *The Land of the Cliff Dwellers*. Boston: Appalachian Mountain Club, 1892.

Charlot, John. *The Hawaiian Poetry of Religion and Politics: Some Religio-Political Concepts in Postcontact Literature*. Honolulu: University of Hawai'i Press for the Institute for Polynesian Studies, 1985.

Chatters, James. *Ancient Encounters: Kennewick Man and the First Americans*. New York: Simon and Schuster, 2001.

Clemmer, Richard. *Roads in the Sky: The Hopi Indians in a Century of Change*. Boulder: Westview Press, 1995.

Clifford, James, and George Marcus, eds. *Writing Culture: The Poetics and Politics of Ethnography*. Berkeley, Los Angeles, and London: University of California Press, 1986.

Collins, James. *Understanding Tolowa Histories: Western Hegemonies and Native American Responses*. New York and London: Routledge, 1998.

Congressional Record. House. 26 October 1990.

Congressional Record. Senate. 22–26 October 1990.

Cooke, George. *Moʻolelo O Molokai: A Ranch Story of Molokai*. Honolulu: Honolulu Star-Bulletin, 1949.

Coombe, Rosemary. "The Properties of Culture and the Politics of Identity: Native Claims in the Cultural Appropriation Controversy." *Canadian Journal of Law and Jurisprudence* 6 (1993): 249–85.

Cordell, Linda, and George Gumerman, eds. *Dynamics of Southwest Prehistory*. Washington and London: Smithsonian Institution Press, 1989.

Cornell, Stephen. *The Return of the Native: American Indian Political Resurgence*. New York and Oxford: Oxford University Press, 1988.

Cox, J. Halley, with William Davenport. *Hawaiian Sculpture*. Rev. ed. Honolulu: University of Hawai'i Press, 1988.

Daws, Gavan. *Shoal of Time: A History of the Hawaiian Islands*. Honolulu: University of Hawai'i Press, 1968.

Deloria, Vine, Jr. *Custer Died for Your Sins: An Indian Manifesto*. New York: MacMillan Company, 1969.

Detienne, Marcel. *The Masters of Truth in Archaic Greece*. Trans. J. Lloyd. New York: Zone Books, 1999.

Dodd, Edward. *Polynesian Art*. New York: Dodd, Mead and Company, 1967.

Dombrowski, Kirk. *Against Culture: Development, Politics, and Religion in Indian Alaska*. Lincoln and London: University of Nebraska Press, 2001.

Dongoske, Kurt, et al. "Archaeological Cultures and Cultural Affiliation: Hopi and Zuni Perspectives in the American Southwest." *American Antiquity* 62, no. 4 (1997): 600–608.

Donham, Theresa. *Data Recovery Excavations at the Honokahua Burial Site.* Report 246-053199. Hilo: Paul H. Rosenthal, Ph.D., Inc., 2000.

Dumont, Clayton, Jr. "The Politics of Scientific Objections to Repatriation." *Wicazo Sa Review* 18 (Spring 2003): 109–28.

Dumont, Louis. *Essays on Individualism: Modern Ideology in Anthropological Perspective.* Chicago and London: University of Chicago Press, 1986.

Eisenstadt, S. N. "Post-Traditional Societies and the Continuity and Reconstruction of Tradition." *Daedalus* 102 (1973): 1–28.

Engler, Steven, and Gregory Grieve, eds. *Historicizing "Tradition" in the Study of Religion.* Berlin and New York: Walter de Gruyter, 2005.

Evans-Pritchard, E. E. *The Nuer.* New York and Oxford: Oxford University Press, 1940.

Feldman, Allen. *Formations of Violence: The Narrative of the Body and Political Terror in Northern Ireland.* Chicago and London: Universi-ty of Chicago Press, 1991.

Fforde, Cressida. "Collection, Repatriation and Identity." In Fforde, Hubert, and Turnbull, *The Dead and their Possessions,* 25–46.

Fforde, Cressida, Jane Hubert, and Paul Turnbull, eds. *The Dead and Their Possessions: Repatriation in Principle, Policy and Practice.* New York and London: Routledge, 2002.

Fine-Dare, Kathleen. "Anthropological Suspicion, Public Interest and NAGPRA." *Journal of Social Archaeology* 5, no. 2 (2005): 171–92.

———. *Grave Injustice: The American Indian Repatriation Movement.* Lincoln and London: University of Nebraska Press, 2002.

Fitzpatrick, Peter. *The Mythology of Modern Law.* New York and London: Routledge, 1992.

Fletcher, Alice, and Francis La Flesche. *The Omaha Tribe: 27th Annual Report of the Bureau of American Ethnology to the Secretary of the Smithsonian Institution, 1905–1906.* Washington: Government Printing Office, 1911.

Flynn, Johnny, and Gary Laderman. "Purgatory and the Powerful Dead: A Case Study of Native American Repatriation." *Religion and American Culture* 4, no. 1 (1994): 51–75.

Fowler, Loretta. *Tribal Sovereignty and the Historical Imagination: Cheyenne-Arapaho Politics.* Lincoln and London: University of Nebraska Press, 2002.

Friedman, Jonathan. *Cultural Identity and Global Process.* London and Thousand Oaks, CA: Sage Publications, 1994.

Friesen, Steven, ed. *Ancestors in Post-Contact Religion: Roots, Ruptures, and Modernity's Memory.* Cambridge: Harvard University Press, 2001.

Gable, Eric, and Richard Handler. "After Authenticity at an American Heritage Site." *American Anthropologist* 98 (1996): 568–78.

Garroutte, Eva Marie. *Real Indians: Identity and Survival of Native America.* Berkeley, Los Angeles, and London: University of California Press, 2003.

Gathercole, Peter, and David Lowenthal, eds. *The Politics of the Past.* New York and London: Routledge, 1990.

Geertz, Armin. *The Invention of Prophecy: Continuity and Meaning in Hopi Indian Religion.* Berkeley, Los Angeles, and London: University of California Press, 1997.

Gonzales, Angela. "The (Re)articulation of American Indian Identity: Maintaining Boundaries and Regulating Access to Ethnically Tied Resources." *American Indian Culture and Research Journal* 22, no. 4 (1998): 199–225.

Goodrich, Peter. "Antirrhesis: Polemical Structures of Common Law Thought." In *The Rhetoric of Law*, ed. Austin Sarat and Thomas R. Kearns, 57–102. Ann Arbor: University of Michigan Press, 1996.

Gramsci, Antonio. *Prison Letters.* Trans. Hamish Henderson. London and Chicago: Pluto Press, 1996.

Greenblatt, Stephen. *Marvelous Possessions: The Wonder of the New World.* Chicago and London: University of Chicago Press, 1991.

Grim, John. "Honoring the Ancestral Bones: The Grave Protection and Repatriation Act and the Algonquian Feast of the Dead." In Friesen, *Ancestors in Post-Contact Religion*, 197–215.

Grimes, Ronald. "Desecration of the Dead: An Inter-Religious Controversy." *American Indian Quarterly* 10 (Fall 1986): 305–39.

Guenther, Mathias, et al. "The Concept of Indigeneity." *Social Anthropology* 14, no. 1 (2006): 17–32.

Gulliford, Andrew. *Sacred Objects and Sacred Places: Preserving Tribal Traditions.* Boulder: University Press of Colorado, 2000.

Hall, Dana Naone, ed. *Mālama: Hawaiian Land and Water.* Honolulu: Bamboo Ridge Press, 1985.

Hall, Stuart. "Gramsci's Relevance for the Study of Race and Ethnicity." *Journal of Communication Inquiry* 10 (1986): 5–27.

Handler, Richard. "On Having a Culture: Nationalism and the Preservation of Quebec's Patrimone." In *Objects and Others: Essays on Museums and Material Culture*, ed. George Stocking, 192–217. Madison: University of Wisconsin Press, 1984.

Handler, Richard, and Jocelyn Linnekin. "Tradition, Genuine or Spurious?" *Journal of American Folklore* 97 (1984): 273–90.

Harden, M. J. *Voices of Wisdom: Hawaiian Elders Speak.* Kula, HI: Aka Press, 1999.

Harding, Sarah. "Defining Traditional Knowledge—Lessons from Cultural Property." *Cardozo Journal of International and Comparative Law* 11 (Summer 2003): 511–18.

———. "Justifying Repatriation of Native American Cultural Property." *Indiana Law Journal* 72 (1997): 723–44.

Harding, Susan F. *The Book of Jerry Falwell: Fundamentalist Language and Politics.* Princeton and Oxford: Princeton University Press, 2000.

Harjo, Suzan Shown. "American Indian Religious Freedom Act after Twenty-five Years." *Wicazo Sa Review* 19 (Fall 2004): 129–36.

Hawaii Island Burial Council. Meeting Minutes for 17 November 2005. State of Hawaii Department of Land and Natural Resources.

Hawaii State Historic Preservation Division. "Nā Iwi Kūpuna: The Bones of Our Ancestors." http://www.hawaii.gov/dlnr/hpd/naiwikupuna.htm.

Herzfeld, Michael. *Cultural Intimacy: Social Poetics in the Nation-State.* New York and London: Routledge, 1997.

Hind, Mehanaokala. "Kakoo for Hui Malama I Na Kupuna O Hawaii Nei." Hawaiian Independence Blog, 22 December 2005. http://www.hawaiiankingdom .info/C259362623/E20051223142150.

———. "Manao about the 'Princess' Abigail." 20 September 2005. Copy on file with author and used by permission.

Hobsbawm, Eric. "The Social Function of the Past." *Past and Present* 55 (1972): 5–17.

Hobsbawm, Eric, and Terrence Ranger, eds. *The Invention of Tradition.* Cambridge: Cambridge University Press, 1983.

Hoig, Stan. *The Sand Creek Massacre.* Norman and London: University of Oklahoma Press, 1961.

Hoʻomanawanui, Kuʻualoha. "Ha, Mana, Leo (Breath, Spirit, Voice): Kanaka Maoli Empowerment through Literature." *American Indian Quarterly* 28 (Winter–Spring 2004): 86–91.

Hultkrantz, Åke. "Mythology and Religious Concepts." In *Handbook of North American Indians,* vol. 11, *Great Basin,* ed. Warren D'Azevedo, 630–40. Washington and London: Smithsonian Institution Press, 1986.

Irwin, Lee. "Freedom, Law and Prophecy," *American Indian Quarterly* 21 (Winter 1997): 35–55.

Johnson, Greg. "Facing Down the Representation of an Impossibility: Indigenous Responses to a 'Universal' Problem in the Repatriation Context." *Culture and Religion* 6, no. 1 (2005): 57–78.

———. "Incarcerated Tradition: Native Hawaiian Identities and Religious Practice in Prison Contexts." In *Historicizing "Tradition" in the Study of Religion,* ed. Steven Engler and Gregory Grieve, 195–210. Berlin: Walter de Gruyter, 2005.

———. "Narrative Remains: Articulating Indian Identities in the Repatriation Context." *Comparative Studies in Society and History* 47, no. 3 (2005): 480–506.

Johnson, Paul. *Secrets, Gossip, and Gods: The Transformation of Brazilian Candomble.* New York and Oxford: Oxford University Press, 2002.

Johnson, Rubellite. "The Hawaiian 'Aumakua: Ancestors as Gods." In Friesen, *Ancestors in Post-Contact Religion,* 29–45.

Jorgensen, Joseph. *The Sun Dance Religion: Power for the Powerless.* Chicago and London: University of Chicago Press, 1972.

Kalakaua, David. *The Legends and Myths of Hawaii: The Fables and Folklore of a Strange People.* 1888. Reprint, Rutland and Tokyo: Charles E. Tuttle, 1972.

Kamakau, Samuel. *Ka Poʻe Kahiko: The People of Old Honolulu.* Honolulu: Bishop Museum Press, 1964.

Kameʻeleihiwa, Lilikalā. *Native Land and Foreign Desires: Pehea Lā E Pono Ai?* Honolulu: Bishop Museum Press, 1992.

Kanahele, Dennis. "Clandestine Manipulation toward Genocide." *Arizona State Law Journal* 34, no. 1 (2002): 63–73.

Kanahele, George. *Kū Kanaka: Stand Tall, A Search for Hawaiian Values.* Honolulu: University of Hawai'i Press and the Waiaha Foundation, 1986.

Kanahele, Pualani. "Rhythms from the Past Beating into the Future." In Friesen, *Ancestors in Post-Contact Religion,* 157–62.

Kapferer, Bruce. *Legends of People, Myths of State: Violence, Intolerance, and Political Culture in Sri Lanka and Australia.* Washington and London: Smithsonian Institution Press, 1999.

Kaulukukui, Guy. "Bishop Museum as a Native Hawaiian Organization Under the *Native American Graves Protection and Repatriation Act.*" 1 July 2004. Copy on file with author.

——. "Sacred Objects in the Collection of Bishop Museum, and Right of Possession as Defined by the *Native American Graves Protection and Repatriation Act.*" 3 July 2004. Copy on file with author.

Kelly, Anne. "Hawaiian Literature and Resistance; Or, How My Ancestors Took on the Stryker Brigade and Joined the Struggle to Demilitarize Hawai'i!" *American Indian Quarterly* 28 (Winter–Spring 2004): 92–96.

Kirch, Patrick. *Feathered Gods and Fishhooks: An Introduction to Hawaiian Archaeology and Prehistory.* Honolulu: University of Hawai'i Press, 1985.

Laclau, Ernesto. "Identity and Hegemony: The Role of Universality in the Constitution of Political Logics." In *Contingency, Hegemony, Universality: Contemporary Dialogues on the Left,* ed. Judith Butler, Ernesto Laclau, and Slavoj Žižek. London and New York: Verso, 2000.

Laclau, Ernesto, and Chantal Mouffe. *Hegemony and Socialist Strategy: Towards a Radical Democratic Politics.* London and New York: Verso, 1985.

Lake, Randall. "Between Myth and History: Enacting Time in Native American Protest Rhetoric." *Quarterly Journal of Speech* 77 (1991): 123–51.

——. "Enacting Red Power: The Consummatory Function in Native American Protest Rhetoric." *Quarterly Journal of Speech* 69 (1983): 127–42.

Li, Tanya Murray. "Articulating Indigenous Identity in Indonesia." *Comparative Studies in Society and History* 42, no. 1 (2000): 149–79.

Lincoln, Bruce. *Authority: Construction and Corrosion.* Chicago and London: University of Chicago Press, 1994.

——. *Discourse and the Construction of Society: Comparative Studies of Myth, Ritual and Classification.* New York and Oxford: Oxford University Press, 1989.

——. *Holy Terrors: Thinking about Religion after September 11.* Chicago and London: University of Chicago Press, 2003.

——. "A Lakota Sun Dance and the Problematics of Sociocosmic Reunion." *History of Religions* 34, no. 1 (1994): 1–14.

——. "Theses on Method." *Method and Theory in the Study of Religion* 8 (1996): 225–27.

Linnekin, Jocelyn. "Cultural Invention and the Dilemma of Authenticity." *American Anthropologist* 93 (1991): 446–49.

———. "Defining Tradition: Variations on the Hawaiian Identity." *American Ethnologist* 10 (1983): 241–52.

———. "On The Theory and Politics of Cultural Construction in the Pacific." *Oceania* 62 (1992): 249–63.

———. "The Politics of Culture in the Pacific." In *Cultural Identity and Ethnicity in the Pacific,* ed. Jocelyn Linnekin, 149–74. Honolulu: University of Hawai'i Press, 1990.

Losch, Tracie. "Hawaiian Issues." *Contemporary Pacific* 17, no. 1 (2005): 203–9.

Malo, David. *Hawaiian Antiquities.* Trans. Nathaniel B. Emerson. Special publication no. 2. Honolulu: Bernice P. Bishop Museum, 1951.

McCutcheon, Russell. *The Discipline of Religion: Structure, Meaning, Rhetoric.* New York and London: Routledge, 2003.

McKeown, Timothy C., and Sherry Hutt. "In the Smaller Scope of Conscience: *The Native American Graves Protection and Repatriation Act* Twelve Years After." *UCLA Journal of Environmental Law and Policy* 21, no. 2 (2003): 153–213.

McNitt, Frank. *Richard Wetherill, Anasazi: Pioneer Explorer of Southwestern Ruins.* Albuquerque: University of New Mexico Press, 1957.

Merrill, William, Edmund Ladd, and T. J. Ferguson. "The Return of Ahayu:da: Lessons for Repatriation from Zuni Pueblo and the Smithsonian Institution." *Current Anthropology* 34 (1993): 523–67.

Merry, Sally Engle. *Colonizing Hawai'i: The Cultural Power of Law.* Princeton: Princeton University Press, 2000.

Mihesuah, Devon, ed. *Repatriation Reader: Who Own American Indian Remains?* Lincoln and London: University of Nebraska Press, 2000.

Miller, Bruce. *Invisible Indigenes: The Politics of Nonrecognition.* Lincoln and London: University of Nebraska Press, 2003.

Miller, Jay. "Numic Religion: An Overview of Power in the Great Basin of Native North America." *Anthropos* 78 (1983): 337–54.

Moriwake, Isaac. "Critical Excavations: Law, Narrative, and the Debate on Native American and Hawaiian 'Cultural Property' Repatriation." *University of Hawai'i Law Review* 20 (Summer–Fall 1998): 261–319.

Morris, Richard, and Phillip Wanderer. "Native American Rhetoric: Dancing in the Shadows of the Ghost Dance." *Quarterly Journal of Speech* 76 (1990): 164–91.

Murray, David. *Forked Tongues: Speech, Writing and Representation in North American Indian Texts.* Bloomington and Indianapolis: Indiana University Press, 1991.

Museum of Natural History. "Summary of the NAGPRA Dispute over Possession of the Hawaiian Support Figure in the Collection of the Museum of Natural History." Providence, RI: Roger Williams Museum, Museum of Natural History, 1998.

Nabokov, Peter. *A Forest of Time: American Indian Ways of History.* Cambridge: Cambridge University Press, 2002.

Nagel, Joane. *American Indian Ethnic Renewal: Red Power and the Resurgence of Identity and Culture.* New York and Oxford: Oxford University Press, 1996.

Native American Graves Protection and Repatriation Act (NAGPRA). Public Law 101-601 (25 U.S.C. 3001), 1990.

Niezen, Ronald. *The Origins of Indigenism: Human Rights and the Politics of Identity.* Berkeley, Los Angeles, and London: University of California Press, 2003.

———. *Spirit Wars: Native North American Religions in the Age of Nation Building.* Berkeley, Los Angeles, and London: University of California Press, 2000.

Nihipali, Kunani. "Stone by Stone, Bone by Bone: Rebuilding the Hawaiian Nation in the Illusion of Reality." *Arizona State Law Journal* 34, no. 1 (2002): 28–46.

NorthSun, Nila. "NAGPRA-Prayer Poem." *American Indian Culture and Research Journal* 23, no. 4 (1999): 187.

Opler, Marvin. "The Character and History of the Southern Ute Peyote Rite." *American Anthropologist* 42 (1940): 463–78.

———. "The Integration of the Sun Dance in Ute Religion." *American Anthropologist* 43 (1941): 550–72.

Orsi, Robert. *Between Heaven and Earth: The Religious Worlds People Make and the Scholars Who Study Them.* Princeton and Oxford: Princeton University Press, 2005.

Ortiz, Simon. *From Sand Creek.* Tucson: University of Arizona Press, 1999.

Ortner, Sherry. "On Key Symbols." *American Anthropologist* 75 (1973): 1338–46.

Osorio, Jonathan. *Dismembering Lahui: A History of the Hawaiian Nation to 1887.* Honolulu: University of Hawai'i Press, 2002.

Park, Willard. *Shamanism in Western North America: A Study in Cultural Relationships.* Chicago: Northwestern University Press, 1938.

Parker, Linda. *Native American Estate: The Struggle over Indian and Hawaiian Lands.* Honolulu: University of Hawai'i Press, 1989.

Pearce, Roy Harvey. *Savagism and Civilization: A Study of the Indian and the American Mind.* Berkeley, Los Angeles, and London: University of California Press, 1988.

Pensley, D. S. "The Native American Graves Protection and Repatriation Act (1990): Where the Native Voice Is Missing." *Wicazo Sa Review* 20 (Fall 2005): 37–64.

Petrich, Matthew. "Litigating NAGPRA in Hawai'i: Dignity or Debacle?" *University of Hawai'i Law Review* 22 (Summer 2000): 545–68.

Povinelli, Elizabeth. *The Cunning of Recognition: Indigenous Alterities and the Making of Australian Multiculturalism.* Durham and London: Duke University Press, 2002.

Providence, Rhode Island, Executive Office. "Hawaiian Artifact Now in Possession of City of Providence." Press release. 21 November 1996. http://www.providenceri.com/press/hawai2.html.

Pukui, Mary Kawena, and Samuel Elbert. *Hawaiian Dictionary.* Honolulu: University of Hawaiʻi Press, 1986.

Pukui, Mary Kawena, E. W. Haertig, and Catherine E. Lee. *Nānā I Ke Kumu: Look to the Source.* Honolulu: Hui Hanai, 1972.

Reagan, Albert. "Collection of Ancient Artifacts from the Ashley–Dry Fork District of the Uintah Basin, with Some Notes on the Dwelling and Mortuary Customs of the Ouray Indians of the Ouray (Utah) Region." *El Palacio* 31 (1931): 407–13.

"Report of the Panel for a National Dialogue on Museum/Native American Relations (Feb. 28, 1990)." *Arizona State Law Journal* 24, no. 1 (1990): 487–500.

Return of the Sacred Pole. Video. Dir. Michael Farrell. Lincoln: Nebraska Educational Television Network, Great Plains National, 1990.

Review Committee. "Draft Recommendations Regarding the Disposition of Culturally Unidentifiable Native American Human Remains and Associated Funerary Objects." Department of the Interior. *Federal Register* 60, no. 118 (20 June 1995): 32163–64.

———. "NAGPRA Review Committee Advisory Findings and Recommendations Regarding a Carved Wooden Figure from the Hawaiian Islands." *Federal Register* 62, no. 84 (1 May 1997): 23794–95.

———. "Native American Graves Protection and Repatriation Review Committee Findings and Recommendations and Minority Opinion Regarding a Dispute between the Royal Hawaiian Academy of Traditional Arts and the Bernice Pauahi Bishop Museum." *Federal Register* 68, no. 161 (20 August 2003): 50179–80.

———. Minutes of the First Meeting of the *Native American Graves Protection and Repatriation Act* Review Committee. Washington, DC. 29 April–1 May 1992. http://www.cr.nps.gov/nagpra/REVIEW/meetings/RMS001.PDF.

———. Minutes of the Second Meeting of the *Native American Graves Protection and Repatriation Act* Review Committee. Denver, CO. 26–28 August 1992. http://www.cr.nps.gov/nagpra/REVIEW/meetings/RMS002.PDF.

———. Minutes of the Fourth Meeting of the *Native American Graves Protection and Repatriation Act* Review Committee. Honolulu, HI. 26–27 February 1993. http://www.cr.nps.gov/nagpra/REVIEW/meetings/RMS004.PDF.

———. Minutes of the Fifth Meeting of the *Native American Graves Protection and Repatriation Act* Review Committee. Washington, DC. 20–22 September 1993. http://www.cr.nps.gov/nagpra/REVIEW/meetings/RMS005.PDF.

———. Minutes of the Sixth Meeting of the *Native American Graves Protection and Repatriation Act* Review Committee. Phoenix, AZ. 23–25 January 1994. http://www.cr.nps.gov/nagpra/REVIEW/meetings/RMS006.PDF.

———. Minutes of the Seventh Meeting of the *Native American Graves Protection and Repatriation Act* Review Committee. Rapid City, SD. 12–14 May 1994. http://www.cr.nps.gov/nagpra/REVIEW/meetings/RMS007.PDF.

———. Minutes of the Ninth Meeting of the *Native American Graves Protection and Repatriation Act* Review Committee. Los Angeles, CA. 16–18 February 1995. http://www.cr.nps.gov/nagpra/REVIEW/meetings/RMS009.PDF.

———. Minutes of the Tenth Meeting of the *Native American Graves Protection and Repatriation Act* Review Committee. Anchorage, AK. 16–18 October 1995. http://www.cr.nps.gov/nagpra/REVIEW/meetings/RMS010.PDF.

———. Minutes of the Eleventh Meeting of the *Native American Graves Protection and Repatriation Act* Review Committee. Billings, MT. 9–11 June 1996. http://www.cr.nps.gov/nagpra/REVIEW/meetings/RMS011.PDF.

———. Official Transcript of the Twelfth Meeting of the *Native American Graves Protection and Repatriation Act* Review Committee. National Park Service. Myrtle Beach, SC. 1–3 November 1996.

———. Official Transcript of the Thirteenth Meeting of the *Native American Graves Protection and Repatriation Act* Review Committee. National Park Service. Norman, OK. 25–27 March 1997.

———. Minutes of the Fourteenth Meeting of the *Native American Graves Protection and Repatriation Act* Review Committee. Washington, DC. 29–31 January 1998. http://www.cr.nps.gov/nagpra/REVIEW/meetings/RMS014.PDF.

———. Minutes of the Fifteenth Meeting of the *Native American Graves Protection and Repatriation Act* Review Committee. Portland, OR. 25–27 June 1998. http://www.cr.nps.gov/nagpra/REVIEW/meetings/RMS015.PDF.

———. Minutes of the Sixteenth Meeting of the *Native American Graves Protection and Repatriation Act* Review Committee. Santa Fe, NM. 10–12 December 1998. http://www.cr.nps.gov/nagpra/REVIEW/meetings/RMS016.PDF.

———. Minutes of the Seventeenth Meeting of the *Native American Graves Protection and Repatriation Act* Review Committee. Silver Spring, MD. 3–5 May 1999. http://www.cr.nps.gov/nagpra/REVIEW/meetings/RMS017.PDF.

———. Minutes of the Eighteenth Meeting of the *Native American Graves Protection and Repatriation Act* Review Committee. Salt Lake City, UT. 18–20 November 1999. http://www.cr.nps.gov/nagpra/REVIEW/meetings/RMS018.PDF.

———. Minutes of the Nineteenth Meeting of the *Native American Graves Protection and Repatriation Act* Review Committee. Juneau, AK. 2–4 April 2000. http://www.cr.nps.gov/nagpra/REVIEW/meetings/RMS019.PDF.

———. Minutes of the Twentieth Meeting of the *Native American Graves Protection and Repatriation Act* Review Committee. Nashville, TN. 11–13 December 2000. http://www.cr.nps.gov/nagpra/REVIEW/meetings/RMS020.PDF.

———. Minutes of the Twenty-first Meeting of the *Native American Graves Protection and Repatriation Act* Review Committee. Kelseyville, CA. 31 May–2 June 2001. http://www.cr.nps.gov/nagpra/REVIEW/meetings/RMS021.PDF.

———. Minutes of the Twenty-second Meeting of the *Native American Graves Protection and Repatriation Act* Review Committee. Cambridge, MA. 17–19 November 2001. http://www.cr.nps.gov/nagpra/REVIEW/meetings/RMS022.PDF.

———. Minutes of the Twenty-third Meeting of the *Native American Graves Protection and Repatriation Act* Review Committee. Tulsa, OK. 31 May–2 June 2002. http://www.cr.nps.gov/nagpra/REVIEW/meetings/RMS023.PDF.

————. Minutes of the Twenty-fourth Meeting of the *Native American Graves Protection and Repatriation Act* Review Committee. Seattle, WA. 8–9 November 2002. http://www.cr.nps.gov/nagpra/REVIEW/meetings/RMS024 .PDF.

————. Minutes of the Twenty-fifth Meeting of the *Native American Graves Protection and Repatriation Act* Review Committee. St. Paul, MN. 9–10 May 2003. http://www.cr.nps.gov/nagpra/REVIEW/meetings/RMS025.PDF.

————. Minutes of the Twenty-sixth Meeting of the *Native American Graves Protection and Repatriation Act* Review Committee. Teleconference. 19 July 2004. http://www.cr.nps.gov/nagpra/REVIEW/meetings/RMS026.PDF.

————. Minutes of the Twenty-seventh Meeting of the *Native American Graves Protection and Repatriation Act* Review Committee. Washington, DC. 17–18 September 2004. http://www.cr.nps.gov/nagpra/REVIEW/meetings/RMS027 .PDF.

————. Minutes of the Twenty-eighth Meeting of the *Native American Graves Protection and Repatriation Act* Review Committee. Teleconference. 2 November 2004. http://www.cr.nps.gov/nagpra/REVIEW/meetings/RMS028.PDF.

————. Minutes of the Twenty-ninth Meeting of the *Native American Graves Protection and Repatriation Act* Review Committee. Honolulu, HI. 13–15 March 2005. http://www.cr.nps.gov/nagpra/REVIEW/meetings/RMS029.PDF.

————. Minutes of the Thirtieth Meeting of the *Native American Graves Protection and Repatriation Act* Review Committee. Albuquerque, NM. 16–17 November 2005. http://www.cr.nps.gov/nagpra/REVIEW/meetings/RMS030 .PDF.

————. Minutes of the Thirty-third Meeting of the *Native American Graves Protection and Repatriation Act* Review Committee. Denver, CO. 3–4 November 2006. http://www.cr.nps.gov/nagpra/REVIEW/meetings/RMS033.PDF

Riding In, James, Cal Seciwa, Suzan Shown Harjo, Walter Echo-Hawk, and Rebecca Tsosic. "Protecting Native American Human Remains, Burial Grounds, and Sacred Places." *Wicazo Sa Review* 19 (Fall 2004): 169–83.

Ridington, Robin. "Omaha Survival: A Vanishing Tribe That Would Not Vanish." *American Indian Quarterly* 11 (Winter 1987): 37–51.

————. "A Sacred Object as Text: Reclaiming the Sacred Pole of the Omaha Tribe." *American Indian Quarterly* 17 (Winter 1993): 83–99.

Ridington, Robin, and Dennis Hastings. *Blessing for a Long Time: The Sacred Pole of the Omaha.* Lincoln and London: University of Nebraska Press, 1997.

Rose, Jerome, Thomas Green, and Victoria Green. "NAGPRA Is Forever: Osteology and the Repatriation of Skeletons." *Annual Review of Anthropology* 25 (1996): 81–103.

Sahlins, Marshall. "Cosmologies of Capitalism: The Trans-Pacific Sector of 'The World System.'" *Proceedings of the British Academy* 74 (1988): 1–51.

————. "Goodbye to *Tristes Tropes:* Ethnography in the Context of Modern World History." *Journal of Modern History* 65 (1993): 1–25.

————. *Historical Metaphors and Mythical Realities: Structure and History in the Early Kingdom of the Sandwich Islands Kingdom.* Ann Arbor: University of Michigan Press, 1981.

———. *Islands of History.* Chicago and London: University of Chicago Press, 1985.

Scherer, Mark. *Imperfect Victories: The Legal Tenacity of the Omaha Tribe.* Lincoln and London: University of Nebraska Press, 1999.

Scott, James C. *Domination and the Arts of Resistance: Hidden Transcripts.* New Haven and London: Yale University Press, 1990.

———. *Seeing like a State: How Certain Schemes to Improve the Human Condition Have Failed.* New Haven and London: Yale University Press, 1998.

Shore, Bradd. "Mana and Tapu." In *Developments in Polynesian Ethnology,* ed. Alan Howard and Robert Borofsky, 137–74. Honolulu: University of Hawai'i Press, 1989.

Sider, Gerald. *Lumbee Indian Histories: Race, Ethnicity, and Indian Identity in the Southern United States.* Cambridge: Cambridge University Press, 1993.

———. "When Parrots Learn to Talk, and Why They Can't: Domination, Deception, and Self-Deception in Indian-White Relations." *Comparative Studies in Society and History* 29, no. 1 (1987): 3–23.

Silva, Noenoe. *Aloha Betrayed: Native Hawaiian Resistance to American Colonialism.* Durham and London: Duke University Press, 2004.

Smith, Anne. *Ute Tales.* Salt Lake City: University of Utah Press, 1992.

Smith, Duane. *Mesa Verde National Park: Shadows of the Centuries.* Lawrence: University Press of Kansas, 1988.

Smith, Huston, and Reuben Snake, eds. *One Nation under God: The Triumph of the Native American Church.* Santa Fe: Clear Light Publishers, 1996.

Smith, Jonathan Z. *Relating Religion: Essays in the Study of Religion.* Chicago and London: University of Chicago Press, 2004.

Stands in Timber, John, and Margot Liberty. *Cheyenne Memories.* New Haven and London: Yale University Press, 1967.

Steiner, Stan. *The New Indians.* New York: Delta, 1968.

Steward, Julian. *Ute Indians I: Aboriginal and Historical Groups of the Ute Indians of Utah.* New York and London: Garland Publishing, 1974.

Stewart, Omer. "Culture Elements Distribution List: XVIII: Ute-Southern Paiute." *Anthropology Records* 6, no. 4 (1940).

Stocking, George, ed. *Objects and Others: Essays on Museums and Material Culture.* Madison: University of Wisconsin Press, 1985.

———, ed. *Observers Observed: Essays on Ethnographic Fieldwork.* Madison: University of Wisconsin Press, 1983.

Stokes, J. F. G. "Notes on Hawaiian Petroglyphs." B. P. Bishop Museum Occasional Paper no. 4. Honolulu: B. P. Bishop Museum Press, 1910.

Stuart, David. *Anasazi America.* Albuquerque: University of New Mexico Press, 2000.

Sullivan, Paul. "Customary Revolutions: The Law of Custom and the Conflict of Traditions in Hawai'i." *University of Hawai'i Law Review* 20 (Summer–Fall 1998): 99–163.

Sullivan, Winnifred. *The Impossibility of Religious Freedom.* Princeton and London: Princeton University Press, 2005.

Thomas, David Hurst. *Skull Wars: Kennewick Man, Archaeology, and the Battle for Native American Identity.* New York: Basic Books, 2000.

Thomas, Nicholas. *Entangled Objects: Exchange, Material Culture and Colonialism in the Pacific.* Cambridge: Harvard University Press, 1991.

———. *In Oceania: Visions, Artifacts, Histories.* Durham and London: Duke University Press, 1997.

Thornton, Russell. "Who Owns Our Past? The Repatriation of Native American Human Remains and Cultural Objects." In *Studying Native America: Problems and Prospects,* ed. Russell Thornton, 385–415. Madison: University of Wisconsin Press, 1998.

Trask, Haunani-Kay. "From a Native Daughter." In *The American Indian and the Problem of History,* ed. Calvin Martin, 171–79. New York and Oxford: Oxford University Press, 1987.

Trope, Jack, and Walter Echo-Hawk. "*The Native American Graves Protection and Repatriation Act:* Background and Legislative History." *Arizona State Law Journal* 24, no. 1 (1992): 35–78.

Tweed, Thomas. "Marking Religion's Boundaries: Constitutive Terms, Orienting Tropes, and Exegetical Fussiness." *History of Religions* 44, no. 2 (2005): 252–76.

U.S. Court of Appeals for the Ninth Circuit. "Memorandum." No. 05-16721. D.C. No. CV-05-00540-DAE. Argued and submitted 6 December 2005; filed 12 December 2005.

U.S. Department of the Interior (DOI). *Native American Graves Protection and Repatriation Act: Final Rule. Federal Register* 60, no. 232 (4 December 1995): 62133–69.

———. National Park Service (NPS). Native American Graves Protection and Repatriation Review Committee: Finding. "Finding Regarding Human Remains Identified as 12-5456 from the Hawaiian Islands." *Federal Register* 58, no 71 (15 April 1993): 19688.

———. NPS. "Notice of Intent to Repatriate Cultural Items from Kawaihae, Kohala, Island of Hawaii, HI, in the Possession of the Bernice Pauahi Bishop Museum, Honolulu, HI." *Federal Register* 66, no. 47 (9 March 2001): 14201.

———. NPS. "Notice of Intent to Repatriate Cultural Items from Nebraska and South Dakota in the Possession of the Fruitlands Museum, Harvard, MA." *Federal Register* 62, no. 42 (4 March 1997): 9801–3.

———. Office of the Secretary. Proposed Rules. *Native American Graves Protection and Repatriation Act* Regulations. *Federal Register* 58, no. 102 (28 May 1993): 31122–34.

U.S. District Court of Hawaii. Status Conference Regarding Na Lei Ali'i Kawananakoa and Royal Hawaiian Academy of Traditional Arts vs. Bishop Museum and Hui Malama I Na Kupuna 'O Hawaii Nei (Civil No. 05-00540 DAE). 17 January 2006.

U.S. House. House Report 101-877 on H.R. 5237, "Providing for the Protection of Native American Graves." 15 October 1990.

———. Interior and Insular Affairs Committee (HIIAC). Hearing 101-62 on H.R. 1381, Native American Burial Site Preservation Act of 1989; H.R. 1646, Native American Grave and Burial Protection Act; and H.R. 5237, Native American Grave Protection and Repatriation Act. 17 July 1990.

U.S. Senate. Senate Report 100-601 on S. 187, "Establishing the Native American Museum Claims Commission." 21 October 1988.

———. Senate Report 101-473 on S. 1980, "Providing for the Protection of Native American Graves and the Repatriation of Native American Remains and Cultural Patrimony." 26 September 1990.

———. S. 2843. "Making Technical Corrections to Laws Relating to Native Americans, and for Other Purposes." 11 October 2004.

———. S. 536. "A Bill Making Technical Corrections to Laws Relating to Native Americans, and for Other Purposes." Introduced by Senator McCain. 7 March 2005.

———. Select Committee on Indian Affairs (SSCIA). Senate Hearing 100-90 on S. 187, Native American Cultural Preservation Act. 20 February 1987.

———. SSCIA. Senate Hearing 100-931 on S. 187, Native American Museum Claims Commission Act. 29 July 1988.

———. SSCIA. Senate Hearing 101-952 on S. 1021 and 1980, Native American Grave Burial Protection Act (Repatriation); Native American Repatriation of Cultural Patrimony Act; and Heard Museum Report. 14 May 1990.

———. SSCIA. Oversight Hearing 103-189 on the Native American Graves Protection and Repatriation Act. 27 May 1993.

———. SSCIA. Oversight Hearing 104-399 on the Implementation of Public Law 101-601, the Native American Graves Protection and Repatriation Act. 6 December 1995.

———. SSCIA. Oversight Hearing on the Implementation of Public Law 101-601, the Native American Graves Protection and Repatriation Act. 20 April 1999.

———. SSCIA. Oversight Hearing on the Implementation of Public Law 101-601, the Native American Graves Protection and Repatriation Act. 14 July 2004.

———. SSCIA. Oversight Hearing 108-768 on the Implementation of Public Law 101-601, the Native American Graves Protection and Repatriation Act. 8 December 2004.

———. SSCIA. Oversight Hearing on the Implementation of Public Law 101-601, the Native American Graves Protection and Repatriation Act. 28 July 2005.

Valeri, Valerio. *Kingship and Sacrifice: Ritual and Society in Ancient Hawaii.* Trans. Paula Wissig. Chicago and London: University of Chicago Press, 1985.

Vecsey, Christopher, ed. *Handbook of American Indian Religious Freedom.* New York: Crossroad Publishing Company, 1991.

Vizenor, Gerald. "Bone Courts: The Rights and Narrative Representation of Tribal Bones." *American Indian Quarterly* 10 (Fall 1986): 319–31.

———. *Manifest Manners: Postindian Warriors of Survivance.* Hanover and London: Wesleyan University Press, 1994.

Walker, James. *Lakota Belief and Ritual.* Ed. Raymond DeMaille and Elaine Jahner. Lincoln and London: University of Nebraska Press, 1991.

Warren, Kay, and Jean Jackson, eds. *Indigenous Movements, Self-Representation, and the State in Latin America.* Austin: University of Texas Press, 2002.

Weaver, Jace. "Indian Presence with No Indians Present: NAGPRA and Its Discontents." *Wicazo Sa Review* 12 (Fall 1997): 13–30.

Welsh, Peter. "Repatriation and Cultural Preservation: Potent Objects, Potent Pasts." *University of Michigan Journal of Law Reform* 25 (1992): 837–65.

Whitney, Scott. "Showdown in Honolulu." *Archaeology,* 27 April 2000. http://www.archaeology.org/online/features/hawaii/.

Wilkinson, Charles. *Blood Struggle: The Rise of Modern Indian Nations.* New York: W. W. Norton, 2005.

Williams, Raymond. *Culture and Society: 1780–1950.* New York: Columbia University Press, 1958.

Wood, Nancy. *When the Buffalo Free the Mountains: The Survival of America's Ute Indians.* Garden City, NY: Doubleday and Company, 1980.

Wroth, William, ed. *Ute Indian Arts and Culture: From Prehistory to the New Millennium.* Colorado Springs: Colorado Springs Fine Arts Center, 2000.

Yellowman, Connie. " 'Naevahoo'ohtseme'—We are Going Back Home: The Cheyenne Repatriation of Human Remains—A Woman's Perspective." *St. Thomas Law Review* (Fall 1996): 103–15.

Young, Kanalu. *Rethinking the Native Hawaiian Past.* New York and London: Garland Publishing, 1998.

Young, Richard. *The Ute Indians of Colorado in the Twentieth Century.* Norman and London: University of Oklahoma Press, 1997.

INDEX

STUDIES IN RELIGION AND CULTURE